POLITICAL CHANGE
IN CALIFORNIA

CONTRIBUTIONS IN AMERICAN HISTORY

SERIES EDITOR

Stanley I. Kutler

University of Wisconsin

NO. 1. Bread and Roses Too: Studies of the Wobblies
Joseph R. Conlin

NO. 2. The Politics of Loyalty: The White House and the
Communist Issue, 1946-1952
Alan D. Harper

NO. 3. The Vanity of Power: American Isolation and the
First World War, 1914-1917
John M. Cooper, Jr.

NO. 4. City and Country: Rural Responses to
Urbanization in the 1920s
Don S. Kirschner

NO. 5. Political Change in California: Critical Elections
and Social Movements, 1890-1966
Michael Paul Rogin and John L. Shover

NO. 6. Negroes and the Great Depression: The Problem
of Economic Recovery
Raymond Wolters

POLITICAL CHANGE IN CALIFORNIA

*Critical Elections
and Social Movements,
1890–1966*

Michael Paul Rogin
John L. Shover

*CONTRIBUTIONS IN
AMERICAN HISTORY*
Number Five

Greenwood Publishing Corporation
WESTPORT, CONNECTICUT

To
James Rector (in memoriam),
Alan Blanshard, and the other victims
of law and order in Berkeley, California,
May 1969

Library of Congress Catalog Card Number: 72-95506
SBN: 8371-2346-1

Greenwood Publishing Corporation
51 Riverside Avenue, Westport, Connecticut 06880

Greenwood Publishers Ltd.
42 Hanway Street, London, W.1., England

Printed in the United States of America

Contents

Figures		vii
Tables		ix
Preface		xiii
Acknowledgments		xix
1	California Populism and the "System of 1896"	3
2	Progressivism and the California Electorate	35
3	The Progressives and the Working-Class Vote in California	62
4	Was 1928 a Critical Election in California?	90
5	The Resurgence of the Democratic Party in California	112
6	Southern California: Right-Wing Behavior and Political Symbols	153
Bibliography		213
Index		227

Figures

1 Populism and Agricultural Wealth, 1894   14

2 Party Realignment in the 1890s   21

3 Ethnic Composition of the Republican
   Presidential Vote, 1884–1908   25

4 Percentage Democratic Vote for President in Most
   Consistently Democratic County in California
   (Plumas) and Most Consistently Republican
   County (Riverside), 1892–1944   96

5 Percentage Democratic Vote for President in the
   5 Counties with the Most Democratic Gain,
   1920–1928, and in the 5 Counties with Greatest
   Democratic Loss (and Least Gain), 1920–1928   98

6 Percentage Democratic Vote for President in 21
   Counties with Most Democratic Gain,
   1908–1916, and in 11 Counties with Least
   Democratic Gain, 1908–1916   99

7 Percentage Democratic Vote for President in the 6 Metropolitan Counties with Most Democratic Gain, 1920–1928, and in the 5 Metropolitan Counties with Least Democratic Gain (or Loss), 1920–1928   101

8 The Regional Pattern of California Politics: Democratic Percentages of the Two-Party Vote, 1920–1966   161

9 Regional Contrasts for Four Counties: Democratic Percentages of the Two-Party Vote, 1920–1966   162

10 Regional Basis of the California Right: Seven Elections   166

11 Regional Differences in Party Realignment, 1964 Compared with 1960   171

Tables

1   Populist Strength, Population Growth, and
Agricultural Wealth, 1892   11

2   Effects of Population Growth and Agricultural
Wealth on Populist Strength, 1894   12

3   Sources of Populist Strength   13

4   Ethnic Cleavages and the Major Party Vote   23

5   Voting Decline in California, 1880–1920   28

6   The Progressive Transformation   38

7   Correlations between Johnson's 1910 Primary
Vote and Demographic Characteristics   40

8   The Shifting Social Basis of Progressive Strength   41

9   Regional Shifts in Progressive Support   42

10   Class and Progressive Support in San Francisco   47

11   Wilson and the San Francisco Working Class,
1916   50

12   Johnson's Percentage Vote in San Francisco   73

13   Correlation Matrix: Johnson's San Francisco Vote   74

14   Johnson Vote and Prolabor Sentiment in San
Francisco   75

15 Correlation: Johnson, Wilson, La Follette   77
16 Correlation: Nativity, Foreign Born, and the
    Progressive Vote   78
17 Percentage Vote for Johnson in Los Angeles
    County   81
18 Ethnic Background, Los Angeles County (in
    percentages)   83
19 Democratic Vote in Eleven Metropolitan Counties,
    1916–1928   93
20 Republican Percentage of Total Vote Cast by
    Assembly Districts in San Francisco, 1920–1928   94
21 Correlation Coefficients between County
    Percentages in Votes for President, 1884–1940   104
22 Reference Factor Loadings in the California
    Democratic Party   106
23 Prohibition and the Democratic Party Vote   116
24 Distribution of Democratic Presidential Votes,
    1928 and 1932   119
25 Regional Contributions to Increase in 'Total
    Vote and Increase in Democratic Vote, 1928
    and 1932   121
26 Correlation Matrix: Democratic Party Presidential
    Vote, 1932–1952   122
27 Regional Distribution of Democratic Presidential
    Vote, 1928–1948   123
28 Regional Distribution of Votes and Contributions,
    1934 Democratic Primary   131
29 Regional Distribution of the Vote for Governor,
    1934   132
30 Comparison of Democratic Vote, General
    Elections, 1932 and 1934   133
31 Regional Distribution of Democratic
    Gubernatorial Vote, 1922–1942   135

32 Correlation Matrix: California Democratic
   Governor's Vote   136
33 Correlation Matrix: California Republican
   Governor's Vote   137
34 Ecological Factors and the Democratic Party Vote   138
35 Relation of Democratic Presidential and
   Gubernatorial Vote, 1932–1952   140
36 Regional Distribution of Democratic
   Gubernatorial Vote, 1950–1966   141
37 Percentage of California Voters Registered
   Democratic   143
38 Intercorrelations among Counties in California
   Presidential Elections, 1936–1960   167
39 Intercorrelations among Right-Wing Causes and
   Republican Candidates   168
40 Right-Wing Sentiment: Southern California and
   the Bay Area   172
41 The Ethnic Basis of the California Right   174

Preface

WE aim, in this book, to continue the tradition of electoral analysis established by the late V. O. Key, Jr. Key's model of "critical elections," originally presented in a seminal article in 1955, provided both the inspiration and organizing principle for our study. Since each of the six chapters that follow makes use of the critical election concept, let us begin with Key's definition:

> Even the most fleeting inspection of American elections suggests the existence of a category of elections in which voters are, at least from impressionistic evidence, unusually deeply concerned, in which the extent of electoral involvement is relatively quite high, and in which the decisive results of the voting reveal a sharp alternation of the pre-existing cleavages within the electorate. Moreover, and perhaps this is the truly differentiating characteristic of this sort of election, the realignment made manifest in the voting in such elections seems to persist for several succeeding elections. All these characteristics cumulate to the conception of an election type in which the depth and intensity of electoral involvement are high, in which more or less profound readjustments

occur in the relations of power within the community, and in which new and durable electoral groupings are formed.[1]

Key's own work, and that of other scholars, indicated that deep voter involvement, durable party realignment, and major shifts in party strength often did not occur once and for all in a single election. The focus broadened, as in our study, to critical periods extending over two or more contests.[2] Even as modified, however, the model of critical realignment focuses unequivocally upon the factor of political change and permits a viable measure of that change in relation to two crucial variables—time and space.

A mutual concern about questions of political and social change brought about collaboration in this book of two authors from different academic disciplines: one, a political scientist, believes that contemporary scholarship in his field tends to ignore unduly the time factor, and the other, a historian, believes that political studies in his discipline have lacked systematic precision and methodological rigor.

This book, however, is designed not merely to test the application of a method. It is rather a book about California politics. California, now the most populous state in the union, exercises a powerful influence upon national politics. The historical development of California political patterns thus assumes far more than local importance. Again, as Key reminded us, contemporary political behavior frequently is determined by the political traditions of an area and reflects decisions made in critical periods long past.[3] In this sense, we are investigating California voting patterns of the past, the better to understand voting behavior in the present.

Like every other scholar who has studied California history, we are struck by the often capricious nature of political change in the state. But mercurial, short-term fluctuations often have lasting electoral effects. This book will focus upon four crucial periods of electoral realignment: (1) The election of 1896. The particular appeals of Bryan and populism reconditioned voting allegiances and set a pattern of alignment relegating the Democratic party to a minority status that prevailed until the depression of the 1930s. (2) The Progressive era. This political reform movement was confined largely to the Republican party and has been viewed by historians as smoothly contoured in its orientation and political support from its origin to its demise. But we find in California a significant realignment of progressivism in midstream that had important repercussions upon major party support and future politics in the state. (3) The 1930s. In this period the depression transformed the moribund Democrats into a majority party that was capable of mustering huge majorities for presidential candidates, but paradoxically was ineffective at the state level. Chapter 5 deals with the importance of this 1930s realignment, but nonetheless we discover important premonitions of the new Democratic constituency in the hitherto neglected elections of 1916 and 1924. Finally (4), we turn to a reorientation still in progress that may have as far-reaching significance as those of 1896 and the depression. Chapter 6 argues that right-wing political appeals in southern California produced a critical realignment starting in the 1960s.

Key, in stressing both critical realignments and the role of political tradition, sought to reemphasize the political determinants of electoral choice. Attention to history, he argued, suggested the reasonableness of political preferences that seemed irrational when taken out of historical context. Key's work became the major defense of the mass electorate's political sensitivity. Over the short term, Key showed, voters responded to the major issues of a campaign.[4] Over the long term they made deeper party political commitments during critical periods and tended to follow them in quieter times. Much of the California historical pattern fits the Key scheme. Individual elections find voters responding to single dominant issues. Durable realignments in major-party support are associated with the rise of ideologically intense third parties or social movements within a major party—populism, the Progressive movement, Upton Sinclair's "End Poverty in California" movement of the 1930s, the New Deal, and the contemporary right wing. A routinized party loyalty thus is periodically upset by infusions from outside the traditional party structure.

But California politics is more issue-dominated than even Key, attending to more stable states, would lead us to believe. Single, divisive issues (for example, prohibition) have affected voting behavior more spectacularly than in states where party loyalties run deeper. Even more striking, the contrast between nonideological traditions and temporary, issue-based sources of change is too straightforward for the California case. In southern California the dominant political tradition itself is an ideologically sensitive one. The right-wing tradition in southern California is by no means the only cause of California political volatility, but it is the factor with perhaps the most lasting and nationally significant impact. Hence in our final chapter we review California electoral patterns from the perspective of southern California, show how its politics created the latest California critical realignment, and investigate the traditional and continuing appeal of right-wing political symbols in the southern part of the state.

Often in the pages that follow we find ourselves in disagreement with previous interpretations. For this reason we assert our conviction that to disagree is not to disparage. We are able to challenge the conclusions of others only because these authors have had the imagination and insight to generate meaningful hypotheses and in so doing provoke further investigation. Our own contribution, which we offer in the same spirit, centers upon the use of quantitative data and statistical techniques. Words of explanation and caution are necessary at the outset.

Often it was desirable to summarize the relationship between voting units (e.g., counties) in two elections or between voting units and demographic measures. Extensive use therefore was made of correlation coefficients; these compare the support for a given candidate or issue in each voting unit with the support for another candidate, measure, or demographic variable. For example, Hiram Johnson's vote in the 1910 gubernatorial primary ranged from 25 percent in tiny Alpine County to 81 percent in Tulare, the percentage of native white stock from 28 percent in San Francisco to 72 percent in Modoc. The correlation between Johnson's vote and the percentage of native white stock indicates the extent to which, the more native the county, the more it favored Johnson.[5] A reasonably high correlation is evidence that Johnson received native, as opposed to immigrant, support.

Other methods, explained as they occur in the text, were also employed to summarize and analyze the mass of data. But as most of the voting units used here are large and heterogeneous, conclusions about the behavior of individuals based on aggregrate data must be drawn with caution. It is important to be sensitive to other factors that may contaminate an apparent statistical relationship between the vote for two candidates or between an election and a demographic measure. Where smaller and more homogeneous units are analyzed, as in Chapter 3, there can be more confidence in the relationships found. Nevertheless, even on the county level the overall patterns, shifts, and relationships are revealing.

This book is a joint effort in the sense that its authors have shared methodological assumptions and materials and consulted constantly in its preparation. Each chapter, however, is the work of one author, and he alone bears responsibility for its strengths and weaknesses. Mr. Rogin is the author of Chapters 1, 2, and 6; Mr. Shover of Chapters 3, 4, and 5.

NOTES

1. V. O. Key, Jr., "A Theory of Critical Elections," *Journal of Politics* 17 (February, 1955): 3-4.
2. Duncan MacRae, Jr., and James A. Meldrum, "Critical Elections in Illinois, 1888-1958," *American Political Science Review* 54 (September, 1960): 669-683; Gerald Pomper, "A Classification of Presidential Elections," *Journal of Politics* 29 (August, 1967): 535-566.
3. V. O. Key, Jr., and Frank Munger, "Social Determinism and Electoral Decision: The Case of Indiana," in *American Voting Behavior*, ed. Eugene Burdick and Arthur J. Brodbeck, pp. 281-299.
4. V. O. Key, Jr., *The Responsible Electorate.*
5. Correlations vary on a scale from 1.00 to —1.00. The higher the number, the more one variable (e.g., election or demographic characteristic) explains the other; the sign (plus or minus) indicates whether the two variables are high in the same counties and low in the same counties, or whether one is high where the other is low. In the example in the text, the correlation of $.52^2$ means that 26 percent (52^2) of the Johnson county-by-county vote can be explained by nativity. Multiple correlations, used here occasionally, permit one to calculate the total effect of two or more variables on an election. For a fuller, mathematical discussion of correlation coefficients in nontechnical language, see V. O. Key, Jr., *A Primer of Statistics for Political Scientists*, pp. 78-153.

Acknowledgments

I~ the course of this study we have incurred numerous obligations to friends and colleagues, who from time to time have encouraged or obstructed, simplified or complicated our efforts. Mr. Shover wishes to acknowledge, in particular, his debt to Professor Ralph Goldman of San Francisco State College, Professor Charles Mayo of the University of Southern California, Professor Samuel T. McSeveney of Brooklyn College, and to students in the graduate seminars in California politics and progressivism at San Francisco State College. Mr. Rogin is indebted to Denis Coughlin and Jeanne Nienaber for statistical assistance, to Sheila Stern Many for bibliographic help, and to Robert E. Burke, Jerry Mandel, Samuel T. McSeveney, Michael Parker, John H. Schaar, James T. Siegel, and Aaron B. Wildavsky for helpful readings of portions of the manuscript. Deborah Rogin, encouraging throughout, helped suggest the formulations in Chapter 6.

In addition, this study was assisted by generous grants to Mr. Shover by the Social Science Research Council, the National Science Foundation, and the Faculty Research Committee of San Francisco State College and to Mr. Rogin by the Institute of Governmental Studies, University of California at Berkeley, and by a Rockefeller Foundation grant to the Department of Political Science, University of California at Berkeley.

Finally, we wish to thank the editors of *The Journal of American History, Western Political Quarterly, Pacific Northwest Quarterly,* and *Labor History* for permission to reproduce chapters which appeared in slightly altered form in their respective journals.

POLITICAL CHANGE
IN CALIFORNIA

1

California Populism and the "System of 1896"

A TWO-PARTY tradition has dominated American politics since the early days of the republic. Normal times see relatively stable competition between the two major parties. Substantial continuity in party program is matched by stable party loyalties at the grass roots. One party can usually be called the "majority party," although over long periods of time the parties often approach a fairly equal distribution of electoral strength.

But periodic political transformations occur within the broad confines of two-party conflict. These "critical periods," as V. O. Key called them, upset party normality. Politics looks very different during and after these periods from how it looked before. Critical periods call forth heightened political interest and political conflict at all levels of the society. New issues become central to party competition, creating durable shifts in party allegiance at the grass roots. The balance of power between the major parties changes, sometimes radically. Third parties, relegated to an insignificant role in normal times, are often crucial in reorienting the issues and constituencies of major-party politics.[1]

The significance of these critical periods is not confined to party politics. The critical period of the 1850s and 1860s coincided with the Civil War; the depression and the New Deal gave the critical period of 1928-1936 its importance. Since the forces bringing these transformations left permanent marks deep in American society, we easily remember the critical periods they created. But the 1890s was also a critical period; perhaps since the forces that created it lost rather than won, it has a less secure place in historical memories. The aim here is to analyze the impact of the 1890s on voting patterns in California. To give the California story its true significance, we must first reexamine the 1896 national election from the "critical period" perspective.

The Critical Election of 1896

The year 1896 marks a watershed in American politics. Mere handfuls of votes had decided national elections for the previous twenty years. Focused on politics by ethnic loyalties, patterns of settlement, Civil War divisions, and perhaps the closeness of the electoral contests, most citizens voted in both presidential and off-year elections.[2] Partisan loyalties were intense, and few voters strayed from their traditional party ties. Those who went to the polls usually marked the straight party ticket, registering a choice from the top to the bottom of the ballot.

In the formal sense, this was a democratic system; the overwhelming majority of male citizens participated, through voting, in a fiercely competitive politics. But this competitive, democratic politics increasingly became a game in which the real social issues of the day were ignored. The "bloody shirt," the tariff, and civil service reform dominated political rhetoric, and corruption permeated political action. Although political traditions were alive for the electorate, they had little relevance to contemporary social and economic developments. Serious social grievances found expression only outside the major parties. Among workers, and in the cities, the major forms of protest were nonpolitical; strikes and urban turmoil marked the twenty years prior to the Bryan campaign.[3] Protest took a more overtly political form in rural areas; a series of short-lived third party revolts culminated in the 1890s with the Populist crusade. The Populist party scored substantial electoral successes in 1890, 1892, and 1894 and mobilized enormous, intense, grass-roots participation in the South and the trans-Mississippi West.

In 1896, major-party politics sought to incorporate substantial social discontent for the first time since the Civil War. With the Populist-Democratic fusion, the social crises entered the major-party system; the results were disastrous for both. Traditional party allegiances, which heretofore had provided political meaning for voters, were shattered. The Democrats, defeated by the largest landslide in a generation, became a national minority party until the 1929 crash; the party became moribund in many states as well. The new party loyalties forged in the Bryan campaign endured for decades, but they reached far less deeply than the old loyalties into the population. Voting participation declined precipitously, never to reach in the twentieth century the heights sustained in the nineteenth. Of those who did vote, more split their tickets, changed parties from one election to another, and failed to vote for all the offices at stake. The interest generated by presidential contests sustained itself less than previously in off-year elections.

At the same time, the movements of radical social protest never recovered from the 1896 defeat. The efforts to remake industrializing America in the image of the pre-Civil War, egalitarian society had failed. Bryan's rhetoric attracted some farmers and native-stock Americans, particularly west of the Mississippi, for whom that Tocquevillian image was real. But it repelled eastern workers, Catholics, and immigrants. After Bryan's defeat, workers and farmers adjusted to a system dominated by giant corporations and, much later, big government. Reform politics in the Progressive period was led by middle-class politicians, not dirt farmers or industrial workers. Workers and farmers, particularly the latter, often supported Progressive reforms, but these were adjustments in the industrial capitalist system rather than assaults upon it. In any case, they left large portions of the electorate uninvolved in politics. The decline in voting participation reflected the irrelevance of the "system of 1896" to the concerns of many rural residents and urban poor. The old party traditions that made politics meaningful had weakened, and the effort to refocus party politics around contemporary social issues had failed. For many voters after 1896, politics was not as central as it had been before. In this sense, and as measured by voting participation, political alienation had increased markedly.[4]

The system of 1896 thus substituted single party dominance for a competitive, two-party politics. Business interests, if they did not rule directly, still did not face the radical social challenge of the 1880s and 1890s. For these political and social reasons, the system involved fewer citizens than had heretofore exercised political options.

Electoral data and more traditional historical evidence support the broad outlines of the picture sketched here. But many details, particularly on a regional level, remain to be filled in. Who supported the social uprisings of the 1870s,

1880s, and 1890s, and why? In particular, who were the Populists, and who were their opponents? To what extent did support and opposition to populism determine the 1896 major-party realignment? What kinds of voters deserted the Democrats to support McKinley? How extensive geographically was the impact of the 1896 campaign in (1) durably realigning major-party support, (2) significantly weakening the Democratic party, and (3) reducing the levels and stability of voting participation? Substantial evidence has accumulated concerning Populist support in the Midwest and South and the impact of the Bryan campaign on states east of the Mississippi.[5] But we know little about developments west of the Rockies.

The present chapter examines electoral patterns in California from the 1880s to 1910. Given its reputation for uniqueness, California participation in the 1896 realignment would suggest further the pervasiveness of the national pattern. Perhaps, also, from the peculiarities of California voting, we can gain some clues about the special characteristics of politics in the Golden State.

California Populism

The Populist movement was the most serious political manifestation of the post-Civil War social crisis. Historians agree that populism was a response to the economic and social dislocation accompanying industrialization. But they disagree on its character. For many, populism was a nativist, fundamentalist rebellion against an increasingly cosmopolitan industrial society. Accordingly, native American countryfolk, nostalgic for an idealized rural past, created the Populist movement. Other historians see populism as an outcry of impoverished farmers against economic adversity and social and political isolation. Instead of emphasizing the status frustrations and ethnic homogeneity of the Populists, these writers look for common economic grievances among the movement's supporters.[6] Electoral evidence alone cannot resolve the meaning of populism in California, but it can indicate who the Populists were.

California populism was weaker than its counterparts on the Great Plains and in much of the South. Populists garnered only 9.4 percent of the 1892 presidential vote, their smallest percentage west of the Mississippi. The vote for governor in 1894 went up to 18 percent, still among the smallest totals in the South and the trans-Mississippi West, although the vote for lesser state offices was considerably higher.[7] California lacked the grinding poverty and authoritarian, personal exploitation that characterized the South. Unlike the other states of the trans-Mississippi West, it had been settled for well over a generation by 1890. The flourishing, established metropolis of San Francisco contained 300,000 people, one-fourth of the state's population; the Great Plains had no such cities. Indeed, California was the seventh most urban state in the country. Moreover, the gold rush boom had petered out by the 1880s, and many mining counties in the northeastern mountains actually lost population during the decade. This contrasts with the population influx on the Great Plains and throughout the West.

But California had its own new frontiers in the 1880s. The land boom in the south, ushered in by the completion of the Sante Fe Railroad in 1886, brought thousands of migrants and skyrocketing real estate values. Like cities further east, such as Wichita, Los Angeles grew up overnight and fell overnight into panic when the land boom collapsed in 1888. California also had a rural frontier; the population of many farming counties increased dramatically between 1880 and 1890. By the latter year, the state was second in the nation in the production of wheat and first in the production of all grains. Much California wheat was produced on gigantic farms rather than on the family operations characterizing the Great Plains. But California also had its small farmers, suffering like other frontier farmers from drought, high mortgages, railroad exploitation, and glutted markets.[8]

Nevertheless, concludes Donald E. Walters, an historian of California populism, the state's political rebelliousness was less a product of poverty than of the restlessness associated with feverish wealth and its exploitation.[9] California populism was indeed rather different from its counterparts on the Great Plains. Its "restlessness" reflected itself in early Populist southern strength and in general support in counties where the population had grown rapidly between 1880 and 1890. In addition, the movement lacked appeal to the foreign-born, and there was a degree of nativism among some Populist leaders. Elements of California populism, moreover, had ties to the anti-Catholic American Protective Association. Perhaps this also reflected the rootlessness of the movement and its lack of grounding in concrete economic grievances. (On the Great Plains, the APA was anti-Populist, allied with local Republicans. Scandinavians, whose support of populism in the Dakotas, Kansas, and Nebraska helped prevent nativism there, were absent in California.)[10]

California populism, however, still had a strong economic component. The party ran best in the poor counties of the state but worst in the wealthy ones. Moreover, socioeconomic factors help explain Populist strength in expanding counties and weakness in declining ones. Let us examine the impact of population growth, nativity, and agricultural wealth on the pattern of Populist support.

CONTINUITIES IN POPULIST STRENGTH

The boom counties of central and southern California were the center of Populist strength in 1892. In these eleven counties, the population increased between 65 percent and 306 percent from 1880 to 1890; nine of them, along with four other counties which had gained population, made up the top quartile of Populist strength.[11] The twelve mining counties that lost population between 1880 and 1890 were beyond their boom days. Many people attracted by the mining boom had gone elsewhere; the remaining inhabitants gave little support to the Populists, who obtained more than 7 percent of the vote in only one county. The boom counties averaged 17.4 percent Populist, and those that had lost population, 5.4 percent. Throughout the state, the greater the increase in population, the greater the Populist vote (see Tables 1 and 3).[12]

Not all counties with equal rates of population change behaved identically, however. For one thing, the foreign-born, concentrated in some mining counties and in the area around San Francisco, were generally unsympathetic to populism. Of the ten counties with the highest percentages of foreign-born in the state, five were in the bottom quartile of Populist strength in 1892, and three more were in the bottom half.

There were still sharp differences in Populist strength among many native-stock counties with similar rates of population change. Examining Table 1, we can compare counties similar in population change, but different in Populist strength. Table 1 gives the average value of farm products per farm entered for individual counties, or averaged for groups of counties of similar population growth and Populist strength. As the table reveals, wealth held down the Populist vote; generally the more Populist the county, the poorer it

TABLE 1
Populist Strength, Population Growth, and Agricultural Wealth, 1892

Percentage Populist

Percentage Populist	Entries (average value of farm products per farm, $)
27.5	574
23.5	1451 1437
17–21	987 1115 1678 2124 1323
14.5–16	1034
11.5–14	766 857
9–11	2907 1541
8	697 1594
2.5–5	2326 2295 1253 1985
.5–3.5	1663

Percentage population growth

Percentage population growth
—9.5 to —26
—1 to 8
8— to 26
24— to 28
38— to 49
51 to 66
65— to 66
76
99
118
228
238— to 246
307

NOTE: Table entries indicate average value farm products per farm (in dollars) for county or group of counties.

was, particularly in comparison to other counties of similar population growth.

The poor counties also supported populism more than the wealthy ones in 1894.[13] Figure 2 reveals the highest Populist counties bunched among the poorest in the state. Populism was strong in only one of the ten wealthiest counties, the only one with a substantial population increase between 1880 and 1890.[14] Similarly, the most Populist of the poor counties had grown rapidly; the least Populist had not. In the nine Populist counties, the median population increase was 51 percent, and only one county had lost population. The median increase in the seven anti-Populist poor counties was—13 percent, and only one county had gained population (see circled dots in Figure 1). Table 2, which compares wealthy and poor counties, expanding and declining ones, presents the same picture.

TABLE 2

Effects of Population Growth and Agricultural Wealth
on Populist Strength, 1894

Population Growth[b]	Wealthy[a]	Poor
Expanding	32.4%	29.7%
Stable	13.5%	23.7%
Declining	—	14.6%

[a] Wealthy counties range from $2,600 to $5,200 in the value of farm products per farm; poor counties range from $491 to $1,115.

[b] Population growth in the expanding counties ranges from 27.8% to 306%. (The median among the seven poor expanding counties is 51.3%.) The nine stable wealthy counties range from population decreases of —4.2% to increases of 27.8%; the median is 13.4%. Population changes in the three stable poor counties range from 6.1% to 13.4%. The seven poor counties losing population range from —2.7% to —25.6%; the median is —13.6%.

As in 1892, counties with high percentages of foreign-born gave little support to populism. Again, five of the ten counties with the most foreign-born were in the bottom quartile of Populist strength; three more were in the bottom half. Moreover, ethnicity explains the contrasts in Populist strength among six counties of middling wealth (see circled dots in Figure 1). The three Populist counties averaged 16.6 percent foreign-born. The three anti-Populist counties, among the ten most foreign-born in the state, averaged 31.4 percent.

California populism was thus a peculiar mixture of the midwestern and southern movements. Like southern populism, it was strong in poor, native-stock counties.[15] Like midwestern populism, it was strong along the settled frontier. Table 3 sums up, through the use of correlation coefficients, the impact of wealth, population growth, and nativity on Populist strength.

TABLE 3
Sources of Populist Strength

Populist Strength	Population Growth	Agricultural Poverty	Native-Born White	Multiple Correlation
1892	.590	.344	.290	.689
1894	.354	.291	.360	.539

Populist strength in poor counties has the obvious economic explanation. Native American support for populism lends credence to interpretations of the movement that stress its ethnic character. But Populist roots in expanding counties are less easy to understand. In part, frontier populism had an economic basis in undiversified agriculture, hard-pressed by falling crop prices, disease, and drought. Frontier farmers

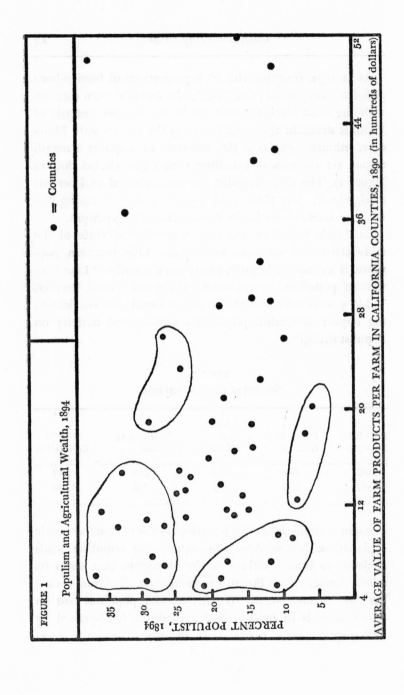

FIGURE 1

Populism and Agricultural Wealth, 1894

● = Counties

PERCENT POPULIST, 1894

AVERAGE VALUE OF FARM PRODUCTS PER FARM IN CALIFORNIA COUNTIES, 1890 (in hundreds of dollars)

lacked resources on which to fall back during hard times. In addition, there were few stable traditions or elites on the frontier to inhibit third party protest. Settlers had come west with high expectations; confronted with adversity, their disappointment could take a political form.[16]

SOUTHERN CALIFORNIA AND THE BOOMER MENTALITY: 1892

The strength of frontier populism has been attributed often to dashed hopes, artificially high to begin with. In southern California, the cycle of optimism and despair was particularly powerful. Frenzied boosterism dominated the settlement of southern California, and the collapse of the land boom in 1888 plunged the area into panic.[17] California populism sprang from this soil.

Populism literally had originated in southern California, organized in the central and southern counties by followers of Edward Bellamy. After publishing *Looking Backward* (1888), Bellamy had formed Nationalist clubs to put its program into effect. Los Angeles was the home of the most flourishing Nationalist movement in the country. Like Bellamy himself, these utopian reformers, with their dream of a classless, conflict-free society, supported populism. The urban, southern California Nationalists were the first organizers of Farmers' Alliances; Nationalists dominated the early days of populism; and the Nationalist movement itself soon disappeared into the People's party. These Nationalists gave California populism an urban, middle-class, "theoretical" flavor, which it lacked elsewhere in the country.[18] They suited the politics of frustrated dreams endemic to southern California. As in northern California, back-country farmers supported populism more than town dwellers; but populism in 1892 also seems to have attracted significant nonfarm southern support.[19] This again was peculiar to California. Thus, in addition to its agrarian roots, California populism grew from the southern California boomer mentality.

By 1894, however, southern California was no longer a center of Populist strength.[20] For one thing the movement had had time to expand beyond its central and southern origins. Second, the south had not been hit so hard as the rest of the state by the 1893 depression. Finally, in the intense, highly personal, factional strife of populism, its southern leader had been expelled for supporting the Democratic senatorial aspirant. The south was poorly represented at the 1894 Populist convention, and only one Populist candidate for statewide office was a southerner.[21] Thus populism lacked staying power in the south. Driven to the party by the panic of 1888, the south did not seem to be a natural home for left-wing, economic protest movements. One is reminded of the short-lived strength of Upton Sinclair's EPIC in the south during the 1930s depression and of southern opposition to left-wing protest in less desperate times.

POPULISM IN THE HINTERLANDS: 1894

The Populist center of gravity in 1894 moved out of the south and into the outlying, northern, Protestant rural counties. Part of the shift was religion-based. Catholics comprised more than 15 percent of the population in eight counties; five were in the bottom quartile of increases in Populist strength. Catholics were unsympathetic to populism even in states where the American Protective Association was anti-Populist. In California, APA influence in the Populist movement grew between 1892 and 1894, and Populist rhetoric occasionally had a nativist flavor. The antiforeign tradition of California reform, rooted in hostility to Orientals among workers and small farmers, may have played a role here.[22]

The APA most often infiltrated the Populist movement in rural areas, and its activities may account for Populist increases in some outlying northern counties. But the Populist economic appeal was probably also important. Farmers were a strong majority in six of the counties with the biggest Populist increases between 1892 and 1894—all outlying northern and central counties with virtually no Catholics. No such counties were in the bottom quartile of Populist increases.[23] And while populism gained on the farms, it barely held its own in the six largest cities of the state. Only Sacramento was in the top quartile of Populist increases. Alameda (Oakland), San Joaquin (Stockton), Santa Clara (San Jose), and Los Angeles were all in the fourth quartile, and San Francisco was at the bottom of the third.

Thus populism by 1894 was shifting to the rural, Protestant hinterlands of California. Never strong among the foreign-born or the wealthy, populism now more than ever was a movement of impoverished, rural, frontier Californians of old-American stock. The question was whether it could attract working-class support so essential in an industrializing country to its success.

POPULISM AND ORGANIZED LABOR

Although populism supported the demands of organized labor, it had no success in the working-class centers of the East. However, railway workers and miners further West often did support the party. When the Pullman boycott erupted in 1894, Populists gave the strikers strong support. This was particularly significant in California, since working-class San Francisco had no counterpart in Populist states further east. The

California Populists worked closely with the strikers, and the San Francisco Populist paper became the official West Coast organ of the American Railway Union. The party sought labor support in other ways as well, nominating a carpenter for lieutenant governor in 1894 and a printing pressman for secretary of state.[24]

These efforts had considerable success. Populist weakness in 1894 in cities other than San Francisco need not indicate working-class opposition; most of these cities were trading centers with little developed working class. Urban antipathy to populism reflected country-town, not farmer-worker, opposition. San Francisco, the only major city in the state, was a center of railway workers, teamsters, and skilled tradesmen. These workers were uninterested in populism in 1892, but under the impact of the Pullman strike and Populist prolabor activity, the party made substantial gains in working-class districts in 1894. Its gubernatorial candidate ran badly, but other Populists on the state ticket did much better. Populist candidates for the state assembly garnered a total of 23 percent of the vote in the working-class districts of the city, more than twice their showing among the middle class. Moreover, one of the two Populist state assemblymen elected in 1894 was from a San Francisco working-class district.[25] Populist strength in working-class San Francisco did not match the successes in a good many farming counties. Nevertheless, by 1894, California populism had incorporated some of the urban, working-class discontent that had culminated in the Pullman boycott.

Tinged at its inception with southern California boomerism, populism was infected at its height with the nativist taint of nineteenth-century California reform. Nevertheless, the Populists had built an economic base among poor, frontier farmers and had made inroads in working-class districts as well. The movement thus represented politically weak social groups with substantial grievances. Seeking political power, these groups transformed the character of major-party politics in unintended ways.

The Transformation of Party Politics

The 1896 presidential contest, the first to focus around the social conflicts accompanying industrialization, transformed California major-party politics at the grass roots. We shall show that the election created a new, lasting pattern of major-party support, influenced substantially by Populist strengths and weaknesses, and signifying the decline of competitive, two-party politics and the atrophy of political consciousness among substantial numbers of citizens.

PARTY REALIGNMENT

When V. O. Key first developed the "critical election" concept, he made it operational in fairly simple terms. In a critical election, more voters than usual changed party allegiances and retained the new loyalties for several succeeding elections. We shall examine other consequences of the 1890s critical period, but first it is necessary to show, in Key's original meaning of the concept, that a critical election occurred in California in 1896. To demonstrate the critical election, we are comparing the counties with the greatest Democratic gains from 1888 to 1896 to those with the greatest Democratic losses. We have plotted the average vote in these two sets of ten counties for the presidential elections of 1884 to 1908. If the two lines diverge widely from each other at any point, like the opening of a scissors, and the divergence perpetuates itself, then a critical election has occurred.[26]

Consider first the Democratic vote. The counties with the greatest Democratic gains were actually more Republican in 1888 than the counties with the greatest Democratic losses. In 1896, the two groups of counties dramatically shifted places (see Figure 2); although the split between them narrowed thereafter, it remained clearly significant.[27] An examination of the Republican vote, however, shows a somewhat different picture. The counties becoming Democratic had deserted the Republican party in 1892, even though, as the graph of the Democratic vote reveals, they did not become Democratic until 1896.

An analysis of the critical election by another method reveals the same pattern. We have obtained correlation matrices of the county percentages for President for both major parties from 1884 to 1944. By an elementary form of cluster analysis, we may discover which groups of elections are most highly intercorrelated, and where breaks between groups of elections occur. For the Democratic vote, this method locates one cluster composed of the elections of 1884, 1888, and 1892, and another for the elections of 1896-1908. For the Republican vote the election of 1892 shows up in both the pre- and post-1896 clusters.[28] Again the critical change in Republican support came in 1892, but the counties that had left the GOP in 1892 did not become strongly Democratic until 1896.

POPULISM AND THE CRITICAL ELECTION

What happened is obvious. Several Republican counties gave the Populists support in 1892[29] and then entered the Democratic party to vote for Bryan. Thus, the major difference between the counties gaining Democratic strength in 1896 and those losing strength was the percentage polled by the Populists. The counties becoming Republican averaged 4.8 per cent Populist in 1892, those becoming Democratic 14.2 per cent; the

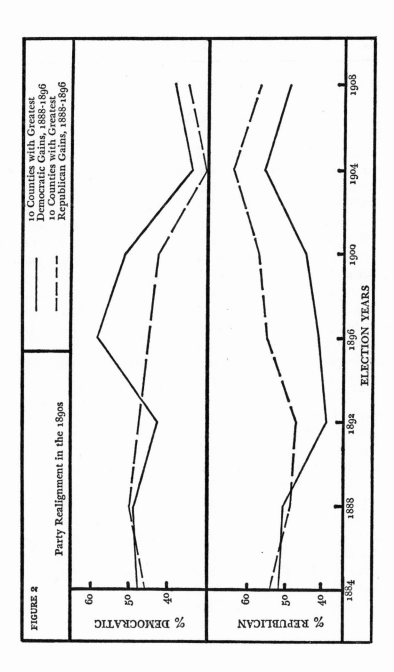

FIGURE 2

Party Realignment in the 1890s

10 Counties with Greatest Democratic Gains, 1888-1896
10 Counties with Greatest Republican Gains, 1888-1896

% DEMOCRATIC

% REPUBLICAN

ELECTION YEARS

1884 1888 1892 1896 1900 1904 1908

60 50 40

averages for 1894 were 12.9 per cent and 27.8 per cent, respectively.

Does this mean simply that the social forces mobilized by populism entered the Democratic party in 1896, while those it antagonized went Republican? From what we know about Bryan and the Democrats, we might expect the story to be more complex. While the Populists offered a broad program of social and economic reform, Bryan was far more moderate. He ignored most of the Populist program and flavor, concentrating to Populist dismay on the single issue of free silver. Bryan's evangelical rhetoric lacked the Populist radical economic edge. An aspiring Democratic politician, he was far more in the political mainstream than the Populists.[30] We might expect, therefore, that the critical election of 1896 focused more around the ethnic character of populism and less around its economic aspects—that it fit more into the ethnic traditions of major-party politics than into the economic, radical egalitarianism of third-party social protest.

The evidence from California sustains this view. We have found Populist strength among poor, native-stock, and Protestant counties and among those gaining population. Populists ran poorly in wealthy, foreign-stock, and Catholic counties and in those losing population. Table 4 contrasts each kind of county with its counterpart (poor counties with wealthy, Protestant with Catholic, etc.) in terms of their support for the Republican party before and after 1896. The table reveals that economic indicators best distinguished Populist from anti-Populist counties. But neither poverty nor population growth contributed to the pattern of stable party realignment.[31] Instead, shifts in party support were related to the ethnic variables, as Catholic and foreign-stock counties moved into the GOP far more than Protestant and native-stock counties. The major-party political system thus found the ethnic cleav-

TABLE 4

Ethnic Cleavages and the Major Party Vote

Counties[c]	Popu-list 1894[a]	Repub-lican 1888[a]	Repub-lican 1900[a]	Polari-zation[b]
Catholic/ non-Catholic	4.0	1.2	6.8	5.6
Foreign/ native	8.6	7.0	12.7	5.7
Popula-tion loss/ gain	10.4	—0.9	—0.3	0.6
Rich/ poor	9.0	—3.5	—2.9	0.6

[a] Cell entries indicate difference between Populist or Republican vote for each group of counties (e.g., Catholic counties in 1888 averaged 1.2% more Republican than non-Catholic counties).

[b] Cell entries indicate extent to which counties were more polarized between the major parties in 1900 than in 1888.

[c] County composition is as follows: ten with highest and ten with lowest percentages of Catholics; ten with highest and ten with lowest percentages of foreign born; eleven counties which lost population, and ten with more than a 60% population increase (since Orange County did not exist in 1888, it was omitted); ten richest agricultural counties (excluding metropolitan Sacramento and San Francisco), and ten agriculturally poorest counties (excluding poor counties which lost population).

ages associated with California social protest more congenial than economic-based discontent.

Other methods also place ethnic cleavages at the center of the party realignment. Figure 3 shows foreign-stock counties moving into the Republican party in 1896, while native counties actually became more Democratic. Unlike those in some eastern states, Democrats in California had always been stronger in native than in foreign-stock counties. The ethnic cleavage became truly pronounced in 1896 and remained greater in the first decade of the twentieth century than it had been in the 1880s.[32]

Prior to 1896, the statewide major-party vote had not been split along religious lines. In 1896, many Catholic Democrats deserted Bryan; the Democratic vote that year was correlated —.44 with the percentage of Catholics, and the correlations were —.39, —.37, and —.42 in the next three presidential elections.[33] Although the Populists had been opposed in strongly Catholic counties in 1894, the number of nonethnic factors influencing the vote kept the overall correlation between populism and Catholicism to —.11; as the economic variables became less significant in 1896, religion became more dominant.

THE DECLINE OF THE DEMOCRATS

The 1896 election seriously weakened the Democrats in other states and nationwide. Unfortunately for the party, the depression of 1893 occurred during a Democratic administration. In addition, Bryan's rural, provincial, Protestant appeal cost the Democrats necessary eastern, urban, minority-group support. The fusion ticket, however, almost carried California for Bryan and elected three of seven Congressmen. In 1902 and 1906, helped by grievances against the Southern Pacific Railroad, Democrats came close to winning the governorship.

Nevertheless, the party's overall competitive position had deteriorated seriously. Democrats had carried California in five of nine elections for president and governor from 1880 to 1896; six elections had been decided by less than 1 percent of the total vote. The Democrats lost every statewide election from 1898 to 1910, only one by less than 1 percent of the total vote. In the seven elections from 1880 to 1892, the Republicans had elected twenty-two Congressmen, the Democrats nineteen.

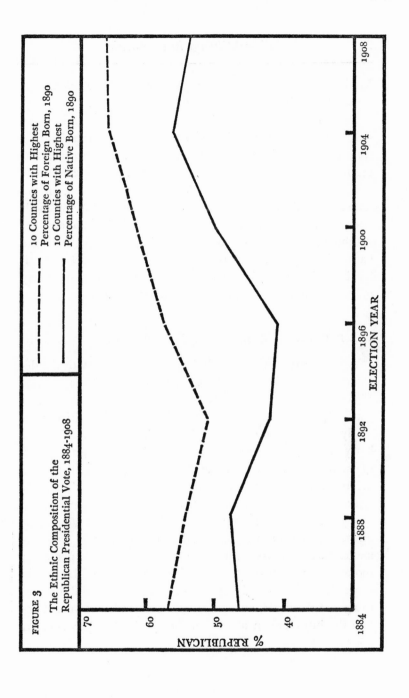

FIGURE 3

The Ethnic Composition of the
Republican Presidential Vote, 1884-1908

- - - - 10 Counties with Highest
Percentage of Foreign Born, 1890

——— 10 Counties with Highest
Percentage of Native Born, 1890

% REPUBLICAN

ELECTION YEAR

1884 1888 1892 1896 1900 1904 1908

40 50 60 70

In the seven elections from 1898 to 1910, the Republicans elected forty-nine Congressmen, the Democrats five.

Some writers have attributed Republican resurgence to southern California's rapidly expanding population migrating from the Republican Midwest.[34] This was surely a contributing factor, but the Democrats failed to carry San Francisco as well as the south in national elections from 1896 on. In the state as a whole, there was a sharp drop in Democratic strength after 1896, rather than a gradual, migration-influenced erosion. Although the Democrats had run well in the state in 1896, the national party thereafter was weak and without appeal. California could not maintain an isolated, competitive two-party politics when one party was crippled nationally.

THE DECLINE IN POLITICAL PARTICIPATION

Voting participation also declined dramatically with the defeat of Bryan and the Populists. Turnout in California prior to 1896 was substantially lower than in settled states back East. In part, population mobility may have made fewer citizens actually eligible to vote. In part, California may have lacked the party traditions that reached so deeply into the electorates of the stabler, eastern states. But if many citizens failed to vote before 1896, many more stayed home thereafter (see Table 5). Averaging 57.1 percent before 1888, turnout rose dramatically that year, reached a high-point of 68.6 percent in 1896, and remained high until 1900. From then on the decline was dramatic. Elections from 1888 to 1898 averaged 66.8 per cent; those from 1900 to 1910 averaged 53.2 percent.[35] The closely contested gubernatorial elections of 1902 and 1906 did nothing to reverse the trend, and most of the decline had occurred before the introduction of woman suffrage in 1912.[36] Moreover, one study has shown that turnout declined substantially in rural, native-stock counties as well as in urban ones.[37] Neither women nor immigrants, the usual culprits in discussions of American voting decline, explain the California figures. Many of the kinds of people who had been voting prior to the impact of the "System of 1896" did not bother to go to the polls thereafter.

Rates of drop-off from presidential to off-year elections also illustrate the declining interest in politics. Prior to 1896, more people usually voted in the off year than in the preceding presidential contest, reflecting the growing population of the state. But although the population expanded even more rapidly after 1896, drop-off also increased markedly (see Table 5). Since drop-off figures are based on actual numbers voting rather than estimates of eligible voters, their evidence about the impact of the 1896 reorientation is indeed persuasive.

The 1896 election thus affected California electoral politics in several fundamental ways. Bryan's campaign durably realigned the sources of support for the major parties. This realignment owed much to the Populist movement, but it exaggerated Populist ethnic cleavages at the expense of the movement's economic base. The farmer and worker social protest movements in the years prior to 1896 failed to transform major-party politics in their own image. Instead, voting turnout declined, party loyalty weakened, and the Democrats offered little sustained opposition to the Republicans.

Historians of California politics have long observed the weakness of both the Democrats and of party loyalty in the years before the New Deal. But they often attribute these consequences to progressivism rather than to the system of 1896. By concentrating all political conflicts within the GOP, the standard argument goes, progressivism made the Democratic

TABLE 5

Voting Decline in California, 1880-1920

Year	Percentage Turnout of Eligible Voters	Drop-Off (Decrease in Off Year as Percentage Previous Presidential Turnout)
1880	58.2	—0.3
1882	54.2	
1884	60.7	0.7
1886	56.7	
1888	68.5	—1.0
1890	65.4	
1892	67.0	
1894	67.9	—5.6
1896	68.6	
1898	63.4	3.9
1900	64.5	
1902	56.4	—0.6
1904	54.3	
1906	45.8	5.9
1908	51.4	
1910	46.9	2.6
1912	43.3	
1914	59.6	—37.6
1916	54.9	
1918	35.2	31.1
1920	45.2	

party irrelevant. Cross-filing, like the party primary, allegedly further weakened the Democrats; voters lost interest in an uncompetitive politics, and turnout declined.[38]

Progressivism, cross-filing, and primaries helped weaken further an already tottering Democratic party, although the decline in Democratic strength after World War I is a complicated story. But historians have generally overlooked the crucial deterioration in both the Democratic party and voting turnout in the first decade of the twentieth century. In this, California participated in the national trend.

It is true that in 1918 cross-filing eliminated the Democratic gubernatorial candidate, and two-thirds of the voters stayed home. But before America entered the war, progressivism had actually revitalized both the Democrats and voter interest in politics. Progressive politics created a voting realignment in 1916, which gave Democrat Woodrow Wilson California and the presidency.[39] Two years earlier, off-year apathy and woman suffrage notwithstanding, turnout was higher than in any election between 1902 and 1930 (see Table 5). We have characterized the system of 1896 by its failure to make politics relevant for many voters, either in terms of the traditional party conflicts of 1876-1892 or in terms of the social questions accompanying industrialization. The Progressives contested the election of 1914 as a third party; for a brief moment social questions came to the surface in a general election offering clear alternative choices. Turnout skyrocketed, and one has at least the sense, for the first time since 1896, that politics was central to the citizens of the state.

NOTES

1. See V. O. Key, Jr., "A Theory of Critical Elections," *Journal of Politics* 17 (February, 1955): 3–18; Charles Sellers, "The Equilibrium Cycle in Two-Party Politics," *Public Opinion Quarterly*, 29 (Spring, 1965): 16–37; Samuel Lubell, *The Future of American Politics*, pp. 1–7, 28–57, 198–226; Gerald Pomper, "A Classification of Presidential Elections," *Journal of Politics* 29 (August, 1967): 533-566.
2. National turnout averaged 78.5 percent in presidential elections from

1876–1898, 62.8 percent in off years. In eastern and midwestern states, the percentages were even higher: 93.1 percent in Indiana presidential elections, 90.4 percent in Iowa, and 87.9 percent in New York. In Michigan, Pennsylvania, and Ohio for roughly comparable periods, presidential turnout was 84.9 percent, 78.5 percent, and 92.2 percent; off-year turnout 74.9 percent, 69.3 percent, and 80.5 percent, respectively. See Walter Dean Burnham, "The Changing Shape of the American Political Universe," *American Political Science Review* 69 (March, 1965): 10, 13–19.

3. Among the highlights were the 1877 railroad strikes and riots; successful strikes by the half-million member Knights of Labor ten years later; the agitation surrounding the Haymarket Affair; the Homestead Steel Strike of 1892; and the 1894 Pullman boycott, in which Grover Cleveland called out troops to break the strike. Almost 300,000 men per year went on strike in the half decade following the 1893 depression. See Harold U. Faulkner, *Politics, Reform, and Expansion, 1890-1900*, p. 88 and passim; Henry David, *The History of the Haymarket Affair;* Norman O. Ware, *The Labor Movement in the United States, 1860-1895*.

4. Much of the argument here is based on these seminal articles: Burnham, "American Political Universe," pp. 10, 13–19, and Key, "Theory of Critical Elections," pp. 3–18, in addition to E. E. Schattschneider, "United States: The Functional Approach to Party Government," in *Modern Political Parties*, ed. Sigmund Neumann, pp. 197–206. See also Duncan MacRae, Jr., and James A. Meldrum, "Critical Elections in Illinois, 1888–1958," *American Political Science Review* 54 (September, 1960): 679–680; Lee Benson, "Research Problems in American Political Historiography," in *Common Frontiers of the Social Sciences*, ed. Mirra Komarovsky, pp. 165–170; Michael Paul Rogin, *The Intellectuals and McCarthy: The Radical Specter*, Chaps. 3–7.

5. On the Bryan election, see the sources cited in note 4. Populist strength is summarized and analyzed, with full citation of sources, in Rogin, *Intellectuals and McCarthy*, Chaps. 4–6, and J. Rogers Hollingsworth, "Populism: The Problem of Rhetoric and Reality," *Agricultural History* 39 (April, 1965): 81–85.

6. For a more complete discussion of the lively contemporary debate over populism, see Rogin, *Intellectuals and McCarthy*, Chaps. 4–6. The most interesting sources are Richard Hofstadter, *The Age of Reform;* Walter R. Nugent, *The Tolerant Populists;* Norman K. Pollack, *The Populist Response to Industrial America;* C. Vann Woodward, "The Populist Heritage and the Intellectual," *American Scholar* 29 (Winter, 1959): 55–72. The best older sources are John D. Hicks, *The Populist Revolt;* Roscoe C. Martin, *The People's Party in Texas*.

7. See Hicks, *Populist Revolt*, pp. 263, 337; Secretary of State, *California Blue Book*, 1893, 1895. All election returns have been taken from the *California Blue Book* for the relevant year. Omitting San Francisco, the Populists polled 11.2 percent of the 1892 vote, 20.9 percent of the 1894 gubernatorial vote.

8. See Donald E. Walters, "Populism in California, 1889–1900" (Ph.D.

dissertation), pp. 1–4; Carey McWilliams, *Factories in the Field,* pp. 5–64; Remi Nadeau, *Los Angeles: From Mission to Modern City,* pp. 71–93; Claude B. Hutchinson, ed., *California Agriculture,* p. 396.

9. Walters, "Populism in California," p. 1.

10. Ibid., pp. 46, 148–151, 276, 285–289, 340, 350. See also Nugent, *Tolerant Populists,* pp. 100–121, 138–144, 154–155, 163–180, 199–200, 211–235; Rogin, *Intellectuals and McCarthy,* pp. 111–112, 118–119, 140, 175–177.

11. Seven of these eleven boom counties were among the first ten in the state in which the Alliance organized. Walters, "Populism in California," pp. 59–61.

12. Because of their tiny size and peculiar characteristics, the four least-populated counties have been omitted from all scatter diagrams, quartilings, and selections of counties to illustrate demographic or political characteristics. Three are the sparsely populated desert counties of Alpine, Inyo, and Mono, generally resembling each other demographically and politically and varying widely from the rest of the state. The fourth, tiny Del Norte County in the northwest corner of the state has had, throughout California history, its own unique behavior patterns. The tiny populations of these counties, which ranged from 667 in Alpine to 3,544 in Inyo, distort behavior patterns in a study such as this one in which each county is treated as a unit. Their omission left, in 1890, fifty counties, which divide into quartiles of thirteen, twelve, twelve, and thirteen.

13. The 1892 and 1894 Populist votes were correlated .67.

14. Its rate of population increase was more than twice that of eight of the other nine, the ninth being urban San Francisco.

15. But the poor California counties were far better off than their Southern counterparts; indeed, they were even wealthier than the middle-income Dakota counties where populism flourished. Perhaps California's greater agricultural wealth helps explain the relative weakness of its Populist movement.

16. The causes of frontier protest are discussed more fully, with citation of sources, in Rogin, *Intellectuals and McCarthy,* pp. 111–115, 188.

17. See Nadeau, *Los Angeles,* pp. 64–80.

18. See Walters, *Populism in California,* pp. 18–23, 45, 102, 115; Arthur Lipow, "Edward Bellamy and the Nationalist Movement: A Study in the Sociology of Authoritarian Ideological Currents in American Socialism."

19. See Walters, "Populism in California," pp. 207–209, 290–293.

20. Only one of six southern counties was in the top quartile of increases in Populist strength; four were in the bottom quartile. Three southern counties were now in the bottom half of Populist strength. (This, incidentally, explains the much lower correlation between population growth and populism in 1894.)

21. See Walters, "Populism in California," pp. 210–220, 229–240, 276–278.

22. There were no Catholics among Populist leaders, and almost all the names in the registers of the suballiances examined by Walters were

Anglo-Saxon. See Walters, "Populism in California," pp. 148–150, and for additional material on Catholics and populism, pp. 46, 276, 285, 289, 340, 350.

The Kearneyite "workingmen's" movement of the 1870s, which almost captured control of the state constitutional convention, had attacked the Chinese. The use of Chinese labor in mining, railway building, and giant corporate farming had brought out racist proclivities among workers and small farmers. Given this history, the Populist movement was impressively free of anti-Oriental rhetoric. There is no record of Populist participation in the anti-Chinese riots which spread through rural California in the 1890s. The Populists adopted a plank in their 1894 platform calling for exclusion of Orientals, but this seems due, as in other states, to union allies' fears of cheap labor. See McWilliams, *Factories in the Field*, pp. 74–76; Ralph Edward Shaffer, "Radicalism in California" (Ph.D. dissertation), pp. 7–45; Alexander Saxton, "San Francisco Labor and the Populist and Progressive Insurgencies," *Pacific Historical Review* 35 (November, 1965): 425; Ralph Kauer, "The Workingmen's Party of California," *Pacific Historical Review* 13 (1944): 278–291.

23. There is no reliable measure of the percentages in each county living on farms. Farms as a percentage of all homes can be computed, and this seems reliable in many states. MacRae and Meldrum, "Critical Elections in Illinois," p. 679n. However, in California this measure produces anomalies, counties with substantially more farms than homes. For that reason it has been used sparingly here, but as a general indication of where farm families are a substantial majority of the population, it does seem usable.

Of the four counties with the smallest Populist increases where farmers were a majority, one was heavily foreign, one Catholic, one southern, and one Catholic and southern.

24. Saxton, "San Francisco Labor," pp. 425–426; Walters, "Populism in California," pp. 247–266.

25. Saxton, "San Francisco Labor," pp. 426–427.

26. Key, "Theory of Critical Elections"; see also Chap. 4 of this book. Normally, to obtain the Republican percentage, one subtracts the Democratic percentages from 1.00; separate graphs for the two parties are required because of substantial minor-party votes in 1892, 1904, and 1908.

27. The critical shift from 1900 to 1908 shows up more sharply in the Republican than in the Democratic vote, since much Populist support that had gone to the Democrats in 1896 went Socialist thereafter. For example, the 1904 Socialist vote for president was correlated .48 with the 1892 Populist vote, and .40 with Populist strength in 1894. There is evidence that, whereas the major parties absorbed the ethnic cleavages called forth by populism (see below), the Socialists acquired populism's economic following.

28. These calculations are reported, and the method explained in Chap. 4 of this book.

29. Thus enabling Grover Cleveland, by a tiny plurality, to carry California.

30. For the national story, see Hicks, *Populist Revolt*, pp. 301–320, 340–375. On California, see Walters, "Populism in California," pp. 308–344. All three California parties favored silver in the early 1890s. See Harold F. Taggart, "California and the Silver Question in 1895," *Pacific Historical Review* 6 (1937): 249–250, 266–269, passim.

31. Agricultural wealth was an important source of cleavage in 1896, but not thereafter. The average value of farm products per farm averaged $1,150 in ten counties with the biggest Democratic gains, $2,190 in the counties with the biggest Democratic losses (excluding the metropolitan counties of Sacramento and San Francisco).

32. There is considerable overlap between foreign-stock and Catholic counties, but the trend sustains itself in the non-Catholic, foreign-stock counties.

Bryan also sustained large losses among immigrants in the states of the Northeast. For a comparable shift in South Dakota, see Michael Paul Rogin, "McCarthyism and Agrarian Radicalism" (Ph.D. dissertation), p. 142.

33. The correlations are with the county percentages of Catholics in 1890. The Protestant-Catholic realignment was also paramount in Wisconsin. See Rogin, "McCarthyism," p. 35.

34. See Harold F. Taggart, "The Party Realignment of 1896 in California," *Pacific Historical Review* 8 (1939): 450.

35. Estimates of the eligible voting population are not highly reliable. From the number of citizens over twenty-one for the census years, the population is estimated for the years between: e.g., Population 1896 equals Population 1890 plus .6 (Population 1900 minus Population 1890). See Chap. 4 of this book.   However, there are no figures for aliens over twenty-one in 1910; therefore estimates had to be made. Moreover, population increase was not evenly spaced over the ten-year intervals between the census. This is particularly serious in the 1880s, when there was substantially more growth in the second half of the decade than in the first. Therefore, the turnout figures in the early 1880s may be artificially reduced.

Since the use of turnout figures follows Burnham ("American Political Universe," pp. 10, 13–19), some differences should be noted. Burnham used congressional totals in the off years, but governors in California are elected in the off years. Table 2 reports the gubernatorial totals, since these reveal the greatest turnout. It is noteworthy that, in the years before 1896, congressional and gubernatorial turnout was virtually identical. (The differences averaged 1.2 percent from 1882–1894, 3.5 percent from 1898–1910.) Although turnout was substantially lower in California than in the states Burnham analyzed, drop-off, whether measured by gubernatorial or congressional totals, was much smaller. Finally, because California turnout was low in the nineteenth century, state turnout has been higher in modern times, at least in presidential elections. (For some figures, see Chap. 4 in this book.) This was strikingly not true in Burnham's states.

36. Turnout in 1912 was also sharply reduced because Taft was not on

the ballot. The Progressives had made Roosevelt the regular Republican candidate in California.

37. See Charles H. Titus, "Rural Voting in California, 1900–1926," *Southwestern Social Science Quarterly* 9 (September, 1928): 199–200, 205–206, 213–214; Charles H. Titus, "Voting in California Cities, 1900–1925," *Southwestern Social Science Quarterly* 8 (March, 1928): 383–399. Titus's methods for estimating eligible voters by counties are far more detailed and sophisticated than the one adopted here.

38. Cross-filing permitted candidates to run in both party primaries without, until the 1950s, giving their own party allegiance. It greatly benefitted incumbent office-holders, whose names were familiar to the voters. See Robert J. Pitchell, "The Electoral System and Voting Behavior: The Case of California's Cross-Filing," *Western Political Quarterly* 12 (1959): 459–484.

39. See Chaps. 2 and 3 in this book.

2

Progressivism and the California Electorate

SHORTLY before the 1906 California Republican convention, the editor of the *Fresno Republican* wrote an attack on machine politics. Mixing wish and prophecy in a formula that Progressive rhetoric was to make commonplace, the editorial declared: "The man to win will be the man who makes his appeal direct to the people."[1] A few years later progressivism did win in California and in other states as well. But the Progressive claim to be a movement of the people has been disputed by modern historians. Progressivism, historians now argue, was a middle-class movement of native-stock Americans.[2] In California, for example, the few dozen leading Progressive politicians were primarily urban, native-born, high-status Protestants from the old independent middle class. Largely journalists and lawyers not employed by the giant corporations, they feared that the political power of capital and labor would introduce class conflict into American politics and subvert traditional moral values.[3]

Virtually all the historical studies, whatever their differences in interpretation, have focused on leading Progressive

35

politicians or intellectuals. Clearly the concerns and backgrounds of Progressive leaders decisively influenced the nature
of the movement. Most Progressive state factions were organized by a small group of leaders from the top down, rather
than by the mass upsurge from below that characterized populism. Therefore, the character of Progressive leaders was particularly crucial. Nevertheless, conclusions that progressivism
was not a movement of "the people" can hardly be sustained
until the behavior of the people is actually examined. And
there is almost no evidence concerning the grass-roots, electoral support for Progressive candidates.[4] Too often, Progressive support is implicitly deduced from the background
and preoccupations of Progressive leaders. We propose in
this chapter and the following to examine the popular support
for California progressivism and to modify, in the light of
this examination, modern interpretations of the movement.

Progressive conceptions of "the people" apparently excluded large sections of the electorate—workers, immigrants,
Catholics, the urban and rural poor. As middle-class moral reformers, Progressives would seem to have fashioned a popular
following in their own image. This, at least, is often the drift
of George Mowry's pioneering study *The California Progressives* (1951). Mowry did not argue explicitly that Progressive
voters were—like their leaders—urban, native-born, and Protestant. But he did locate Progressive strength in urban, native-
stock, Anglo-Saxon southern California.

Mowry's thesis, diffused throughout the book, was that progressivism sought political reform in the service of moral re-
generation; it was therefore strongest in the south. In the
early years of the twentieth century, southern California was
stricter on moral issues like temperance than the north, but
more willing to support such political experiments as woman
suffrage. The Lincoln-Roosevelt League was weaker in the

north than in the south, not only organizationally but electorally as well. The southern citrus belt was "the very heart of progressive strength" in 1910, and Hiram Johnson was strongest in the primary in the San Joaquin Valley and "throughout all southern California." In the 1910 general election, Johnson carried every southern county, but lost twenty-one of forty-nine northern counties. In 1912, Theodore Roosevelt and Johnson lost San Francisco but carried Los Angeles and the state. Johnson lost southern California for the first time in the 1920 presidential primary, but by then he was supported by anti-League of Nations conservatives and opposed by old Progressives.[5] For other writers besides Mowry, southern California had been the home of moralistic uprisings. In his penetrating study of California prohibitionism, Gilman Ostrander wrote: "California Progressivism, like California temperance, drew its greatest strength from Los Angeles county. It was there that the movement originated in the good-government movement of 1906, and it was there that the heaviest majorities for the Progressive ticket were registered in the next ten years."[6]

As a middle-class, southern California movement, progressivism was unsympathetic to organized labor, argued Mowry. He attributed the ultimate failure of progressivism to Johnson's lack of sympathy for working-class problems. He also stressed the business orientation and antilabor biases of the Los Angeles reformers. Even most northern Progressives, Mowry believed, were critical of unions, although many San Francisco labor leaders supported Progressive politicians. Early Progressive legislatures passed considerable labor legislation, but defeated or watered down perhaps the most significant measures. Nevertheless, Mowry found workers consistently pro-Johnson on election day. "Johnson regularly rolled up majorities" in the San Francisco "labor wards south of Market

Street," although he could not deliver the labor vote to
Roosevelt in 1912. In 1914 and 1916, Mowry argued, Johnson
himself continued to get strong labor backing.[7]

But the most striking fact about Progressive support was its
dramatic transformation after Johnson's initial victory. Southern California had never been a Progressive stronghold, as
northern rural voters supported Johnson most heavily in 1910;
nevertheless, Johnson was far stronger in the south than in
the northern urban centers, and he was particularly unpopular
in the San Francisco working-class district. But by 1916, southern California was the stronghold of anti-Progressive sentiment, as the movement received powerful backing from San
Francisco workers, and throughout the Catholic, foreign-
stock counties of the Bay Area. Progressives remained strong
here in the 1920s, foreshadowing the working class, immigrant-
based New Deal coalition.

A simple table, based on the characteristics Mowry and
Ostrander associate with Progressive leaders, indicates the
contrast between Progressive voters in 1910 and 1916 (see
Table 6).

TABLE 6
The Progressive Transformation

Johnson	Urban	Native-Born	Protes-tant	Middle Class	Prohibi-tionist	Southern
1910 primary	no	yes	yes	yes	yes	relative
1916 primary	relative	no	no	no	no	no

Although Mowry's references to Progressive voters are misleading, he does provide insight into the transformation of
its social base. Mowry argued that their antagonism to class

consciousness disguised, even from the Progressives themselves, their own intense class loyalties. What would happen, he asked, after the Progressives took power in 1910 and, in trying to act politically, saw their illusion of a class-free, neutral government shattered?[8] Perhaps Progressive leaders would seek to maintain the illusion of neutrality. But in the process of governing, Progressives took steps that would reorient the behavior of the electorate.

The Johnson Vote: 1910

In its first contest for public support—Johnson's campaign in 1910—progressivism appealed most strongly to rural, native-stock Protestant counties and least strongly to Catholics, immigrants, and Bay Area residents.[9] The Mowry view prepares us, as older interpretations had not, for the Protestant, native-born, prohibitionist character of this initial Progressive support.[10] (See Table 7.) The antirailroad Johnson campaign naturally attracted farmers, although "urban" interpretations of the Progressive movement tend to overlook the rural basis of Progressive strength.[11] The rural support for Johnson in the San Joaquin Valley[12] and in a sparsely populated group of counties in the northeast was particularly striking (see Tables 8 and 9).

How did workers vote in 1910? The northern and northeastern counties, where lumbering was the most important industry, supported the Progressive candidate, but we cannot be certain that the lumberjacks and woodworkers living in those counties actually voted for him. The working class in San Francisco opposed Johnson. In the primary, he received 32 percent of the vote in the working-class section of the city and 38 percent in the middle-class section. In November, Johnson

TABLE 7

Correlations between Johnson's 1910 Primary Vote and Demographic Characteristics

Percent Native	Percent Farm Homes	Percent German	1916 Prohibition Referendum	Hired Farm Labor	Percent Catholic	Percent Urban	Value Land Per Acre	Multiple Correlation
.52	.42	−.38	.35	−.33	−.31	−.29	−.26	.64

NOTE: Religious figures are from the 1916 census of religion; all other census data is from the 1910 census.

TABLE 8

The Shifting Social Basis of Progressive Strength

Types of Counties	1910 Johnson Primary % of Vote	1912 Roosevelt and La Follette Primary % of Vote	1914 Johnson % of Vote	1916 Johnson Primary % of Vote	1922 Johnson Primary % of Vote	1924 La Follette % of Vote	1926 Young Primary % of Vote
Farming	63.7	77.5	41.9	51.1	64.4	36.9	44.0
Urban	46.6	76.3	51.7	52.3	60.9	30.2	45.9
Immigrant	49.1	68.7	47.8	53.9	64.1	39.8	49.9
Native Stock	60.3	77.4	43.5	48.4	64.4	35.8	42.4

NOTE: This table reports county averages in selected Progressive elections for four different types of counties. The farming counties are the top quartile of counties (fourteen) in the percentage of farm dwellings—31%–46%. The urban counties are the eleven more than 50% urban in 1910. The immigrant counties are the sixteen whose population of foreign-born and their children was more than 50%. In the fourteen native counties, white Americans of native stock comprised more than 60% of the population. (For a description of these characteristics, see note 9.) Since the Catholic and immigrant, Protestant and native, counties are substantially the same, religion was not included in this table. There is also considerable overlap between farming and native counties. (Tiny Alpine County, with a population of only 309 in 1910, was excluded from this table.)

TABLE 9

Regional Shifts in Progressive Support

Regions	1910 Johnson Primary % of Vote	1912 Roosevelt and La Follette Primary % of Vote	1914 Johnson % of Vote	1916 Johnson Primary % of Vote	1922 Johnson Primary % of Vote	1924 La Follette % of Vote	1926 Young Primary % of Vote
Southern California	45.6	72.4	46.5	41.5	52.1	28.7	35.3
Bay Area	40.6	68.0	53.4	58.0	62.6	39.2	46.4
San Joaquin Valley	63.0	79.9	44.6	56.8	64.9	36.0	44.8
Lumber Region	60.2	75.7	46.4	51.9	70.8	46.5	53.4
Northwest Grape	52.3	72.3	37.4	43.6	62.5	35.5	44.1

NOTE: The basis for selecting the seven counties of southern California is described in note 14. These were generally urban counties (five of seven more than 50% urban; all less than 30% farm), with small percentages of Catholics and immigrants (averages 12.6% and 36.5% respectively). The six counties bordering on the San Francisco Bay had few farmers (all less than 15%). They ranked 1-4 and 7-8 in the percentage of foreign stock, averaging 62.1% foreign stock and 24.8% Catholic. The eight counties of the San Joaquin Valley in central California were, in 1910, heavily farm (31.8%), native (55.8%), and Protestant (13.4% Catholic). The sixteen lumbering counties are a block of northern counties where lumbering was the most important industry in 1911, and where its quarterly payroll was more than $2,000,000, excluding two counties bordering the Pacific Ocean. See Secretary of State, *1911 California Blue Book* (Sacramento, 1913), pp. 591-891; Donald J. Bogue and Calvin L. Beale, *Economic Areas of the United States* (New York, 1964), pp. 557-559. Six counties north of San Francisco generally voted as a unit, although they do not define, by themselves, a clear economic region. All were farm counties (average 32.2%) in which the number of grape vines in 1910 was more than half of the total value of all crops. For sources and descriptions of the demographic data, see note 9.

received 38 percent of the working-class vote and 46 percent of the middle-class vote. In both elections, middle-class voters were more likely than working-class voters to support Johnson. It should be noted, however, that the Republican party had always run better in middle-class than in working-class neighborhoods.[13]

What, finally, of Johnson's southern California strength in 1910?[14] Not a single southern county was in the top half of the counties supporting Johnson in the primary. True, many of the counties most strongly for Johnson were small and sparsely populated. Moreover, the southern counties were far more for Johnson than those in the Bay Area; he received majorities of the total Republican vote in Los Angeles and Orange counties, and large pluralities elsewhere in the south. However, Johnson's overall percentage of the northern vote was just as high as his percentage in the south, and he would have been easily elected had there been no southern California.[15] Johnson's vote in the 1910 primary was peculiarly rural, not peculiarly southern.

Johnson's southern vote, however, was certainly reduced by the presence on the ballot of former assembly speaker Philip Stanton. Stanton polled virtually no votes north of the Tehachapis, but received 28 percent of the southern vote. But the two northern machine candidates did very poorly in the south, and there is no assurance that the Stanton vote would have gone to Johnson rather than to them had Stanton not been on the ballot.[16]

In the general election, Johnson won every southern county while losing twenty-one northern counties. However, Johnson carried the south because he was a Republican, not because he was a Progressive. The south was traditionally Republican, and although party allegiances weakened substantially during the Progressive period, they continued to exert an important

influence on voting patterns. Indeed, party allegiance was invariably the most important single predictor of a candidate's support in a general election.[17] Johnson's vote in November 1910 clearly had a Progressive component,[18] but it remained rooted in traditional party allegiances, correlating .63, for example, with Taft's vote in 1908. In the primary, on the other hand, Johnson had actually been stronger in Democratic than in Republican counties.[19] Many progressive voters left the Democratic party to vote for Johnson in 1910, and many conservative Republican regulars defected to the Democrats. However, even after this realignment, Johnson's November vote remained slightly *negatively* correlated with his vote in August.

To take the November vote as an indication of Progressive strength, then, is unwarranted. Our aim, instead, is to discover areas of Johnson strength and weakness after the influence of the regular Republican vote is eliminated. To that end, Johnson's percentage in each county was plotted against the 1908 Taft vote. Taft ran far better than Johnson in the state, but in some counties Republican strength fell off less than in others. The counties where the Republican vote fell off least between 1908 and 1910 had been peculiarly pro-Johnson in the primary. Counties where the Republican vote fell off most were likely to be strongly anti-Progressive.[20] The sharpest decline in Republican strength occurred in several Bay Area, Catholic, and north coast counties. In Los Angeles and two other southern counties, the Republican vote also fell off disproportionately. Republican strength held its own best in ten counties; none of these was southern. The traditionally Republican south remained Republican in 1910, but Johnson's vote was less peculiarly southern than that given orthodox Republican candidates.

Roosevelt and Johnson: 1912

In the 1912 primary and general election, progressivism generally retained its 1910 character. Roosevelt in November did run impressively in the south, but this southern strength may well indicate the difference between Roosevelt and state Progressives.

The three-cornered Republican presidential primary of 1912 pitted two Progressives—Roosevelt and La Follette—against President Taft. Taft, who received only 27 percent of the vote, was generally strongest where Johnson had been weak, notably in the Bay Area and the south (see Table 9). The Johnson and Taft votes were correlated —.47.[21] In November, the Progressives kept Taft's name off the ballot and made Roosevelt and Johnson the official Republican ticket. Roosevelt polled a vote that was in part Republican, in part Progressive, and in part peculiarly southern.

Roosevelt's vote had a Republican component, though it was much less related to previous Republican presidential elections than these were to each other.[22] Compared to regular Republican strength, the Roosevelt-Johnson ticket did best in areas of Progressive strength and worst in areas of Progressive weakness—except in the south. There Roosevelt picked up the kind of support that Johnson had failed to get in 1910. In thirteen counties, the Republican vote dropped more sharply than was typical between 1910 and 1912; these counties had averaged only 50 percent for Johnson in the 1910 primary. In fifteen counties the Republican vote fell off least; ten of these were northern counties that had averaged 68 percent for Johnson.[23] The remaining five were southern counties that had averaged only 49 percent for him. Thus five of the seven southern counties, although not Progressive, showed a special fondness for Roosevelt.

In speculations about why Roosevelt attracted more southern support than Johnson, additional information should be kept in mind. Roosevelt did not receive a typically Progressive vote in at least three midwestern states.[24] The specific character of the Roosevelt vote has yet to be examined in detail, but the electoral evidence questions whether the Bull Moose party was typically Progressive. Was the southern California vote mobilized by Roosevelt Progressive, or did it have some other character? The behavior of the south in subsequent Progressive elections should help resolve that question.

The Progressive Transformation: 1914–1916

Workers, Catholics, and immigrants in the Bay Area re-elected Johnson governor in 1914 and nominated him for senator in the 1916 Republican primary. The Bay Area had switched from the center of Progressive weakness to the area of its greatest strength. Southern California, less for Johnson than the Bay Area in 1914, voted strongly against him in 1916. Had progressivism been forced to rely on its southern strength, it might have disappeared from California politics before World War I.

The six Bay Area counties averaged 54 percent for Johnson in 1914 and were among the highest Progressive counties in the state (see Table 9). Johnson's vote in San Francisco increased markedly in both working-class and middle-class neighborhoods, indicating that whatever their class, the Catholics and immigrants who dominated the city had moved into the Progressive camp. Throughout the state, Catholic and foreign-born counties were no longer anti-Progressive, and counties favoring prohibition were no longer supporting Johnson (see Table 8). Johnson's strength in the Bay Area, and among Catholics and immigrants, was somewhat more striking in 1916 (see Tables 8 and 9).

The sharpest shift in Johnson support in 1914 occurred among San Francisco workers. These were now clearly more for Johnson than their middle-class neighbors, and the gap widened somewhat in 1916 (see Table 10). The Socialist vote had been a force in California politics during the early Progressive years. Largely nonrural and (at least in San Francisco) working class, the Socialist vote disappeared into the Progressive party in 1914.[25]

TABLE 10

Class and Progressive Support in San Francisco

Type of Assembly District	1914 Johnson % of Vote	1914 Republican % of Vote	1914 Democratic % of Vote	1914 Socialist % of Vote	1916 Johnson Primary % of Vote
Working class	63	17	13	7	69
Middle class	51	33	12	4	55

As the Bay Area became an important source of Progressive strength, the movement lost its rural character. Indeed, in 1914 many rural Progressive counties remained in the major parties, while the grape-growing region north of San Francisco, never strongly Progressive, voted heavily against Johnson (Table 9). Johnson's 1914 strength was as disproportionately urban as it had been disproportionately rural four years previous. His vote was correlated .50 with the 1910 urban population, and —.55 with the percentage of farm residents.[26] By

1916, the San Joaquin Valley, at least, had returned to the Progressive fold, and progressivism thereafter was equally strong in rural and urban counties (see Tables 8 and 9).

What, finally, of the south? In 1914, Johnson ran as well in Los Angeles as in the urban counties to the north. In the other six southern counties, with a far smaller working-class population than Los Angeles, his showing was much worse. Five of these counties were among the bottom half of all the counties in their support for Johnson, and the average of his percentages in the seven southern counties was well below his average in the Bay Area (see Table 9). In 1916, Johnson's southern vote fell precipitously as the south became the major area of opposition to Johnson. Johnson's conservative opponent was from Los Angeles, which no doubt contributed to the Progressive's southern failure. But whatever the contributing factors, the results are clear: the well-organized conservative campaign to defeat Johnson in the Republican primary succeeded in the south and failed badly in the north. Never a Johnson stronghold, southern California was becoming the center of anti-Johnson sentiment.

The shift in the economic basis of Progressive strength was not limited to California. In South Dakota, for example, 1916 gubernatorial candidate Peter Norbeck was the first Progressive whose support was not concentrated among the wealthy counties. In North Dakota, the Non-Partisan League began to break through the resistance of Russian-German farmers, poorest in the state, to left-wing candidates.[27] Little attention has been paid to these developments, perhaps because they were nipped in the bud by World War I. But before the war shattered the new, nascent Progressive coalition, this coalition carried California, and therefore the nation, for Woodrow Wilson.

Wilson's narrow California victory further demonstrates the

significance of the Progressive realignment. In explaining Progressive defections to Wilson, some historians emphasize standpatter control of Hughes' California itinerary, his failure to meet Johnson, and the bad feeling between the two men. Alternatively it is argued that California Progressives were generally pro-Wilson, and that Johnson could not have delivered the Progressive vote to Hughes even had he so desired.[28] Election returns cannot resolve this question, but they do show that Progressive voters put Wilson in the White House.

To determine whether Progressive voters deserted Hughes in 1916, the Hughes vote was subtracted from the November Johnson senatorial vote in every county in the state. This indicated where Hughes had run closest to Johnson and where he had run furthest behind. And Hughes ran worst relative to Johnson in counties that had voted Progressive in 1914 or in the 1916 primary; the correlations were .51 and .55.[29] Many progressive voters had thus voted for Johnson but not for Hughes in 1916; in crossing party lines they helped elect Wilson.

In addition to Progressives, workers have also been credited with defeating Hughes. He antagonized organized labor in the Bay Area, it is said, by associating with the leaders of the San Francisco open-shop campaign. Labor was particularly sensitive because of the Preparedness Day bombings that were to send Tom Mooney and Warren Billings to jail. In addition, unionists felt indebted to Wilson for the passage of the Clayton and Adamson Acts.[30] San Francisco labor supported Wilson, who was the first Democrat since the advent of the Progressive movement whose vote was significantly more working class than middle class. The contrast with Hughes is particularly striking (Table 11). San Francisco workers had voted progressive in 1914 and in the summer of 1916; in November, they voted again for the more Progressive candidate.[31]

TABLE 11

Wilson and the San Francisco Working Class, 1916

Type of Assembly District	Hughes % of Vote	Wilson % of Vote	Socialist % of Vote
Working class	35	60	5
Middle class	46	50	4

There is, however, an alternative explanation for Wilson's victory: "It might be argued that Wilson won because he appealed to the small towns and countryside. In the six most populous counties in the state, which included every sizable city, Hughes had a majority of 10,000 votes." But, this hypothesis concludes, he lost the rural counties and the state.[32] California Republicans, however, had run better in the cities than on the farms since the Bryan election campaign of 1896.[33] In 1912, Wilson himself had run much worse in cities than in nonurban areas. In 1916, Wilson actually reduced his 1912 deficit in the six most populous counties. And his vote was the *least* disproportionately rural of any Democratic presidential candidate since Bryan.[34]

Workers and Progressives voted for Wilson; the south did not. The Hughes vote was even more concentrated in southern California than the support given previous Republicans. As the Democratic party became more Progressive, the Republican party became more southern. Nor was the southern shift the only change in the base of the major parties between 1908 and 1916. Progressivism did not simply shatter party allegiances, as many historians have alleged, it also realigned them. The biggest increases in Democratic support between

1908 and 1916 came in Progressive counties. Working-class counties also tended to be more Democratic in 1916 than in 1908, while rural counties were somewhat more likely to be Republican.[35]

What, in sum, was the electoral significance of the 1916 campaign? Woodrow Wilson, by attracting workers to the Democratic banner, reduced the traditional urban Democratic deficit. In switching parties in 1916, workers and Progressives elected Wilson. In the face of these changes, the Republican party became more exclusively southern than it had been before the rise of progressivism. The difference between the party vote before progressivism and the vote in 1916 indicates the impact of the movement on party allegiances in California.

1920s Progressivism: The Realignment Sustained

The shift in Progressive support extended beyond the 1914-1916 period into the 1920s. World War I, the prohibition issue, and personal rivalries confused party patterns in the 1920s, limiting the impact of the 1916 party realignment on Democratic-Republican conflict.[36] But Progressive candidates remained strong among northern workers and weak in the south. Running in the 1920 presidential primary and in the 1922 senatorial primary, Johnson encountered little opposition outside the south.[37] La Follette in 1924 and C. C. Young in the 1926 Republican gubernatorial primary were also much weaker in the south than elsewhere in the state (see Table 9). Both La Follette and Young ran very well in California with La Follette polling 35 percent of the state vote and Young winning the gubernatorial primary and general election two years later. Their support was fairly similar (r = .58), as both candidates were strongest among workers and poor farmers.[38]

Perhaps progressivism faltered in the 1920s because it could depend less on the support of substantial middle-class citizens than previously in its history, not because it failed to appeal to the more deprived strata of the population. California progressivism may have died because it could not understand the problems faced by workers and low-income groups. But the La Follette and Young elections were rooted in economic grievances. Perhaps the Young vote was less the last gasp of progressivism than a precursor of the New Deal.

Interpretations of Progressive Support

The electoral patterns raise more questions about California progressivism than they answer. The most interesting issues— the character of Johnson's original appeal, the significance of its transformation, and the relation between the shifting social base and the unchanging rhetoric—cannot be resolved with quantitative data. Nevertheless, some tentative reinterpretations seem in order.

The California Progressives appealed to "the people" against outside interests and special privileges. Such an appeal is hardly as universal as its proponents believe, but it functions as more than mere verbiage. If a few vested interests and alien outsiders can be blamed for the existing social evils, there is no need to recognize and choose between concrete, diverse groups with conflicting points of view. Perhaps Shasta County Progressive lawyer Jesse Carter, later a state Supreme Court Justice, was typical. He could see himself defending the "common man" against the railroad and the power companies, while many of his clients owned thousands of acres, and others were local businessmen. But these were the "honest countryfolk" fighting against outside corporations and "city slickers."[39] In the same spirit Johnson ran his 1910 campaign solely on the issue of the Southern Pacific Railroad; even his Democratic opponent had a more well-rounded reform program. But antirailroad sentiment was diffused throughout the population, from poor farmers to San Francisco merchants and industrialists.[40] The community could be mobilized against a common foe; no need to stir up more divisive feelings.

Neverthelesss, a purely antirailroad, consensus campaign had more appeal to some of "the people" than to others. Farmer grievances against Southern Pacific were concrete and deeply rooted. Moreover, there was less diversity in native-stock, rural areas; an appeal to "the people" made more instinctive sense there. Native, rural residents could feel they were members of a community, undivided by issues, and vote overwhelmingly for Johnson. In the more diverse urban areas it was difficult to mobilize a united populace. Catholics and immigrants may well have felt threatened by a politics appealing to unified community standards, and in any event railroad control over politics was most firmly established there. Moreover, the Union Labor party graft trials of 1906-1911, in which Johnson had become chief prosecutor, had become unpopular by 1910 in both labor and middle-class San Francisco neighborhoods. In the absence of concrete antirailroad grievances of the type that moved farmers, Johnson's campaign had least appeal to workers and ethnic minorities.

Southern California was largely urbanized by 1910, and its residents lacked local roots. In the south a politics of community had to be more strident than in the countryside. Such a politics was further removed from actual experience; it required that moral standards be imposed rather than simply maintained. Southern political moralism could not unite the community against powerful authorities like the railroad; immigrants, saloons, and radicals were more comfortable targets.

The moralistic politics of southern California was always rooted in orthodox, Protestant conservatism, and the region as a whole was never strongly Progressive.

In 1910, an appeal to the people against the Southern Pacific octopus made a certain sense. Although communal in its feeling, such a politics did not need to impose radical standards of moral virtue on a corrupt populace. It could appeal to the public interest without seeking to wipe out the wide variety of conflicting private interests. But, as Mowry points out, the Progressives once in power would have to make concrete decisions, and the illusion that these could be made in the interests of all must necessarily be threatened. Then choices would have to be made—choices of program and rhetoric that would affect the sources of support for the movement.

The general framework of "classless" politics used so effectively in 1910 could blossom in many different—and opposing—directions. Mugwump former Senator Thomas Bard, not wanting to forsake the morally unified 1910 world, would leave the movement instead. For Jesse Carter, Progressive politics would come to mean support for the demands of labor unions, opposition to Upton Sinclair but support of Culbert Olson in the 1930s, and a role on the California Supreme Court in the 1950s protecting freedom of speech, civil liberties, and the rights of Negroes and aliens.[41] Other Progressives might stridently insist on a communal politics, enforcing conformity—prohibition, antiradical campaigns, immigration restriction—on an increasingly hostile world.

This is not the place to detail the choices and programs of leading California Progressives in the years following 1910. But to workers and labor leaders the record was clear. The 1911 state legislature passed a workmen's compensation statute and required an eight-hour day for women. A child labor law, a factory inspection act, and other pieces of prounion legislation all followed two years later. Although workers also suffered compromises and defeats, the prolabor achievements were unprecedented. The San Francisco labor press expressed enormous, highly visible enthusiasm for Johnson; this translated itself, in his campaign for reelection, into working-class support at the polls.[42]

The alliance Johnson forged with the Bay Area working class did not cost him middle-class votes there. But to voters in southern California, progressivism quickly became too left-wing and experimental. In addition, the successful open-shop campaign and the dynamiting of the *Los Angeles Times,* preventing the growth of a union-based, Progressive constituency, further conservatized the south. Anglo-Saxon, moralistic southern California felt more at ease with regular Republicans and increasingly opposed the Progressive movement.

Thus, a decade before the Al Smith "revolution" foreshadowed immigrant, working-class support for New Deal reform, Hiram Johnson also depended on immigrant, working-class votes. This alliance between reformers and workers elected Woodrow Wilson president in 1916 and remained a cohesive force in California politics during the 1920s. California voting patterns thus suggest that the New Deal coalition had roots in the Progressive period. Perhaps prohibition and the war interrupted a class-based party realignment; perhaps party patterns in the 1920s were an interlude in a secular realignment stemming from progressivism, rather than the "norm" for pre-New Deal party politics.[43] California may be an exception; if not, interpretations that contrast middle-class, Anglo-Saxon progressivism with the working-class, immigrant-based New Deal will have to be revised.[44]

Progressive social support shifted after 1910. But most historians agree that the language of progressivism remained "classless," oriented toward moral virtue and fearful of conflict. How, then, explain working-class and immigrant support for the movement? It is possible that California progressivism was not typical, both because of traditions peculiar to California and the largely skilled character of the San Francisco labor force. Nevertheless, in California at least, working-class, immigrant support for "classless" American rhetoric must be explained.

Perhaps certain versions of these classless appeals are diffused throughout American politics and are not simply middle class in any narrow sense. Perhaps workers are also fearful of class conflict and concerned with Americanism—as comparison with the European examples suggests. Progressive rhetoric, in short, may not have had as narrow an appeal as middle-class interpretations of the movement would have us believe. Given concrete evidence of prolabor activity, workers may well have found middle-class sentiments of public harmony more congenial than proletarian slogans of class war.[45] The incorporation of workers into liberal, middle-class American politics, a major achievement of the New Deal, may have had its beginnings in the Progressive era.

NOTES

1. Quoted in Alice Rose, "The Rise of California Insurgency" (Ph.D. dissertation), pp. 96–97.
2. Among other works, see George E. Mowry, *Theodore Roosevelt and the Progressive Movement*; Richard Hofstadter, *The Age of Reform*; Henry May, *The End of American Innocence*; Charles Forcey, *The Crossroads of American Liberalism*; Samuel P. Hays, *Conservation and the Gospel of Efficiency*; Samuel Haber, *Efficiency and Uplift*.
3. George E. Mowry, *The California Progressives*. See also George E. Mowry, "The California Progressive and His Rationale: A Study in Mid-

dle Class Politics," *Mississippi Valley Historical Review* 26 (September, 1949): 239–250.

4. But see the following older studies: George A. Lundberg, "The Demographic and Economic Basis of Political Radicalism and Conservatism," *American Journal of Sociology* 32 (March, 1927): 719–732; Jerry A. Neprash, *The Brookhart Campaigns in Iowa, 1920–1926;* Stuart A. Rice, *Farmers and Workers in American Politics.*

5. Mowry, *California Progressives,* pp. 8, 105, 128, 129, 133, 189, 281–284.

6. Gilman M. Ostrander, *The Prohibition Movement in California, 1848–1933,* p. 105.

7. Mowry, *California Progressives,* pp. 27–54, 92–94, 140–153, 214, 271.

8. Mowry, "The California Progressive," pp. 245–249.

9. County election returns were taken from State of California, Secretary of State, *Statement of Vote,* issued after each election. Demographic data, unless otherwise cited in the text, come from the following sources: U.S., Department of Commerce, Bureau of the Census, *Thirteenth Census of the United States Taken in the Year 1910,* vol. 2, pp. 148–153 (number of farms, type and value of crops, value of land per acre), p. 166 (value of wages paid to hired labor per farm); U.S., Department of Commerce, Bureau of the Census, *Religious Bodies 1916,* part I, p. 244 (Catholic church members).
Several of the categories used here require further explanation. "Native white stock" refers to the descendants of Caucasians born in this country; "immigrants" or "foreign white stock" indicate Caucasians born abroad or the children of at least one foreign-born parent. The percentage of Catholics in a county was determined as follows: county population was estimated for 1916, the year of the religious census, from the populations of 1910 and 1920. Dividing this figure into the number of Catholic church members gave the percentage of Catholics in each county. (A city like San Francisco clearly had innumerable nonchurch members of Catholic stock; thus the percentage of Protestants should by no means be taken as the difference between the Catholic percentage and 1.00.) The number of farmers was not reported directly in the 1910 census. Instead, the percentage of farmers was estimated by dividing the number of farms by the total number of dwellings. The percentage urban, as defined by the census, is the percentage living in cities of 2,500+ population.

10. The prohibitionist nature of Johnson's support is actually less striking than might have been expected. In part—though only in part—this is explained by relative progressive weakness in the south, home of prohibitionist sentiment. Except for one or two small and isolated counties, the southern counties were the only ones to support prohibition significantly more than they supported Johnson.

11. Progressivism was also not based in the cities in Wisconsin and North and South Dakota. See Michael Paul Rogin, *The Intellectuals and McCarthy: The Radical Specter,* pp. 116, 144–146, 303.

12. Leading Progressive Chester Rowell owned and edited a Fresno

newspaper, which may account in part for the persistence of Progressive strength in the San Joaquin Valley.

13. In 1908, for example, Taft polled 70 percent of the middle-class vote and 49 percent of the working-class vote; his support was actually more concentrated in the middle class than Johnson's. Note also that the Socialists polled one-fourth of the working-class vote in 1910, and that Johnson's vote was no more middle class than the Democratic vote.

For most of the San Francisco data reported in this chapter, see Alexander Saxton, "San Francisco Labor and the Populist and Progressive Insurgencies," *Pacific Historical Review* 34 (November, 1965): 422–424, 432–433. Saxton was able to divide San Francisco into working-class and middle-class assembly districts, although there is no exact indication of just how "working class" the working-class districts were. He also reported the vote along class lines in the general elections of 1910 and 1914. Working-class support for progressivism is fully explored, with more precise data, in Chap. 3 of this book.

14. Southern California is defined for this period as the seven counties south of the Tehachapi Mountains other than Imperial. The Imperial Valley was separated from the rest of southern California culturally and economically, and authorities argued it was not truly part of the south. By the modern period, Imperial was more fully integrated into southern California; Chaps. 5 and 6 in this book include it in the region. Other writers have identified anywhere from eight to fourteen counties. Mowry uses nine (unspecified) counties, but for all practical purposes his southern California is used here.

15. The forty-five northern counties with no large cities gave Johnson more votes than he received in the south, as did the thirty-seven northern counties more than 17.5 percent rural-farm in 1910.

16. The computations for a multiple correlation also indicate which counties lower the correlation most drastically. (These are the counties whose actual vote differs most from that predicted by the multiple correlation.) Of the thirteen counties deviating more than ten percentage points, four were southern; each was less Progressive than its demographic characteristics alone predicted. (Almost all the other deviating counties were small and sparsely populated.) This might be further evidence for the peculiar anti-Progressive character of the south, or it might indicate that Stanton reduced Johnson's southern vote below what it would otherwise have been.

17. In the table of intercorrelations among Republican and Democratic votes for President and governor from 1884 to 1908, correlations range from .49 to .92. Not one election is correlated more highly with a demographic variable than with some previous party vote. During the Progressive years from 1910 to 1916, party correlations were lower, but party still exerted a greater impact than any single demographic factor.

18. Johnson's primary vote was correlated about —.45 with most Republican general elections from 1896 to 1908; the correlation with his own vote in November was still negative, but much lower (—.12).

19. This is not surprising, since the Democratic party had actually been the home of progressivism in California since 1896. Johnson's primary vote was correlated about .45 with the vote given most Democratic candidates from 1896 to 1908.

20. The method of measuring decreases in the Republican vote, as employed here and elsewhere in the chapter, requires explanation. The Republican county percentages in two elections (here, 1908 and 1910) were plotted against each other. The scattergram revealed a general pattern of relationships between the two elections, but with a number of deviant counties. These were the counties in which the Republican vote fell off either less or more than was typical, and it is these deviant counties that are referred to in the text.

21. Robert La Follette's vote in the 1912 primary was concentrated in the mountain and lumbering counties of the northeast and among the San Francisco working class. He received 28 percent of the vote in the city's working-class assembly districts. In two counties where the IWW had recently waged free-speech fights, La Follette received far more support, however, than anywhere else in the state. He garnered 39 percent of the San Diego vote and 48 percent of the San Joaquin (Stockton) total. Voting returns from the Midwest indicate that La Follette progressivism was generally radical and economically based. See Rogin, *Intellectuals and McCarthy*, pp. 70–80, 116–120.

22. The correlations between the elections of 1900, 1904, and 1908 ranged from .90 to .92. Roosevelt's correlations with these three elections dropped to an average of .6.

23. Among these was Imperial County, although its vote for Johnson was far lower than that in the other counties.

24. See Rogin, *Intellectuals and McCarthy*, pp. 71, 145–148, 288.

25. The correlations between Johnson's 1914 vote and various Socialist votes were as follows: 1910, .53; 1912, .41; 1920, .41; 1922, .53. The four Socialist votes averaged —.49 with the percentage of farm homes in 1910. Note that Johnson's 1914 vote was related to the Socialist vote for governor in 1910 rather than to his own vote. Chap. 3 in this book discusses the shift in working-class support more fully, using much finer data.

26. Because many California counties had neither a significant farming population nor any towns with a population as large as 2,500, relating elections both to the farming population and to the urban population does not simply report two sides of the same coin. The correlation between the percentage of the population living in cities and the percentage living on farms was only —.47. When each was held constant, the relation between the other and the Progressive vote remained above .3.

Perhaps in the absence of severe economic shocks, party traditions were stronger in rural than in urban areas. That might explain the relatively low Progressive party vote in the rural counties as well as the greater party stability there in the presidential elections of 1908 and 1916. Today, party loyalty is most fragile in rural areas, but fifty years ago the reverse may have been true. See Angus Campbell et al., *The American Voter*, pp. 402–408; Walter Dean Burnham, "The Changing Shape of the American Political Universe," *American Political Science Review* 59 (March, 1965): 10–26.

27. See Rogin, *Intellectuals and McCarthy*, pp. 120, 148. On the Midwest generally, see Benton Harold Wilcox, "A Reconsideration of the Character and Economic Basis of Northwestern Radicalism" (Ph.D. dissertation), pp. 110–114, passim.

28. Mowry, *California Progressives*, pp. 269–270; Spencer C. Olin, Jr., "Hiram Johnson, the California Progressives, and the Hughes Campaign of 1916," *Pacific Historical Review* 21 (1962): 303–304; Frederick M. Davenport, "Did Hughes Snub Johnson? An Inside Story," in *The Politics of California*, ed. David Farrelly and Ivan Hinderacker, pp. 208–211.

29. The multiple correlation between the two Johnson votes and the defections from Hughes was .63.

30. Mowry, *California Progressives*, pp. 270–271; Davenport, "Did Hughes Snub Johnson?" p. 211.

31. See Chap. 3 in this book.

32. Mowry, *California Progressives*, p. 272.

33. From 1896 through 1912, Republican presidential votes correlated about —.45 with the percentage of farm dwellings, and all were correlated above .3 with the percentage of urban residents.

34. The correlation with percentage of farm homes was only .27.

35. A 1908/1916 scattergram identified the counties whose percentages of Democratic votes had increased most and those whose percentages had increased least. The Democratic counties (all northern) averaged 56 percent for Johnson in 1916 and 54 percent in 1914. The Republican counties (even omitting five southern) averaged 45 percent in both years. The Democratic counties averaged 13 percent of their males in manufacturing industries in 1930 (the first year when such figures are available); the Republican counties averaged 4 percent. The Democratic counties were 18 percent rural-farm in 1910, the Republican counties 26 percent.

The shift of the south into the Republican party can be seen when the 1916 Republican presidential vote is plotted against the Republican votes of 1908 and 1912. On the 1908/1916 scattergram, five of the seven southern counties registered large relative Republican gains; none registered a large loss. On the 1912/1916 scattergram, four registered large gains, one a large loss.

36. The prohibition issue had at least as destructive an impact as progressivism on party loyalties in the 1920s. See Harold F. Gosnell, *Grass Roots Politics*, p. 85; Ostrander, *Prohibition Movement in California*, pp. 144–150. Tables of correlation co-efficients provide further evidence. There is no relationship at all between the Republican votes for senator and governor in 1922, senator and governor in 1926, and president in 1928 and governor in 1930. In each case, one election in the pair is highly positively correlated with the 1926 referenda against prohibition, the other highly negatively correlated.

37. The correlation between the two elections was .71. Johnson could hardly be considered a Progressive candidate in either year. He ran in alliance with anti-League of Nations conservatives, and many of the old Progressives supported Johnson's opponents in both years. Mowry, *California Progressives*, pp. 281–285. But rooted southern animosity to Johnson, rather than a temporary southern "Progressivism," seems best to explain the southern vote.

38. The La Follette election was correlated —.43 with the farm family level-of-living index for 1930; the Young correlation (in the primary) was —.29. The two elections correlated .34 and .40 with the percentage of males employed in manufacturing industries in 1930. See Margaret Jarmon Hagood, *Farm-Operator Family Level-of-Living Indexes for Counties of the United States, 1930, 1940, 1945, and 1950*; U.S., Department of Commerce, Bureau of the Census, *Fifteenth Census of the United States Taken in the Year 1930*, vol. 3, pp. 273–276. In part these correlations reflect the strength of both candidates in the northern and northeastern lumbering counties (see Table 4). It might also be noted that the La Follette and Young elections were correlated —.52 and —.48 with a 1926 prohibition referendum, even though Young had been active in temperance circles for decades.

39. Corinne Lathrop Gilb, "Justice Jesse W. Carter, An American Individualist," *Pacific Historical Review* 29 (1960): 149–151.

40. Mowry, *California Progressives*, pp. 19–21, 111–121; Lee Benson, *Merchants, Farmers, and Railroads*.

41. Mowry, *California Progressives*, p. 16; W. H. Hutchinson, "Prologue to Reform: The California Anti-Railroad Republicans, 1899–1905," *Southern California Quarterly* 44 (1962): 180–208; Gilb, "Jesse W. Carter," pp. 151–156.

42. This argument is more fully developed in chapter 3. See also Saxton, "San Francisco Labor," pp. 427–435; Mowry, *California Progressives*, pp. 143-153.

43. See Chap. 4 in this book.

44. Hofstadter, *Age of Reform;* Samuel Lubell, *The Future of American Politics;* Duncan MacRae, Jr. and James A. Meldrum, "Critical Elections in Illinois, 1888–1958," *American Political Science Review* 54 (September, 1960): 669–683.

45. Gilb ("Jesse W. Carter," pp. 145–146) reports on the similarity in political views between Progressives and San Francisco labor leaders. The labor leaders had the mentality of skilled artisans, she suggests, not class-conscious proletarians. Saxton ("San Francisco Labor," p. 437) notes the lessening of labor militance by 1916, concomitant with the Progressive-labor alliance. More generally, see Louis Hartz, *The Liberal Tradition in America;* Richard Hofstadter, *The American Political Tradition*.

3

The Progressives and the Working-Class Vote in California

WAGE earners were the forgotten men of the Progressive years, if current historical interpretations are to be accepted. Progressivism was a middle-class movement, and while its leaders might strive to remedy the crassest abuses of industrial society, they were as fearful of concentrated labor power as of unregulated monopoly capitalism. In their zeal for moral reform and efficiency they often were thrown into conflict with labor and immigrant-dominated political machines in cities. Consequently, we should expect few labor leaders to declare their sympathy for the reformers' cause; we should anticipate far less voting strength for Progressive candidates in working-class districts than in middle-class or exclusive residential neighborhoods.[1]

The case is made even stronger for California. The leading authority on the California reformers writes: "Admitting in theory that the union was a necessary organization in the industrial world, the progressives' bias against labor was always greater than against the large corporation." One of the most influential interpreters of the Progressive movement asserts: "And wherever labor was genuinely powerful in politics—as it was, for instance, in San Francisco, a closed-shop town where labor for a time dominated the local government—Progressivism took on a somewhat antilabor tinge."[2] The Progressive leaders of southern California were affected by the open-shop militancy of the *Los Angeles Times;* when they faced political crises in 1911 and 1913, they joined forces with reactionaries to defeat the mayoralty candidacy of a labor-backed Socialist candidate.[3]

The legislatures of 1911 and 1913, guided by Progressive Governor Hiram Johnson, passed significant legislation for the benefit of California working people, but Mowry stresses that any concessions to labor were always ringed with compromises. In the 1911 session, legislation was approved limiting the working day for women to eight hours, but only after the bill had been amended to exclude farm labor and cannery and packinghouse workers. A labor-endorsed anti-injunction bill passed the Senate but died in the assembly.[4] The 1913 legislature made workmen's compensation compulsory; established an Industrial Welfare Commission empowered to regulate maximum hours, minimum wages, and standard working conditions for women and children; and set a minimum wage for contract work done for the state. However, legislation legalizing peaceful picketing, a bill to provide jury trials in contempt cases arising from labor disputes and a second anti-injunction measure were defeated.[5]

Even this moderate labor legislation distressed Progressive leaders from the conservative southland; some of the early and prominent supporters of reform attempted to foil the tempered eight-hour day measure and they vigorously resisted the anti-injunction bills.[6] Governor Johnson dispatched four companies of the National Guard to Wheatland, north of Sacramento, after migratory farm workers organized by the IWW had clashed with a sheriff's posse. When "General" Charles T. Kelley's latter-day version of Coxey's Army of the unemployed was dispersed and driven from the capital city by volunteer deputies, the governor remained silent. Mowry adds, however, "there is no question that his sympathies were with the city officials."[7]

The interpretation of progressivism as a political movement of a disaffected middle class, frightened by the power of monopolistic corporations and fearful of organized labor, rests upon inferences drawn from public statements and, in a few instances, private thoughts, of a leadership elite. Chapter 2 has advanced the hypothesis that a distinct realignment of voting patterns took place in California midway in the period of Progressive ascendancy. Although Hiram Johnson was elected in 1910 with strongest support from areas preponderantly rural, native stock, and Protestant—the pattern of support that would be anticipated from the interpretations of Mowry and Hofstadter—a distinct change took place by 1914, and Progressive appeals henceforth were most effective in areas more urban, more working class and with greater foreign-born populations.

This hypothesis, supported in Chapter 2 by data drawn from counties and ecological areas of California, merits more specific analysis. The present chapter will explore the nature of progressivism's political support; it will not only turn from consideration of leadership to consideration of voters, but will add two additional sources of data to the evidence in the last chapter. First, we will examine the response of labor leaders and the labor press to progressivism. Second, we will attempt to determine the distribution of support for Progressive candidates and measures in California's two major metropolitan counties, San Francisco and Los Angeles.

Progressive insurgency and the factionalism it wrought in the dominant Republican party were the central issues in California politics from 1910 until 1930. California progressivism was greater than Hiram Johnson, but there can be little doubt that the forceful governor and senator was the prime representative of the movement in the state. Although Progressive leadership was fractured after 1920, Johnson still laid claim to the mantle of reform leadership, and neither his supporters nor his enemies were inclined to deny him the title. A focus primarily upon the political support for Johnson therefore provides a good index of the nature of the Progressive voting constituency. During the period considered here, 1910 to 1924, Johnson appeared as a candidate on the California ballot ten times: in the Republican primary for governor, 1910; Republican candidate for governor, 1910; Progressive vice-presidential nominee in 1912; Progressive candidate for governor, 1914; candidate in two Senatorial primaries and Republican nominee in two general elections, 1916 and 1922; delegations pledged to him were entered in two presidential primaries, 1920 and 1924. He lost the state in only one election, the presidential primary of 1924.[8]

Labor Leaders, the Labor Press, and Hiram Johnson

If California Progressives harbored a bias against labor, it was never obvious to contemporary labor or political leaders. No labor leaders were numbered among the top advisers of Hiram Johnson, but this apparently had little effect upon their support for the governor. Paul Scharrenberg, longtime executive secretary of the California State Federation of Labor and a central figure in the San Francisco labor movement, was asked in 1954: "Do you think Johnson was prolabor generally?" He replied:

> Oh, there was no question about it. Some of Mowry's statements in here are perfectly ridiculous. Hiram Johnson was started on his career by the Teamsters' Union of San Francisco. He'd been their attorney for some time. And John P. McLaughlin, who was secretary of the Teamsters' Union and was later appointed Labor Commissioner by him, he was the boy that rounded them up. And I was one of the first converts. (I was inclined to be for Bell, you know.[9] I was a Democrat then.) I swung in line and so did all the other leaders, but the rank and file in the labor districts of San Francisco, they were Democrats. And they couldn't just switch over because some new guy appeared on the horizon and said, 'Here, vote for me.' So when someone told Mowry that the leaders of labor were not for Johnson, he's got the thing upside down. The leaders of labor were for Johnson, they dragged the rank and file along. After the election and one or two sessions of the legislature, then the rank and file didn't have to be persuaded any more. They came along all right—on state issues. On national issues, that's something else again.[10]

Scharrenberg also recalled that the labor movement in San Francisco had backed the Progressive initiative and referendum measures.[11]

Franck Havenner, who served as Hiram Johnson's private secretary, managed his California campaign in the presidential primary of 1924 and later served as congressman from a San Francisco district, commented:

> Johnson through his policies as governor won strong support from organized labor and I think that after that the organized labor forces of San Francisco supported Johnson. . . . As Hiram John-

son gradually acquired the support of organized labor in Northern California . . . he began to lose some of his old anti-labor so-called Progressive support in Southern California.[12]

Chester Rowell, once designated by Johnson as his heir apparent but by 1920 at bitter odds with the senator over the League of Nations, appraised the political situation in California prior to the Hoover-Johnson presidential primary of 1920.[13] He noted that Johnson had the labor vote and that of the political Irish and Catholics. He had the support of all important labor leaders and both the Old Guard and Progressive machines in San Francisco,[14] while Hoover commanded the support of the women, the Protestant church, the anti-Irish and anti-Catholics, and both the Old Guard and Progressive machines in southern California.[15]

Organized labor, particularly in San Francisco, generally refrained from partisan political endorsements. Nevertheless, the sympathies of the labor press for Hiram Johnson were scarcely veiled. The *Labor Clarion,* organ of the San Francisco Central Labor Council, quoted Scharrenberg that Johnson's "uncompromising attitude for an effective Workmen's Compensation Act . . . should ever endear him to the men and women of labor."[16] The *Clarion* refrained from comment during the campaign of 1914, but after the balloting it "rejoiced" in the reelection of Governor Johnson.[17] The paper had discreet blessing for Johnson during his first senatorial campaign in 1916.[18]

When the California State Federation of Labor took a political stance in the 1920s, its support for Senator Johnson was unequivocal. During the 1924 presidential primary, a flyer signed by the president and secretary of the State Federation urged all members who registered Republican to vote for Johnson.[19] The *Southern California Labor Press* (Los Angeles) editorialized on March 21: "The labor movement of California always has supported Mr. Johnson, on account of his record as governor." The four labor councils of Los Angeles—central labor, building trades, metal trades, and allied printing trades—unanimously endorsed Johnson's presidential candidacy. The *Sacramento Bee* noted that the labor councils had taken this stand "in every campaign in which Senator Johnson has figured."[20]

Did the workers of California, organized and unorganized, follow the lead of union leaders and the labor press? The extent of working-class support for Johnson and progressivism can be determined best by examining voting statistics from California's two major metropolitan centers, San Francisco and Los Angeles.[21]

Labor Politics: San Francisco and Los Angeles

The two counties provided upwards of 40 percent of the total vote cast in any California election.[22] Both cities contained a sizable working-class population, but there the similarity ended. San Francisco was predominantly Catholic and ethnically diverse; 28 percent of its population in 1920 was foreign-born, with Irish and Italians predominating. Los Angeles was peopled by immigrants, but they were Protestant Anglo-Saxons from the small towns and farms of the South and Midwest. Only 18 percent of the county's population was foreign-born, and a quarter of these were from England and Canada.[23] San Francisco was a closed-shop town; union membership at its peak in 1918 totaled approximately 100,000.[24] In contrast, Los Angeles was virtually an open-shop city; 40,000 belonged to unions in 1919.[25] Labor influence loomed large in San Francisco city politics. Abe Reuf's Union Labor party, built independently of formal union support, was broken by the 1906 graft prosecutions, but P. H. McCarthy, head of the powerful Building Trades Council, managed to pick up the pieces and win election as mayor in 1909.

By 1911, however, the San Francisco Labor Council, a rival organization that had supported the graft prosecutions and opposed McCarthy, emerged as the dominant power group in San Francisco labor. More cosmopolitan than the locally centered Building Trades, the Labor Council lobbied in Sacramento, and its leaders, such as Scharrenberg, identified with the Progressive administration of Johnson.[26] Los Angeles labor, on the other hand, locked in a futile battle with powerful antilabor interests, assumed a radical posture lacking in San Francisco. Job Harriman, a Socialist supported by labor, barely lost the race for mayor in 1911, and several Socialist assemblymen won seats in Sacramento. Although weak, Los Angeles labor was not politically impotent. Labor-endorsed candidates usually held several posts on the city council and in May, 1925, eight of eleven approved candidates were elected.[27]

The Changing Progressive Constituency: San Francisco

San Francisco was allotted thirteen assembly districts in the reapportionment of 1911. Voting returns were tabulated by assembly district, and since there was no further reapportionment until 1929, political boundaries remained fixed through the Progressive period. To characterize the political constituency of the various San Francisco assembly districts is relatively easy. Tradition has it that the working class lived south of Market Street along the bay shore and in the Mission District, while the nabobs peered down upon them from Nob

Hill, Russian Hill, and Pacific Heights in the north, and an upwardly mobile middle class resided in the trim row houses of Sunset and Richmond on the ocean side of the city. The accuracy of these impressions can be confirmed by such indexes as the vote on an antipicketing referendum in 1916 (an indication of where labor sentiment was strongest), the vote for Socialist candidates, and ethnic data from the 1920 census tabulated by assembly district.[28]

When Hiram Johnson, prosecutor of the Reuf machine and opponent of the Southern Pacific Railroad, first sought the governorship in 1910, he was not popular in his home town. Contesting with five other candidates in the Republican primary, he ran second with 36 percent of the vote while he was carrying Los Angeles County by a clear majority of 52 percent.[29] Johnson carried, all by plurality, only three of San Francisco's eighteen assembly districts[30]—these three encompassed the Sunset and Richmond areas, Pacific Heights, and an apartment house district stretching north from the present Civic Center toward Nob Hill. He ran weakest in the working-class areas south of Market Street and in the Mission District. His 43 percent won him San Francisco County in a three-way race in November, but at the same time he garnered 46 percent in Los Angeles. Johnson carried ten assembly districts but won a majority only in A.D. 41 and 42, the silk-stocking Pacific Heights, and midtown apartment house areas.

The election was complicated by the presence on the ballot of a Socialist[31] who received 8 percent of the city's vote but won more than 20 percent in five of the "south of the slot" working-class districts.[32] Although Johnson carried five of the districts south of Market Street, the votes that won for him ranged from a low of 38 percent to a high of 44 percent. Johnson's victories in 1910 owed little to San Francisco; he had won the "better" neighborhoods, but the vast majority of the working-class population had voted their preference for Democratic or Socialist candidates.[33]

An abrupt change in the Progressive voting constituency took place in 1914. Campaigning as a Progressive party candidate in his bid for reelection and opposed by both major parties, Johnson polled 55 percent of the vote in San Francisco and 53.5 percent in Los Angeles. More important was the vote distribution.[34] Johnson secured a majority in nine of the thirteen assembly districts including all those south of Market Street and in the Mission District. In 1910, for example, Johnson polled 38 percent of the vote in the assembly district situated in the Potrero Hill area; in 1914 in the new A.D. 22, which circumscribed much the same area, he received 67 percent of the vote. The Socialist vote there in 1910 had been 24 percent; in 1914 it was 7 percent. Johnson's poorest showing in the entire city (39.5 percent) was in A.D. 31, located in the Pacific Heights area, its boundaries only slightly modified from the district that had given him 52 percent of its vote in 1910. In addition he ran below his city average in A.D. 27 (Sunset), 28 (Richmond), 32 (Russian Hill, downtown apartment house area), 30 (Western Addition), and 33 (Italian, North Beach). Johnson won San Francisco with a base of support quite different from that which placed him in the state house four years earlier. His success resulted from strong new support in working-class districts, which more than compensated serious losses in the more exclusive residential areas.

The votings patterns of 1914 became a permanent part of the San Francisco political landscape. As Table 12 indicates, in seven contests between 1914 and 1924, Johnson's landslide victories derived most from the vote in A.D. 21 through 26 and 29, all but two of them south of Market Street or in the Mission District.[35] With minor exceptions, Johnson's vote was always below the mean of his San Francisco vote in A.D. 27,

28, 31, 32, and 33—the Sunset, Richmond, Pacific Heights, Nob Hill–Russian Hill, and North Beach areas.[36] The differential was most obvious in primaries, less so in general elections because of traditional party loyalty. Even so, by 1922 working-class districts were casting a more preponderant vote for Hiram Johnson when he was a Republican party candidate than the residents of Pacific Heights.[37]

The Johnson voting constituency in San Francisco can be defined more precisely by correlating the percentage votes in the thirteen assembly districts over a series of elections.[38] Correlations with votes before 1911 is impossible, owing to the reapportionment that took place that year. However, comparison of the votes for Theodore Roosevelt, first in the presidential primary and then in the general election of 1912, with the vote for Hiram Johnson in 1914, strongly suggests that a major realignment took place between these two elections. The vote for Roosevelt in the Republican presidential primary of 1912 correlated a low .484 with the vote for Johnson in the general election of 1914, and the vote for Roosevelt, the Republican presidential candidate in California in 1912, correlated negatively (—.48) with the Johnson vote in the general election of 1914.[39] The alignment first evident in 1914 was amazingly stable. As Table 13 indicates, it persisted regardless of embroilments and defections within the Progressive leadership. For example, Johnson's vote for governor in 1914 correlated a high .93 with his vote in the presidential primary of 1924.

Most important, the correlation figures underscore the close relationship of the vote for Hiram Johnson with prolabor sentiment in San Francisco. In the election of 1916, the city's voters passed by a narrow margin Charter Amendment #8, an antipicketing ordinance modeled on that of Los Angeles and supported by business interests determined to limit union

TABLE 12

Johnson's Percentage Vote in San Francisco

	Governor 1914 % of Vote	Senator (Primary) 1916 % of Vote	Senator 1916 % of Vote	President (Primary) 1920 % of Vote	Senator (Primary) 1922 % of Vote	Senator 1922 % of Vote	President (Primary) 1924 % of Vote
City Total	54.6	59.2	71.9	73.4	60.7	67.9	59.7
Working-class A.D.s							
21	60.0	70.1	68.2	80.5	70.8	64.5	67.5
22	67.7	77.3	77.5	84.2	75.6	70.2	78.8
23	66.3	75.2	72.7	87.5	78.7	70.4	79.9
24	66.5	72.9	74.3	84.1	73.5	71.8	70.6
25	62.6	64.2	74.9	84.9	73.6	75.6	75.2
26	56.2	60.0	73.8	79.7	67.0	69.0	64.3
29	59.4	63.3	70.7	80.3	71.6	71.4	70.4
Middle- and upper-class A.D.s							
27	53.7	55.9	71.1	71.8	58.7	67.6	50.7
28	51.1	53.6	70.8	68.8	50.7	68.0	43.5
30	46.5	57.5	67.7	74.8	61.7	65.7	57.4
31	39.5	42.2	71.3	52.7	38.7	60.7	31.5
32	45.4	49.1	70.0	62.0	48.0	62.6	38.6
Italian working-class A.D.							
33	47.4	57.0	74.3	63.7	52.3	67.1	48.0

TABLE 13
Correlation Matrix: Johnson's San Francisco Vote

	(1) Governor 1914	(2) Primary 1916	(3) Senator 1916	(4) Primary 1920	(5) Primary 1922	(6) Senator 1922	(7) Primary 1924
(1)							
(2)	.944						
(3)	.514	.683					
(4)	.939	.909	.330				
(5)	.938	.936	.351	.994			
(6)	.818	.649	.583	.801	.764		
(7)	.936	.939	.427	.983	.996	.782	

power.[40] The vote for Johnson in the primary correlated .949 with the votes "No" on this crucial index of labor sentiment. In the general election of 1914 and in each primary in which Hiram Johnson was a candidate, the correlation of his vote with the vote "no" on the antipicketing ordinance was above .90.

TABLE 14

Johnson Vote and Prolabor Sentiment in San Francisco

	Governor 1914	Senator (Primary) 1916	Senator 1916	President (Primary) 1920	Senator (Primary) 1922	President (Primary) 1924
Charter Amendment No. 8	.921	.949	.358[a1]	.914	.947	.959

The fact that Johnson absorbed the Socialist vote in San Francisco indicates further the political inclinations of areas in which he gathered his most loyal supporters. His percentage in 1914 correlated .67 with the percentage for Eugene V. Debs in the 1912 election; in 1920 when Johnson was a candidate in the May presidential primary and Debs in the November election, the correlation was .88.

Johnson's working-class backers in San Francisco recognized Progressives regardless of the party label they wore. Woodrow Wilson carried the city in 1916 with 52 percent of the vote; Robert La Follette, listed on the California ballot in 1924 as a Socialist, won 46 percent of the San Francisco vote. The distribution of Wilson's 1916 vote by assembly district correlated .905 with that of Johnson in the Republican primary and .245 with his Republican senatorial vote in November (Table 15). The latter figure is especially significant: against the normal expectation of a close identity between a party's presidential and senatorial candidate, Johnson's vote correlated positively with that of Wilson and negatively (—.245) with that of Hughes.[42] Given the decisive importance of the close California vote in 1916, could Charles Evans Hughes have ridden on Johnson's coattails in San Francisco, he would have become president of the United States.

The high correlation of .986 between the backing given Johnson in the 1924 presidential primary and the vote for La Follette in the general election evidences almost a complete identity of support. Examined in time series (Table 15), La Follette's strength in San Francisco was in the same districts that had overwhelmingly endorsed Johnson, opposed the antipicketing ordinance, and voted most heavily for Wilson in 1916.[43]

There was an important ethnic element in Hiram Johnson's vote. In general, the greater the number of foreign-born and first-generation immigrants in an assembly district, the higher the vote for Johnson (Table 16). Most striking was the high relationship between the number of foreign-born Irish[44] and the Johnson vote. The Irish population was diffused throughout San Francisco with slightly higher concentrations in A.D. 21, 24, and 25, the former south of Market Street on the bay shore and the latter two in the Mission District. All three were Johnson political strongholds.[45] One ethnic group, representing the largest foreign-born component in the city, was little attracted to progressivism. Assembly District 33, where 19 percent of the population were native Italians, ran consistently below the city average for Johnson and voted 60.2 percent "Yes" on the 1916 antipicketing ordinance.[46] The Irish, foreign born, and first generation were concentrated in working-class districts; whether they voted as they did because they were members of a nationality group or because they

TABLE 15

Correlation: Johnson, Wilson, La Follette

	Governor 1914	Primary 1916	Wilson 1916	Charter Amendment #8	Primary 1920	Primary 1922	Primary 1924
La Follette 1924	.888	.935	.922	.971	.926	.967	.986
Wilson 1916	.911	.905		.912	.943	.953	.931

were part of the laboring class cannot be determined accurately. However, the higher correlation figures indicate that the vote against the 1916 antipicketing ordinance would have been a better predictor of the future political behavior of a district than the percentage of Irish or nonnative white population.

TABLE 16

Correlation: Nativity, Foreign Born, and the Progressive Vote

	Nativity[a] 1920	Foreign-Born Irish	Foreign-Born German
Johnson, Governor, 1914	.545	.796	.545
Johnson, Primary, 1916	.756	.692	.455
Johnson, Senator, 1916	.432	.469	.07
Wilson, 1916	.522	.751	.630
Charter Amendment #8	.703	.733	.530
Johnson, Primary, 1920	.524	.780	.686
Johnson, Primary, 1922	.687	.747	.613
Johnson, Senator, 1922	.305	.604	.414
Johnson, Primary, 1924	.644	.735	.578

[a] "Nativity" refers to the percent of the total population of the city or an assembly district who were *not* native whites of native white parentage.

San Francisco voting returns lend scant support to any hypothesis that progressivism in California was sustained by middle-class votes. Alleged bias against unions did not deter the great majority of these San Franciscans who voted "No" on the antipicketing ordinance from at the same time marking their ballot for Hiram Johnson. As governor and senator, Johnson had amazing drawing power in San Francisco and did win middle- and upper-class votes, particularly in general elections. Yet, as 1910 demonstrated, his base became weak when these constituted his principal support. A new Progressive constituency centered in working-class assembly districts emerged in 1914. It carried the city for Johnson every time he was a candidate; it won the city—and the presidency—for Woodrow Wilson in 1916; and it provided the core of La Follette's support in 1924. As the Progressives gained strong labor support, they were deserted by voters in "better" neighborhoods. Had Johnson lacked the urban lower-class support that allowed him to garner huge majorities in San Francisco to offset losses in southern California, his political career would have been terminated at an early date.

The Changing Progressive Constituency: Los Angeles

Analysis of the support for Hiram Johnson in Los Angeles County must take into account that the original enthusiasm southern California voters demonstrated for progressivism waned rapidly after 1914.[47] In the 1910 primary, Johnson ran twenty percentage points ahead of the strongest of his four opponents and carried Los Angeles County with a 52 percent majority. In the general election, his 46 percent was ten percentage points above that of the Democratic candidate.[48] In 1914, the governor far outdistanced the field, winning 53.5 percent of the county's vote against Republican, Democratic, Prohibition, and Socialist opponents. In the four ensuing primaries—two senatorial and two presidential—while Johnson was winning more than 60 percent of the San Francisco Republican vote in each, he carried Los Angeles County in not one.[49]

The study of Los Angeles County voting returns is complicated by methodological problems.[50] Any conclusions drawn from the returns must be more generalized and less precise than those from San Francisco data. However, a few comparisons are possible. Votes within the city of Los Angeles, the urban heart of the county, can be distinguished from the combined vote of the suburbs. It is also possible to extract from the voting ledgers the approximate vote of the two largest suburban communities, Long Beach and Pasadena.

The impressive majority that Hiram Johnson compiled in Los Angeles County in the 1910 primary owed more to votes cast in the suburban communities than in the urban central city. In Pasadena, a wealthy garden city, he amassed 58 percent of the vote; in Long Beach, largest of the suburbs and haven for midwestern émigrés, he won 61.4 percent. The voting pattern was comparable to that of San Francisco in 1910; Johnson ran proportionately better in middle- and upper-class districts.

Changes in the distribution of votes in Los Angeles are less dramatic than those in San Francisco, but a similar trend appears. Between 1910 and 1914, support for Johnson increased sharply in the city. Table 17 shows that as Johnson's voting percentage dwindled throughout the county after 1916, the greatest losses were in the suburbs and were most severe in Pasadena and Long Beach. By 1920, Johnson was distinctly a more popular candidate among the residents of the older, less exclusive homes and apartments in the heart of the city than with the more affluent in Pasadena or Long Beach.

Other variations in voting behavior suggest differences between the city of Los Angeles and the suburbs. The city tended to be more favorable to Socialist candidates: J. Stitt Wilson tallied 20 percent of the city vote in 1910, 12 percent in the suburbs. Los Angeles County was a Republican stronghold, but the city was less so than the suburbs. Woodrow Wilson's percentage in the city in 1916 was 47.4 percent; in the suburbs, 42.6 percent.[51] The most distinct difference was the vote on a 1916 state prohibition initiative: the city voted 46 per-

TABLE 17
Percentage Vote for Johnson in Los Angeles County

Location	Primary 1910 % of Vote	Governor 1910 % of Vote	Governor 1914 % of Vote	Primary 1916 % of Vote	Primary 1920 % of Vote	Primary 1922 % of Vote	Primary 1924 % of Vote
Los Angeles County	51.9	45.7	53.5	41.8	49.7	44.1	34.5
City	49.7	41.5	54.9	41.0	53.7	47.0	37.6
Suburbs	55.7	52.1	51.5	43.2	44.5	40.0	30.8
Long Beach	61.4	54.1	52.9	46.7	46.4	34.2	25.7
Pasadena	58.0	55.9	52.8	49.7	33.0	30.2	19.8

cent in favor; the suburbs, 64 percent. Johnson received his best support in Los Angeles County after 1916 from areas that tended to be against prohibition, slightly more Democratic, and more inclined to vote for an attractive Socialist candidate.[52]

Ethnically, Los Angeles County was more homogeneous than San Francisco; population distinctions between city and suburbs represent shadings rather than clear differences. Of the county's residents in 1920, 55 percent were native whites born of native parents, compared to 33 percent in San Francisco. Nonetheless, a few variations appear in this predominantly white, Anglo-Saxon mosaic. Table 18 shows that Los Angeles City was slightly more diverse than the suburbs and particularly more so than Long Beach and Pasadena. Even the figures of 15 percent and 12 percent foreign born in the latter two cities are deceiving, for 39 percent in Pasadena and 47.5 percent in Long Beach of the foreign born were natives of England or Canada.[53] Nativity statistics from Los Angeles County, although indecisive, support the conclusion that Hiram Johnson ran proportionately stronger after 1916 in more ethnically diverse areas—for example, urban Los Angeles—and, in general, the greater the percentage of native whites of Anglo-Saxon background, the weaker the support for Johnson.

To determine if there were differences in the extent of support for Johnson within the boundaries of the city, an attempt was made in one election—the primary of 1922—to equate the official vote tabulations by precinct with the seven assembly districts in the city.[54] By this estimate, the percentage vote for Johnson was greatest in A.D. 71 (61 percent compared to 47 percent in the city as a whole), located to the south of the city's center adjacent to Long Beach, incorporating the harbor area at San Pedro and stretching north in a narrow corridor

TABLE 18

Ethnic Background, Los Angeles County, 1920

(in percentages)

	Native White	Native White of Native Parentage	Foreign Born
San Francisco County	69.0	33.0	27.7
Los Angeles County	77.4	55.1	17.8
City	75.4	51.1	19.4
Suburbs	79.7	60.0	14.8
Long Beach	86.8	68.2	12.1
Pasadena	81.5	61.7	15.0

SOURCE: *California Compendium, 1920*, pp. 34–35, 39–43.

along Main Street and Central Avenue.[55] Johnson ran above his city average by more than 10 percentage points in two assembly districts just south of the present Civic Center. His weakest showing in the city was in the two districts located west of Figueroa Street, a traditional boundary line that separates the "better" residential areas to the west from those downtown. In general, Johnson's vote in the city was greatest in the most distinctly working-class areas to the south and near the city center and diminished westward across the city.

Los Angeles voting returns reveal a pattern similar to, although less distinctive, than that of San Francisco. Whether this less distinctive pattern is the result of actual voting returns or of the more generalized data from Los Angeles County employed here cannot be determined. Suburban voters in increasing numbers, particularly in Pasadena and Long Beach, like those in San Francisco's Richmond District and Pacific Heights, abandoned Hiram Johnson on election day. As his popularity in the state's largest county declined, those who remained his most steadfast supporters were residents of urban neighborhoods, which not only impressions but more concrete data, such as skepticism toward prohibition, occasional support for Socialists, and diverse ethnic composition, would identify as working class.[56]

Conclusion

To accept the conclusion of this chapter and the preceding one, coupled with a recent and complementary study by Alexander Saxton[57] would require a recasting of widely accepted interpretations of the Progressive movement. Neither the statements of political and labor leaders nor the voting records from California's two major metropolitan centers sustain the thesis that it was primarily a middle-class movement. The rank-and-file urban voters who consistently backed Progressive candidates lived in working-class areas. In consequence, the hypothesis that the California Progressive represented a particular strain of middle-class individualism and became militant when he felt himself hemmed in between the battening corporation and the rising labor union, seems scarcely tenable. Any antilabor tinge in the thought of leaders of California progressivism appears to have had little political significance.

A reevaluation of progressivism taking into account its urban lower-class support would necessitate a new focus upon the social reform program of Progressive governors and legislators, certainly in California and perhaps elsewhere.[58] Between 1911 and 1915, *some* factor transformed working-class voters from apathy to vigorous support of progressivism, and by the same token, *some* factor incited the suspicions of middle- and upper-class electors, causing them to drift away.

If the testimony of labor leaders and the evidence from the labor vote are to be accepted, the working class and its leaders considered the social legislation of the Progressives a major and positive achievement. While this legislation was often qualified and tempered, the labor constituency obviously was more impressed by the gains they had made, rather than by the demands—such as an anti-injunction bill—they had lost.

In like fashion, it would appear that in 1910 when the Progressive program was largely a negative one aimed at destroying the power of the Southern Pacific machine, there were among its leaders—and perhaps voting supporters—individuals, particularly from southern California, who had little sympathy with the demands of labor. As the Johnson legislative program unfolded, these antilabor elements fell by the wayside, and by 1916 the main line of California progressivism was firmly tied to a working-class base. In this perspective, the humanitarian and labor legislation of the first Johnson administration assume major political significance.

A reinterpretation that credits the urban laboring population with a central political role in the Progressive movement will restore a sense of continuity to the study of American reform. Hence, the upsurge of working-class and immigrant power that dominated American politics during the depression, and at least a decade thereafter, would no longer appear as a sudden phenomenon that burst forth in an Al Smith revolution in 1928.[59] In California, the political upheaval of the 1930s marked the augmenting and coming to power of the same groups that had sustained Johnson, Wilson, and La Follette, buttressed the Progressive reforms two decades earlier, and kept what remained of reform politics alive through the 1920s.

NOTES

1. George E. Mowry, "The California Progressive and His Rationale: A Study in Middle Class Politics," *Mississippi Valley Historical Review* 36 (September, 1949): 239–250; Richard Hofstadter, *The Age of Reform,* pp. 131–270.

2. George E. Mowry. *The California Progressives,* p. 92; Hofstadter, *Age of Reform,* p. 239.

3. Mowry, *California Progressives,* pp. 51, 143, 201.

4. Ibid., pp. 144–147.

5. Ibid., p. 155.

6. Ibid., pp. 144, 146–147.

7. Ibid., pp. 195, 198.

8. Johnson won reelection by a landslide in 1928; in 1932 and 1940, he cross-filed and won both Republican and Democratic nominations. Eugene C. Lee, *California Votes, 1928–1960,* pp. A-50, A-55, A-60.

9. Theodore Bell, Democratic candidate for governor, 1910.

10. Paul Scharrenberg, "Paul Scharrenberg Reminiscences" (transcript of tape-recorded interviews), pp. 54–55.

11. Ibid., pp. 56–61.

12. Franck R. Havenner, "Franck Roberts Havenner Reminiscences" (transcript of tape-recorded interviews), p. 61.

13. Hiram Johnson to Chester Rowell, 19 March 1916, Johnson Papers, Bancroft Library, Berkeley.

14. The 1920 election was the only one in which the San Francisco "Old Guard" endorsed Johnson. See *San Francisco Chronicle,* 1, 2 May 1920.

15. Rowell to Mark Sullivan, 29 April 1920, Rowell Papers, Bancroft Library, Berkeley.

16. *Labor Clarion,* 16 May 1913.

17. Ibid., 6 November 1914.

18. Ibid., 1 September 1916, 27 October 1916.

19. Copy in Johnson Papers, part 3, carton 10, Bancroft Library, Berkeley.

20. Ibid., 12 April 1924.

21. Boundaries of the city and county of San Francisco are contiguous.

22. For example, in the 1918 gubernatorial election, 38.7%; 1920 presidential, 42.8%; 1922 gubernatorial, 40.2%; 1924 presidential, 47.6%.

23. U.S., Department of Commerce, Bureau of the Census, *Fourteenth Census of the United States, State Compendium: California,* pp. 39–40, 41, 43 (hereafter cited as *California Compendium, 1920*).

24. Robert Edward Lee Knight, *Industrial Relations in the San Francisco Bay Area, 1900–1918,* p. 369.

25. Louis B. Perry and Richard S. Perry, *A History of the Los Angeles Labor Movement, 1911–1941,* pp. 107–108.

26. Alexander Saxton, "San Francisco Labor and the Populist and Progressive Insurgencies," *Pacific Historical Review* 34 (November, 1965): 427–430.

27. Perry and Perry, *Los Angeles Labor Movement*, p. 215.

28. See Table 14 above. Saxton ("San Francisco Labor," pp. 423–424) uses different indices and arrives at almost the same characterization.

29. All San Francisco voting statistics are from Official Statement of Vote, City and County of San Francisco (in the files of Registrar of Voters, City Hall). Maps of assembly districts are in the same office. Percentages have been calculated by the author; all figures in the text except those ending in .5 have been rounded to nearest whole number.

30. The 1910 election preceded reapportionment; San Francisco had eighteen assembly districts.

31. J. Stitt Wilson, elected mayor of Berkeley in 1911.

32. Refers to the cable car "slot" that ran down Market Street.

33. A vote for the Democrat, Bell, was not a vote against reform. His platform denounced the Southern Pacific. See Mowry, *California Progressives*, p. 130.

34. The primaries of 1914 are ignored; Johnson was unopposed for the Progressive party nomination.

35. Assembly District 29 was intersected by Market Street west of City Hall; the bulk of the district lay south in the upper Mission. Assembly District 26 was immediately west and extended north from Market to Fulton Street.

36. On Assembly District 33, see Table 12 above.

37. The "better" residential areas had not lost their Republican loyalty. Harding polled more than 70 percent in Assembly Districts 27, 28, 31, 32, and 33; his city mean was 65 percent. The victorious Republican gubernatorial candidate in 1922, conservative Friend W. Richardson, lost the city but carried Assembly Districts 28, 31, and 32.

38. A correlation coefficient measures the relationship between two variables. The higher the number, the closer the relationship. A high coefficient would indicate that where one variable was high, the second would be high, and where the first was low, the second would also be low. Coefficients for San Francisco election returns are very high. As a rule of thumb, a coefficient of .90 would explain 81 percent of the variance. All computations are by the author.

39. Woodrow Wilson carried every San Francisco assembly district in 1912; his largest margins were in nonworking class Assembly Districts 30, 31, and 32. Like Johnson's, his support diverged; the vote that won Wilson the city in 1916 correlated —.88 with his vote in 1912.

40. An adjunct of this same campaign was the Preparedness Day parade in July, 1916, at which the bomb exploded that led to the Mooney-Billings case. See Knight, *Industrial Relations in the Bay Area*, pp. 304–318.

41. This correlation is low since votes in the general election might include loyal Republicans unsympathetic to labor.

42. Where there are two candidates only, a positive correlation with

the vote of the Democrat would mean the inverse, a negative correlation with the vote of the Republican.

43. The same constituency also supported Progressive initiative and referendum measures. One of the most important of these, the Water and Power Act of 1922, was designed to put state credit behind public ownership of water and hydroelectric facilities. It was defeated, but in San Francisco the vote "Yes" correlated .94 with the "No" vote on anti-picketing and .97 with Johnson's vote in the 1922 primary. On the act itself, see Franklin H. Hichborn, "California Politics, 1891-1939" (unpublished manuscript), pp. 1958-2013.

44. An inference is made that the larger the number of foreign-born Irish, the more Irish a district. See *California Compendium, 1920,* p. 43.

45. See Table 12 in this chapter.

46. Any explanation of the deviation in the Italian community is beyond the scope of this chapter. Assembly District 33 voted nearly as strongly for Old Guard Republicans as Pacific Heights, but the district shifted in 1928.

47. See Chap. 2 of this book.

48. There were three candidates in the 1910 general election.

49. All Los Angeles County returns are from Minutes of the Board of Supervisors, County of Los Angeles, Record of Elections (in Files Section, Board of Supervisors, County Administration Building).

50. Election results are not totaled for assembly districts but are tallied in units of 60 precincts, the number recorded on a single page of the voting ledger. Precincts are arranged in numerical order for the city of Los Angeles; for outlying areas of the country, all cities with the return from each of their precincts are listed alphabetically. Since precinct boundaries were often modified and new precincts added, correlations are possible only in the rare cases when no changes were made between a primary and general election in the same year. This study made use of the recapitulation of the vote in the ledgers only.

51. Johnson's November vote in 1916 correlated .509 with Wilson's November vote, a coefficient higher than in San Francisco.

52. Differences still exist. In 1966, Governor Brown in losing the county won 53 percent of the vote in the city but only 36 percent in the suburbs. See Frank M. Jordan, comp., *California Statement of Vote and Supplement: November 8, 1966 General Election,* pp. 86-87.

53. In the city of Los Angeles, only 22 percent of the foreign-born were native to England or Canada.

54. No attempt was made to recompute the 600-odd precincts into assembly district totals. Totals used were from the ledger pages and are approximations—for example, Assembly District 74 consisted of precincts 65-104 and 275-282. The totals used here to approximate Assembly District 74 are 61-120, therefore including twenty precincts contiguous to, but not a part of, Assembly District 74 and eliminating eight precincts. Precinct maps are not available. For assembly district boundaries in Los Angeles, 1911-1929, see Don A. Allen, Sr., *Legislative Sourcebook: The California Legislature and Reapportionment, 1849-1965,* p. 140.

55. This area is now inhabited largely by Negroes.

56. Thomas Zach, a graduate student at San Francisco State College, found the same trends apparent in San Francisco and Los Angeles counties to be replicated in California's third metropolitan county, Alameda. For example, correlating the vote for Hiram Johnson in the 1910 governor's primary in eight Alameda County communities (Oakland, Berkeley, Alameda, San Leandro, Hayward, Piedmont, Emeryville, and Livermore) with nine subsequent elections in which Johnson was a candidate, he obtained the following results:

	Governor Primary 1910
Governor, 1910	.96
Presidential Primary, 1912 (Roosevelt)	.72
Roosevelt, 1912	.84
Governor, 1914	.00
Senate Primary, 1916	—.43
Presidential Primary, 1920	—.86
Senate Primary, 1922	—.72
Senate, 1922	—.50
Presidential Primary, 1924	—.81

57. See Chap. 2 in this book; Saxton, "San Francisco Labor," pp. 421–438.

58. The characterization of progressivism as a "middle class" movement rests almost exclusively upon studies of leadership, not voting constituency. This widely accepted view has been challenged by J. Joseph Huthmacher, "Urban Liberalism and the Age of Reform," *Mississippi Valley Historical Review* 49 (September, 1962): 231–241 and more convincingly by John D. Buenker, "The Urban Political Machine and the Seventeenth Amendment," *Journal of American History* 56 (September, 1969): 305–322. A parallel reappraisal of California progressivism is suggested in Spencer C. Olin, Jr., "The Social Conscience of the Hiram Johnson Administration" (Paper delivered at the Annual Meeting of the Organization of American Historians, Chicago, April 27–29, 1967 and in Olin's subsequent book, *California's Prodigal Sons: Hiram Johnson and the Progressives, 1911–1917* (Berkeley, 1968). The extent to which labor's legislative demands were satisfied by Progressive measures is suggested in Gerald D. Nash, "The Influence of Labor on State Policy, 1860–1920: The Experience of California," *California Historical Society Quarterly* 47 (September, 1965): 241–257. Saxton, "San Francisco Labor," pp. 43–45.

59. See Chap. 4 in this book.

4

Was 1928 a Critical
Election in California?

BOTH Samuel Lubell, in his widely read book *The Future of American Politics,* and V. O. Key, Jr., in his seminal article on the critical election phenomena, have attached special significance to the election of 1928.[1] This election, it is argued, marked a critical realignment of American voting patterns, particularly manifested by the fact that the Democratic party for the first time in its history marshaled a plurality of the total vote cast in the twelve largest metropolitan centers of the United States.

Most students of American political behavior concur with Lubell: "Smith's defeat in 1928, rather than Roosevelt's 1932 victory, marked off the arena in which today's politics are being fought." Key was more circumspect and offered an interpretation of voting behavior in only one section: "In New England, at least, the Roosevelt revolution of 1932 was in large measure an Al Smith revolution of 1928, a characterization less applicable to the remainder of the country."[2]

The Key Model and California Voting Behavior

This chapter attempts to apply Key's critical election model directly to California voting data to determine if the same trends Key detected in Massachusetts and Lubell extrapolated into a nationwide phenomenon are equally evident in California.

Any analysis of California voting data is complicated by such vexing factors as population mobility, a tradition of weak political parties, and the compilation of official returns by county units only. Regardless of what qualifications these factors impose, one point is certain: a voting revolution took place between 1928 and 1936. In 1928, Republicans constituted 72 percent of the state's 2,313,816 registered voters; in 1930, 78 percent of California's 2,245,228 voters were registered as Republicans. Then, during the first six years of the 1930s, the Democratic party added nearly 1,500,000 registrants, an increase of 313 percent. During the same interval, the Republicans lost 394,000 registrants, a decrease of 24 percent.[3] In 1934, Democratic registration for the first time exceeded that of the Republicans.

Dramatic increments in registration, however, do not necessarily indicate shifts in distribution of power. Political interest, as manifested by the percentage of the eligible adult population who actually voted, had been increasing for two elections before 1932. In 1916, 58 percent of eligible adults voted; in 1920, 47 percent; in 1924, 51 percent; in 1928, 59 percent; and in 1932, 63 percent.[4] While the Democratic gains in the 1930s marked a phenomenal increase in the party's potential voting strength, in an important context there was no significant realignment of Democratic party support. As Eugene C. Lee has noted:

> Even in the upheaval which occurred between 1928 and 1936, the relative position of the counties tended to be maintained. . . . The 25 most Democratic counties in 1936 were all among the most Democratic counties in 1928, although not all of the 1928 Democratic counties are included in the later figure. . . . Of the 15 most Democratic counties in 1960, all were among the most Democratic counties in 1936.[5]

This would indicate that the increments of the early 1930s were a part of a voting cycle that had been established earlier.

If there was an "Al Smith revolution" in California, it should be clearly evidenced in the support for the Democratic candidate in the metropolitan centers of the state. The eleven largest counties in California contributed 79.8 percent of the total vote cast in 1928, but only 78.1 percent of Smith's vote. The remaining less urban counties contributed 20.1 percent of the total vote, but 21.8 percent of the Democratic presidential total.[6] These inconclusive figures scarcely point to the type of urban revolution Lubell suggests.

Such first suspicions are further confirmed if the Democratic vote in the eleven metropolitan counties in 1928 is compared with the Democratic vote there in the three preceding elections[7] (see Table 19).

In all of the eleven countries, Smith's percentage was less than that for Wilson in 1916 or for the combined La Follette–Davis vote in 1924. The election of 1920 may be aptly classified as a "deviant election"; in all eleven counties Democratic percentages fell off sharply from 1916, but the losses were regained in 1924. It is ironic that most analyses of the 1928 election have been based on comparisons with the deviant election of

TABLE 19

Democratic Vote in Eleven Metropolitan Counties, 1916-1928

County	1916	1920	1924	1928
Alameda	45.9	20.7	37.8	33.6
Contra Costa	48.4	25.0	45.6	43.4
Fresno	54.8	37.5	55.4	44.3
Los Angeles	45.7	22.4	33.4	28.7
Orange	37.9	20.7	31.3	19.8
Sacramento	52.1	30.1	58.5	48.2
San Bernardino	44.1	29.5	41.4	24.1
San Diego	49.7	18.1	50.5	32.0
San Francisco	55.3	22.4	51.6	49.4
San Joaquin	59.3	33.8	50.5	37.9
Santa Clara	46.0	23.4	41.2	35.4

1920. A comparison with 1916 and 1924, therefore, indicates a falling off rather than a Democratic upsurge in California in 1928.

An examination of local voting statistics in the city of San Francisco, which Lubell cites as manifesting the alleged upsurge of 1928, lends no confirmation to the theory. In six of the thirteen assembly districts in San Francisco, the percentage Republican vote in 1928 was greater than that in 1924; in two, it remained constant; and it decreased in five. Most important, however, five of the districts where the Republican vote increased were those in the Mission and South of Market areas—the working-class and immigrant districts where the Al Smith revolution was supposed to have happened. In contrast, the greatest falloff in Republican vote (12 percentage points) between 1924 and 1928 occurred in the 31st, which was the strongest Republican assembly district in San Francisco and encompassed the upper-class Pacific Heights and Marina

TABLE 20

Republican Percentage of Total Vote Cast by Assembly Districts
in San Francisco, 1920-1928

	Assembly District	*1920*	*1924*	*1928*	*Gain or Loss 1924-1928*
21	South of Market	52	29	31	+2
22	South of Market	55	28	31	+3
23	South of Market	57	26	35	+9
24	Mission	61	37	45	+8
25	Mission	62	33	37	+4
26	Western Addition	64	44	44	0
27	Sunset Addition	70	57	55	—2
28	Richmond and Sea Cliff	73	64	57	—7
29	Downtown	59	34	37	+3
30	Downtown	63	45	45	0
31	Pacific Heights and Marina	74	72	60	—12
32	Nob–Russian Hill	71	64	58	—6
33	North Beach	72	55	44	—11

areas. Only one district, the 33d in the heavily Italian and Catholic North Beach area, where the Republican vote declined 11 percent, performed in the fashion that would be expected from the Lubell analysis.

All this is sufficient to raise considerable doubt about the significance of the 1928 election. If 1928 does not meet the test of a critical election, is there some earlier or later point when a genuine realignment appears to have taken place? To answer this question, it is necessary to revert to the basic components of Key's model.

First, the counties with the greatest gains and the greatest losses for one party, in this case, the Democratic, are determined for a particular time span, for example, 1908 to 1916. Then, the average Democratic vote for each set in a series of presidential elections, in this instance from 1892 to 1944, is computed. These average figures for the two sets of counties are then represented in line graph form, and, as the time sequence is surveyed, it may be possible to determine an election in which the two "average" lines diverge widely from each other, like the opening of a scissors. If this separation persists in time, it may be concluded that the particular point where the scissors opened represented a critical election where a realignment that persisted over time first appeared.

If such a cleavage appears, it should be evident in the most extreme cases. Accordingly, a first step is to chart the most consistently Republican county and the most consistently Democratic county in California—Riverside and Plumas counties, respectively. As Figure 4 indicates, from 1896 to 1912 these two counties were separated by a margin of about 10 percent, and in one election—that of 1896—Riverside was more Democratic than Plumas. The first wide difference appears in 1916, when the Democratic percentage in Plumas County rose 18 percent and that in Riverside only 5.6 percent. Omitting momentarily the deviant election of 1920, the two counties were separated by a wide margin of about 30 percent from 1924 through 1944. This represents an ideal type model for the critical election phenomena. Judging from the most extreme cases, one can observe that a readjustment widening the division of political preference in these two counties had occurred in the election of 1916, and that this alignment remained over a twenty-year period. The election of 1928 was but a part of a process already underway.

As Key discovered in New England, the data for the extreme case should represent, in exaggerated form, the patterns occurring in other combinations of data. However, to con-

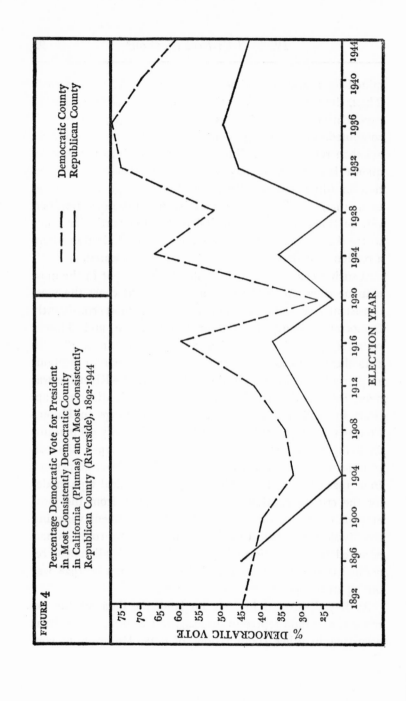

FIGURE 4   Percentage Democratic Vote for President
in Most Consistently Democratic County
in California (Plumas) and Most Consistently
Republican County (Riverside), 1892-1944

Democratic County
Republican County

firm the existence of the pattern, a number of related tests have been conducted, using different base periods and different combinations of counties.

Figure 5 represents a comparison of the five counties with the fewest and the five counties with the most Democratic party gains, using the base years 1920 to 1928. If the election of 1928 were a critical one, it should be manifest in this example. Rather, the pattern is remarkably parallel to the ideal type. The average Democratic vote in the five counties with the most gain rose sharply in 1916, fell off precipitously in 1920, then surged back close to the 1916 total in 1924; the Smith percentage actually was less than that in either 1916 or 1924 for Democratic and Socialist candidates.[8] Again the scissors appears to diverge in the election of 1916 and, with the exception of 1920, the cleavage persists until 1944.

Since the election of 1916 appears to take on a special significance, an appropriate test is to chart in the same manner the counties with the most and the least Democratic gains between the base years 1908 and 1916. Here the number of examples has been expanded, and averages have been computed for the twenty-one counties with the most Democratic increase and the eleven with the least during this period. Nonetheless, the pattern first observed in the ideal type is not significantly modified in Figure 6. It is, however, worthy of note that the counties with the least gain were actually more Democratic than the counties with the most gain prior to the 1916 election. Again, with less sharp differentiation due to the increased number of cases, the alignment of 1916 basically prevailed through 1944.

Inasmuch as many of the counties used in the foregoing analyses were sparsely populated rural counties, it is desirable to examine patterns of change in the eleven metropolitan counties of California. These counties contributed 59 percent

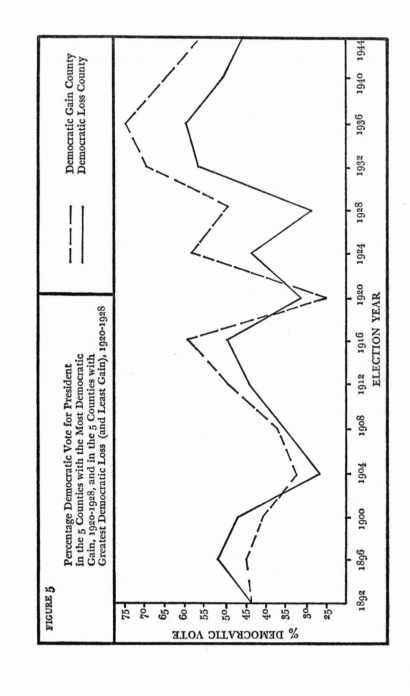

FIGURE 5

Percentage Democratic Vote for President in the 5 Counties with the Most Democratic Gain, 1920-1928, and in the 5 Counties with Greatest Democratic Loss (and Least Gain), 1920-1928

— — — Democratic Gain County
——— Democratic Loss County

% DEMOCRATIC VOTE

75 70 65 60 55 50 45 40 35 30 25

ELECTION YEAR

1892 1896 1900 1904 1908 1912 1916 1920 1924 1928 1932 1936 1940 1944

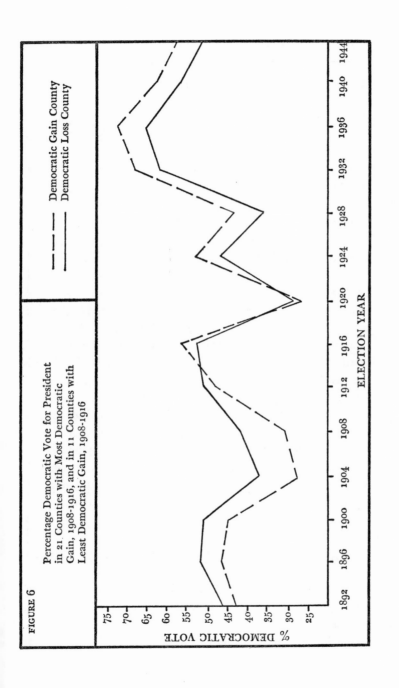

FIGURE 6

Percentage Democratic Vote for President in 21 Counties with Most Democratic Gain, 1908-1916, and in 11 Counties with Least Democratic Gain, 1908-1916

— — — Democratic Gain County
————— Democratic Loss County

% DEMOCRATIC VOTE

ELECTION YEAR

1892 1896 1900 1904 1908 1912 1916 1920 1924 1928 1932 1936 1940 1944

75 70 65 60 55 50 45 40 35 30 25

of the total two-party vote in 1896; 70 percent in 1916, 78 percent in 1932, and 82 percent in 1944. The counties are divided into the six with the largest Democratic gains, 1920 to 1928, and the five with the least.[9] Again, as Figure 7 indicates, the pattern is replicated. After a seesawing of political allegiances from 1892 forward, a cleavage emerged in 1916 that remained relatively constant through 1944.

Our analysis thus far has avoided one extremely important variable: the election of 1920. Although some of the foregoing discussion would seem to point to the Wilson–Hughes election of 1916 as a critical one, Democratic strength was not stable enough to survive the complex of new issues, such as the League of Nations, the Treaty of Versailles, and prohibition, which were interjected into the 1920 campaign. Neither is it accurate to designate the 1924 La Follette–Davis–Coolidge election as critical, since this would overlook the very close relationship of the 1924 vote to that of 1916. While the disastrous desertion from the Democratic party in 1920 does not qualify our hypothesis that there was no "Al Smith revolution" in California, it does make it difficult to identify just when a definite and permanent realignment occurred. However, more than any other election in the time sequences presented, that of 1920 would appear to be a deviant one, in which voters were responding to short-term stimuli not present four years earlier and not present four years later.

Correlation Data and California Voting Behavior

One further methodological device, supplementary to Key's critical election model, can be employed to test the hypothesis of this chapter. This is a measure of multiple correlations developed a number of years ago by the political scientist Har-

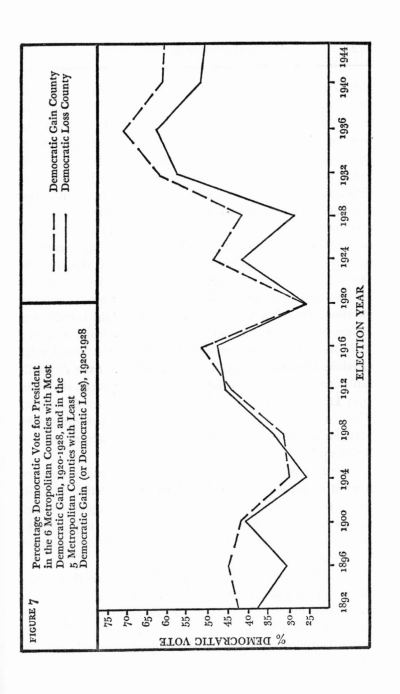

FIGURE 7   Percentage Democratic Vote for President
in the 6 Metropolitan Counties with Most
Democratic Gain, 1920-1928, and in the
5 Metropolitan Counties with Least
Democratic Gain (or Democratic Loss), 1920-1928

Democratic Gain County
Democratic Loss County

% DEMOCRATIC VOTE

ELECTION YEAR

old F. Gosnell and adapted by Duncan MacRae, Jr., and James A. Meldrum to apply to the Key model.[10] It best may be explained by an example. Taking as an illustration the vote for the Republican candidate, Charles Evans Hughes, in 1916, we correlate the percentage vote for Hughes in each of the fifty-eight counties with the percentage vote in each identical county for Warren G. Harding in 1920. In the rare circumstances that the percentages were exactly the same, a correlation coefficient of 1.00 would be produced. Obviously, any correlation coefficient at the .80 level or above represents extremely close parallelism in the distribution of the votes in the two elections. Then, in the same fashion, the percentages for 1916 and 1920 are correlated with percentages for ensuing elections. By using a computer, we can obtain correlations among more than one hundred separate election contests. This chapter employs correlations between the presidential elections from 1884 to 1940, fifteen elections for the Republican party matrix, sixteen for the Democratic party, since the 1924 La Follette vote is included in the Democratic matrix. The correlation coefficients between county percentages in votes for president by both parties, 1884–1940, are set forth in Table 21.[11]

Before we present the results of these calculations, we offer a word of caution. Given the disparate population of California counties, the correlations reflect a geographical rather than a numerical distribution of the vote; hence, any generalizations from the correlation coefficients should be considered as suggestive, not conclusive.

When all the correlations covering the presidential elections from 1884 to 1940 are arranged in the two matrices, fifteen by fifteen and sixteen by sixteen, it is possible to observe those that cluster into high correlations blocs. A voting realignment would be indicated when a sharp drop-off in correlations appears over a short time interval. MacRae and Meldrum point out that "All the elections before the reorientation should show high correlations with one another; all elections afterward should also be highly correlated; but any election before the critical transition should show a lesser correlation with any election afterward."[12] Visual analysis of the matrix can be supplemented with a more refined statistical technique, that of elementary factor analysis, which identifies those elections that cluster together around some common relationship and permits us to estimate the extent to which each election is "loaded" with some particular factor, such as the "Bryan vote" or the "New Deal vote."[13]

Examining Republican party correlations first, one notes that the factor analysis reveals four clusters of highly interrelated elections: first, 1884 and 1888; second, all elections between 1892 and 1908 and the election of 1920; third, the elections of 1912, 1916, 1924, 1928, and 1932; and finally, the elections of 1936 and 1940. This analysis would point to the election of 1912 (when Theodore Roosevelt, although a Progressive nationally, was the Republican nominee in California) as an important turning point, when an older Republican constituency present since 1892 gave way to a different alignment which, except for the election of 1920, prevailed until the depression. It therefore seems appropriate to conclude on the basis of this data that the geographical distribution of the Republican party voting constituency was relatively well established, that the sharpest break had come in 1912, and that the election of 1928 marked no major change.

Analysis of the Democratic party matrix presents a similar, although less clear picture. The three elections from 1884 to 1892 form one bloc. Then, there is high correlation between the five elections from 1896 to 1912. For the purposes of this analysis, the next bloc is the most important. The election of

TABLE 21

Correlation Coefficients between County Percentages in Votes for President, 1884-1940 (decimals deleted)

Republican Party Matrix

	1884	1888	1892	1896	1900	1904	1908	1912	1916	1920	1924	1928	1932	1936	1940
1884															
1888	85														
1892	72	76													
1896	69	52	58												
1900	74	69	76	79											
1904	73	72	76	74	92										
1908	70	68	62	75	90	90									
1912	31	26	22	54	56	61	62								
1916	42	47	42	48	63	69	78	63							
1920	52	44	58	54	70	75	70	54	71						
1924	26	31	30	34	49	59	65	64	86	66					
1928	10	26	23	15	36	42	49	52	75	51	85				
1932	34	42	25	44	53	55	66	56	83	57	82	81			
1936	39	17	47	14	20	27	39	39	66	43	68	76	75		
1940	42	18	12	21	27	36	46	35	71	50	75	76	74	89	

Democratic Party Matrix

	1884	1888	1892	1896	1900	1904	1908	1912	1916	1920	1924 (D)	1924 (S)	1928	1932	1936	1940
1884		85	69	69	74	82	70	47	42	66	62	03	10	34	04	04
1888	85		80	52	69	83	68	43	47	56	51	13	26	42	17	18
1892	69	80		31	56	76	63	47	58	57	43	14	54	51	37	32
1896	69	52	31		79	67	75	52	48	65	68	05	15	44	14	21
1900	74	69	56	79		84	90	55	63	77	62	27	36	53	20	27
1904	82	83	76	67	84		89	65	70	70	64	33	46	62	33	35
1908	70	68	63	75	90	89		64	70	78	62	10	49	66	39	46
1912	47	43	47	52	55	65	64		57	49	60	10	45	52	38	24
1916	42	47	58	48	63	70	70	57		71	48	29	75	83	66	71
1920	66	56	57	65	77	70	78	49	71		64	73	46	60	40	45
1924D	62	51	43	68	62	64	62	60	48	64		52	29	53	19	24
1924S	03	13	14	05	27	33	10	10	29	73	00		80	67	66	71
1928	10	26	54	15	36	46	49	45	75	46	29	80		81	76	76
1932	34	42	51	44	53	62	66	52	83	60	53	67	81		75	74
1936	04	17	37	14	20	33	39	38	66	40	19	66	76	75		89
1940	04	18	32	21	27	35	46	24	71	45	24	71	76	74	89	

TABLE 22

Reference Factor Loadings in the California Democratic Party

Year	Pre-Bryan	Bryan Period	1916 Shift	New Deal
1884	69	82	42	04
1888	80	83	47	18
1892	100	76	58	32
1896	31	67	48	21
1900	56	84	63	27
1904	76	100	70	35
1908	63	89	78	46
1912	47	65	57	24
1916	58	70	100	71
1920	57	70	70	45
1924D	43	64	48	24
1924S	14	33	73	71
1928	54	46	75	76
1932	51	62	83	74
1936	37	33	66	89
1940	32	35	71	100

NOTE: Conclusions should be drawn from this data only with extreme caution. Its principal value is for comparative purposes. For example, the "New Deal" factor, the highest column total in the cluster bloc that includes the elections of 1936 and 1940, is more closely related to the Democratic constituency most evident in the "1916 shift" than to the constituency of either the pre-Bryan or the Bryan period. Also, comparing the column entries, the 1924 Socialist vote is more parallel to the "New Deal" factor than to the 1924 Democratic vote for John W. Davis.

1916 does not fit into the earlier set; rather, four elections—1916, the 1924 Socialist vote for La Follette, 1928, and 1932—form a set of their own. The 1920 vote and the vote for John W. Davis in 1924 appear as a part of the older pre-1912 orientation. This would suggest again the same conclusions reached through the Key model. A new Democratic alignment, harbinger of the New Deal coalition, appeared in the vote for Wilson in California in 1916, was temporarily shattered in 1920, only to emerge hesitantly in the Socialist vote of 1924 and the Smith vote in 1928. With the 1940 vote as 100 representing a "New Deal" factor, the 1916 vote shows a loading of 71; the 1920 vote only 45, the Davis vote only 24. The La Follette vote, loading at 71, shows the same relationship as that of 1916 to the New Deal vote, and the Smith vote loads at 76.

It is probably neither necessary nor possible to identify any single California presidential election as the "critical" one. The alignment in 1916 does not qualify, for it was not permanent; to choose the 1924 Socialist vote would overlook the close correlation of the Wilson percentage to later Democratic votes. But if any single election could be classed as critical, it is clear that either 1916 or 1924, not 1928, constituted a crucial realignment point in California politics. This conclusion is consistent with the suggestion of MacRae and Meldrum that electoral realignments may take place over an extended "critical period," rather than being sharply manifested in any single critical election.

Conclusions

It is not the purpose of this chapter to inquire into motives and to ask what caused voter alignment or lack of it in California. Nevertheless, one possible clue is provided by comparing the correlations of Democratic party votes subsequent to 1900 with such ecological factors as the rural and urban population, males in manufacturing, and such sample reference factors as the "No" vote on the Hot Cargo referendum in 1942 representing prolabor sentiments. Although these correlations are not high, they indicate in general an increasing relationship of the Democratic vote to the urban population, to the percentage of industrial workers in a country and sympathy for organized labor. It is no startling hypothesis, but it can be suggested that the California Democratic party was gradually shifting from a rural base and was becoming an urban party with substantial labor support. This evolution began around 1916 and was still in process in 1940.

One final question is appropriate. Is an interpretation that identifies significant political realignments that took place in California before 1928 consistent with what has been learned about the politics of the state from nonstatistical methods? The years between 1912 and 1924 marked the zenith and the nadir of the Progressive party in California. After a brief third party flurry, the Progressives had returned as unwelcome guests to the Republican party, and from 1916 until the early 1930s the bitter factional battles within the Republican party constituted the most significant political contests in California. The Progressives, more than the weakened and ineffective California Democratic party, represented the major political alternative. Except in 1920, the Progressive leaders were lukewarm supporters of the national Republican party presidential candidates. Given this shattering of traditional party organizations in California, it is not implausible to conceive that large numbers of voters, either from confusion or choice, made new political commitments between 1916 and 1928.

In summary, to prove that the election of 1928 was critical in California, it would be necessary to demonstrate that new alignments took place in that year unlike those in immediately preceding elections. It would be necessary to show that the percentage distribution of votes by counties correlated higher with all elections after 1928 than with any elections before 1928. It is the conclusion of this chapter that such proof cannot be found. In California, the election of 1928 brought Democratic losses from their totals in two preceding elections, and these losses were particularly evident in the metropolitan areas where the ostensible Smith revolution was supposedly most manifest.

The election of 1928 in California was a backward step in the process that led in 1932 to the emergence of a Democratic constituency whose existence was presaged in the elections of 1916 and of 1924.

A single case study of this type is insufficient to challenge the widely held assumption that a nationwide political realignment occurred in 1928. However, two facts should be noted: first, the conclusions about the Smith election are based upon analysis of only the largest urban centers; and second, most of these studies compare 1928 only with the deviant election of 1920. If the conclusions of this chapter can be sustained, it would be wise to suspend final judgment about the importance of the election of 1928 until detailed studies of other metropolitan states identify more clearly the patterns of voting behavior.

NOTES

1. Samuel Lubell, *The Future of American Politics*, 2nd ed., rev., pp. 32–35; V. O. Key, Jr., "A Theory of Critical Elections," *Journal of Politics* 17 (February, 1955): 3–18.

2. Lubell, *American Politics*, p. 36; Key, "A Theory of Critical Elections," p. 4.

3. Eugene C. Lee, *California Votes, 1928–1960*, p. 28.

4. The estimated percentage of eligible adults voting is as follows: 1912—46 percent; 1916—57.6 percent; 1920—47.2 percent; 1924—50.5 percent; 1928—58.5 percent; 1932—63.4 percent; 1936—65.3 percent; 1940—74.1 percent; 1944—64.3 percent; 1948—62.5 percent. To estimate the eligible adult population in any given election year, the number of

adults over 21, excluding aliens, in a census year was determined. Intercensal population was estimated as follows: population for 1924 equals the population of 1920 plus .4 times the population of 1930 minus that of 1920. This formula was borrowed from Burton R. Brazil, "Voting in California, 1920–1946" (Master's thesis).

5. Lee, *California Votes*, p. 71.

6. A metropolitan county is defined as one that includes a city of 50,000 or more (in the 1930 census) or is adjacent to such a county and has 10,000 or more persons in nonagricultural employment. This definition is from Thomas A. Flinn, "The Outline of Ohio Politics," *Western Political Quarterly* 13 (September, 1960): 703 note.

All state statistics used in this paper for elections before 1928 are from State of California, Secretary of State, *Statement of Vote*, for each respective election; after 1928, from Lee, *California Votes*. San Francisco figures are from the files of the Registrar of Voters, City Hall. Rather than an urban-rural differentiation in 1928, the main significance was a north-south division. Northern California contributed 47.6 percent of the total vote cast, but 56.7 percent of Smith's total vote, while the eight counties of southern California contributed 52.3 percent of the total vote and only 43.2 percent of Smith's vote.

7. Lubell, *American Politics*, uses a different computation—a listing of the respective pluralities in a series of elections. His figures are as follows for the twelve largest U.S. cities:

Year	Net Party Plurality
1920	1,638,000 Republican
1924	1,252,000 Republican
1928	38,000 Democratic
1932	1,910,000 Democratic

Plurality figures for the eleven metropolitan counties in California are:

1916	12,766 Republican
1920	302,823 Republican
1924	175,120 Republican
1928	458,738 Republican
1932	361,917 Democratic

8. Since the Progressive electors were barred from the California ballot in 1924, to vote for La Follette one had to cast a vote for the Socialist party electors.

9. No major differences appear if the 1908–1916 rather than the 1902–1928 base is used in this example.

10. Harold F. Gosnell, *Grass Roots Politics: National Voting Behavior of Typical States* (Washington, D.C., 1942).

11. Each entry in the matrix represents a correlation coefficient between two elections. For example, the figure 85 in row 2, column 1 of the Republican matrix is the correlation between the distribution of votes

for the presidential candidate in 1884 and the distribution of votes for the presidential candidate in 1888.

12. MacRae and Meldrum, "Critical Elections in Illinois," p. 670.

13. The method used here is a highly simplified form of factor analysis that selects "reference factors" rather than the more complex computation. It is outlined in Louis L. McQuitty, "Elementary Factor Analysis," *Psychological Reports* 9 (1951): 71-78. The "clusters" are determined by marking the highest entry in each row of the matrix, then selecting the highest single duo of entries in the entire matrix (e.g., in the Democratic party matrix, the highest is the 90 correlation between the 1900 and 1908 votes). These are the first two members of the first cluster. Then by reading across the rows for each of these first entries, we can bring in all other elections that have their highest single correlation with one of these elections. These entries are then checked to bring in all elections that have their single highest correlation with one of them. This is done until all possible elections are incorporated.

The specific clusters are as follows:

Republican

    I. *1884*—1888
    II. 1892—1896—1900—1904—*1908*—1920
    III. 1912—*1916*—1924—1928—1932
    IV. 1936—*1940*

Democratic

    I. 1884—1888—*1892*
    II. 1896—1900—*1904*—1908—1912—1920—1924D
    III. *1916*—1924S—1928—1932
    IV. 1936—*1940*

The reference factor for each of these clusters is the column in each cluster with the highest total when all correlations are added. These are italicized above.

5

The Resurgence of the Democratic Party in California

THE depression of the 1930s transformed a faction-torn Democratic party into the majority party in California. From 20 percent in 1930 the party's registration spiraled to 40 percent of total registrants in 1932 and in 1934 surpassed the Republican total.[1] In the same four-year interval the number of actual votes cast in the Democratic primary multiplied seven times over; the Republican primary vote declined by one-third.

Yet the Democratic party never mobilized this majority in state politics. Franklin D. Roosevelt swept the state with a 58 percent majority in 1932; the unsuccessful Democratic gubernatorial candidate two years later marshaled only 38 percent of the vote. In 1938, Culbert Olson won a 53 per cent majority to become the state's first Democratic governor in the twentieth century, but two years earlier 67 percent of the state's vote had been given to Roosevelt in his successful bid for a second term. In 1940, Roosevelt carried the state a third time by a substantial 57 percent majority, yet two years later Earl Warren won all but one of the 58 counties and 57 percent of the votes to usher in a period of Republican dominance in Sacramento that lasted until 1958. Between 1930 and 1958, the Democratic party never controlled the California senate and held a majority in the assembly only from 1937 to 1943.[2]

What groups within the electorate produced this Democratic resurgence? Did changes in party leadership parallel the change in voting constituency? Why was the party that claimed 60 percent of the registered voters and whose presidential candidates swept the state by landslides in four of the six elections from 1932 to 1952 the minority party at the state level? To answer these questions we must focus upon the crucial campaigns of 1932 and 1934, when the dramatic revival of Democratic strength occurred. An understanding of the scope of these changes requires a brief examination of Democratic politics in the decade before the transformation, and an understanding of the consequences of these changes requires a projection of the party's successes and failures through the 1950s.

The Moribund Party: California Democrats in the 1920s

No one would have disputed the assertion of the Democratic national committeeman that California in 1924 was a "rock-ribbed Republican state."[3] In a total of 555 electoral contests, 1920 to 1930, Democratic candidates won only twenty-five.[4] Not a single Democrat was elected to a statewide executive office, and no gubernatorial candidate polled more than 36 percent of the vote. Al Smith, the party's most successful presidential nominee, won only 34.2 percent of the California vote.[5]

California Democratic leadership was polarized into two loose factions that reflected in microcosm the deep schisms within the national party. One wing, centering around William Gibbs McAdoo, who went to Los Angeles in 1922, identified with southern Democrats in their stand for prohibition and their hostility to the increasing influence of urban-based machines.[6] Opposed was a faction associated with former Senator James D. Phelan of San Francisco and led by Isidore Dockweiler, a Los Angeles attorney and Democratic national committeeman, and Justus Wardell, publisher of the *Daily Journal of Commerce* in San Francisco. Strongest in northern California, this faction's tightest link was to the Irish and labor-based Democratic machine in San Francisco. Its opportunistic leaders could usually be found in alliance with James Rolph, the Republican mayor of San Francisco.[7]

The central issue that immobilized the party and kept it fragmented was prohibition. The rival groups joined to support McAdoo's presidential bid in 1924, but the party collapsed after the convention debacle at New York, and there was virtually no campaign for John W. Davis in the state.[8] The party typically divided senatorial and gubernatorial nominations between wets and drys. In 1922 a wet Democratic candidate for governor won 53 percent of the votes in San Francisco but only 29 percent in Los Angeles County and 21 percent in Orange and Riverside—the prohibition centers of the south. In the same election, San Francisco gave only 23 percent of its votes to a dry Democrat opposing Hiram Johnson.

The schism widened in 1926: the nominee for governor was Justus Wardell, a wet; for senator, John B. Elliott, a southerner and ally of McAdoo, a dry. Wets controlled the party machinery, but the platform contained a dry plank. The two factions did not assist each other in the campaign. In the 1928 presidential primary, an Al Smith slate headed by Dockweiler defeated a slate pledged to Senator Thomas J. Walsh of Montana backed by the McAdoo wing. The defeated faction reluctantly supported Smith—making clear their opposition to his anti-prohibition stance; even so, a number of prominent McAdoo lieutenants, including John B. Elliott, supported Herbert Hoover.[9]

In 1930, although portents of the Depression crisis were apparent, the Democratic party rode the dying prohibition issue to the low point in its history. Traditional party roles were reversed. A north-south split in Republican dry ranks handed the gubernatorial nomination to Mayor "Sunny Jim" Rolph, an uncompromising wet. Milton Young of Los Angeles, the Democratic nominee, in an ill-starred maneuver to win dry votes, ran on a prohibition platform. He established a campaign committee independent of the party machinery, split with the nominee for lieutenant-governor, and for his efforts captured 24 percent of the state's votes. Most leaders identified with the Dockweiler-Wardell faction defected to Rolph.[10]

Traditional party loyalty was insignificant for the California Democrats in the 1920s (see Table 23). The party was usually strongest in northern California, but only if it presented a wet candidate. The party's constituency, as the correlation figures show, varied in each election according to the prohibition stance of the candidate.

Political paralysis was not a fate thrust unalterably upon the party, for a potential Democratic voting constituency existed in California. As it had since 1914, the still viable Progressive wing of the Republican party presented voters with clearer alternatives than the ineffective Democrats. Save for Woodrow Wilson's 1916 campaign, the Republican Progressives absorbed the economic and ethnic groups that otherwise could have made up a Democratic voting constituency. Throughout the 1920s, potential Democratic voting strength, as it had appeared in the 1916 Wilson vote, was as much re-

TABLE 23

Prohibition and the Democratic Party Vote

	Governor 1922 (Wet) % of Vote	Governor 1926 (Wet) % of Vote	Senator 1926 (Dry) % of Vote	President 1928 (Wet) % of Vote	Governor 1930 (Dry) % of Vote
CALIFORNIA	35.9	24.6	36.8	34.2	24.1
Southern California	28.0	17.4	42.3	28.4	32.4
Northern California	40.8	30.2	33.5	40.4	12.9
Five wet counties	51.6	36.5	32.5	48.3	10.5
Five dry counties	25.1	22.1	41.9	24.7	34.8
Prohibition Correlation	—.38			—.63	.73

NOTE: Southern California is defined to include the following counties: Imperial, Los Angeles, Orange, Riverside, San Bernardino, San Diego, Santa Barbara and Ventura. All others are included in northern California.

The measure for the prohibition correlation is the vote "No" on a 1926 referendum to repeal the Davis Act, California's "Little Volstead" Act. A "No" vote would indicate support for prohibition. The five wet and five dry counties are those casting the greatest percentage for repeal and the greatest percentage opposed.

flected in the votes for Progressive Republicans in that party's primaries as in the votes for Democrats.[11]

A vigorous campaign for Robert M. La Follette in 1924 waged by Progressive Republicans, a few prominent Democrats (including such former luminaries as Francis J. Heney and such future luminaries as Culbert Olson), and enthusiastic political amateurs overcame a quagmire of obstacles to win 34.5 percent of the state's vote. The vote for La Follette was a Democratic party vote never successfully mobilized by the party.[12] Democratic registration figures rose slightly after the 1924 election, but the percentage vote for the party's candidate for governor declined from the 1922 figure both in 1926 and 1930.[13]

Roosevelt in 1932 did what the California Democrats had failed to do throughout the 1920s: he reconstituted the voting constituency of 1916. And like the vote for Wilson, the Roosevelt vote was distributed by counties in a pattern that paralleled Progressive Republican votes in the 1920s more than Democratic votes.[14]

The Upsurge of the 1930s: Presidential Politics

Roosevelt in 1932 swept fifty-five of California's fifty-eight counties; Smith four years earlier had won only four. On the eve of the most dramatic reversal of party fortunes in the state's history, the Democratic leadership was still snared in the debilitating factional controversies of the 1920s.

Slates pledged to three candidates competed in the Democratic presidential primary of May 1932. A year earlier, Roosevelt organizers had courted and won the Dockweiler-Wardell faction that controlled the state's party machinery. A delegation pledged to John Nance Garner was backed by one of the strangest alliances in California political history: William Randolph Hearst, ardent foe of prohibition, fearful of Roosevelt's alleged internationalist sympathies, lent his support to McAdoo's dry faction in their attempt to wrest party control away from their traditional wet rivals. A third slate was pledged to Alfred E. Smith. Control of the Democratic party, not the identity of the party's nominee, was the issue in the 1932 Democratic presidential primary.[15]

The 222,000 votes cast for the Garner delegation, compared with 175,000 for Roosevelt and 142,000 for Smith, gave it a plurality victory. Roosevelt carried thirty-five counties, most of them in the inland agricultural and mountain areas; Smith won a clear majority in San Francisco and carried four additional Bay Area counties. Seventy-four percent of the support for the Garner ticket came from ten southern counties; Garner's 79,300 margin of victory in Los Angeles County more than accounted for his statewide plurality.[16] McAdoo rode the crest of the Garner victory to replace Dockweiler as the national committeeman and defeat Wardell for the senatorial nomination in August.

The California delegation played a critical role in the Democratic convention at Chicago in June. The dramatic shift of California from Garner to Roosevelt—the result of political pressures exerted upon Garner, Hearst, and McAdoo—set in motion the bandwagon that carried Roosevelt over the required two-thirds margin on the fourth roll-call. The resulting prestige gained by the McAdoo faction assisted its leader to his election as United States senator in November.[17]

Democratic victories in 1932 aggravated rather than assuaged the internecine warfare in the California party. Both factions demanded priority in the allotment of patronage—the McAdoo faction because of their major contribution at the Chicago convention; the Dockweiler-Wardell faction because they were the original Roosevelt supporters in the state.[18] Even so profound a reversal in party fortunes had thus failed to transform the entrenched party leadership at a time when the party's opportunities were the most propitious in the twentieth century. New leaders and new issues were overtaking a tired party leadership. Most important, the full extent of the depression-engendered protest vote was not yet manifest.

The voting revolution of 1932 was the result of the political participation of hundreds of thousands of California citizens who had never cast a ballot before. Between 1928 and 1936, the state's population increased 15.6 percent, but Democratic registration leaped 219 percent, while Republican registration declined 19 percent.[19] The Democrats retained the loyalty of these new voters in the 1932 election and made deep inroads into Republican ranks. The voter/registration ratio, the statistic produced by dividing the party's percentage of the two-party vote by the party's percentage of the two-party registration was 143.2, the high for any election between 1928 and 1960.[20]

The actual Democratic vote rose from 614,365 (34.2 percent) in 1928 to 1,324,157 (58.4 percent) in 1932. This Democratic upsurge affected every county in the state, the percentage shift ranging from a low of 15 percent to a high of 34 percent. The gains, however, were most pronounced in counties that had been predominantly Republican and dry. The 1932 election (see Table 24) erased the wide differential that had separated southern from northern California and subsumed the wet-dry issue as a factor in California politics.

TABLE 24

Distribution of Democratic Presidential Votes, 1928 and 1932

	1928 % of Vote	1932 % of Vote	Percentage Increase
CALIFORNIA	34.2	58.4	24.2
Southern California	28.4	56.2	27.8
Northern California	40.4	61.1	20.7
Five wet counties	48.3	63.2	14.9
Five dry counties	24.7	51.7	27.0
Los Angeles County	28.7	57.2	28.5
San Francisco County	49.4	64.8	15.4

The 707,792 new Democratic voters in 1932 were predominantly southern Californians. Forty-eight percent came from Los Angeles County and 60.4 percent from the eight counties of southern California. This was an increase in Democratic votes of 261 percent in southern California and 264 percent in Los Angeles County, compared to a 215 percent increase in the state.

As Table 25 shows, southern California contributed 53.4 percent of all the votes cast in 1932, but 62.9 percent of all those added to the voting rolls since 1928. Los Angeles County accounted for 42.7 percent of all the ballots marked, but for 50.5 percent of the new voters. Southern California in 1932 accounted for 52.4 percent of the votes cast for Roosevelt, but for 60.4 percent of the new Democratic voters. Los Angeles provided 41.8 percent of Roosevelt's California votes, but for 48.5 percent of the state's new Democratic voters.[21]

The increase in Democratic votes in the region that had been most consistently Republican does not mean that the counties there had become the leading Democratic counties in the state. In fact, since Democratic strength grew in all counties, including those like San Francisco that had been relatively strong Democratic centers in the elections of 1916 and 1928, the upsurge in the 1930s produced little rearrangement of California's counties when ranked in the order of Democratic strength.[22]

The election of 1932 set the stage for Democratic victories in California in four succeeding presidential elections (see Tables 26 and 27). However, correlations of 1932 with succeeding Democratic elections are less than those for 1936. The election of 1932 was more a protest vote than later elections; the new Democratic constituency solidified when it reached its peak strength in 1936. The linkage analysis introduced in Chapter 4 demonstrated that the 1932 Democratic distribution paralleled

TABLE 25

Regional Contributions to Increase in Total Vote and Increase in Democratic Vote, 1928 and 1932

	California	Southern California	Northern California	Los Angeles County	San Francisco County
Total vote cast, 1932	2,265,822	1,235,520	1,080,302	968,580	222,446
Total vote cast, 1928	1,796,696	940,334	856,362	731,301	195,468
Increase	469,126	295,186	173,940	237,179	26,978
Percent contribution, 1932		53.4	45.5	42.7	9.8
Percent contribution, 1928		52.3	47.7	40.7	10.8
Percent contribution to increase, 1932 over 1928		62.9	37.1	50.5	5.7
Democratic vote, 1932	1,324,157	694,625	629,532	554,476	144,236
Democratic vote, 1928	614,365	265,873	348,492	209,945	96,632
Increase	709,792	428,752	281,040	344,531	47,604
Percent contribution, 1932		52.4	47.6	41.8	10.8
Percent contribution, 1928		43.2	56.8	34.1	15.7
Percent contribution to increase, 1932 over 1928		60.4	39.6	48.5	6.7

the Democratic vote of 1916, the La Follette vote in 1924, and the Smith vote in 1928 more closely than it paralleled the vote in any election after 1932. The highest single correlation for the 1932 election was the .83 with the Wilson vote in 1916.

TABLE 26
Correlation Matrix:
Democratic Party Presidential Vote,
1932-1952

	1932	1936	1940	1944	1948	1952
1936	.75					
1940	.74	.89				
1944	.53	.81	.89			
1948	.59	.78	.88	.93		
1952	.43	.71	.77	.90	.95	

The sharp regional differentials of the 1920s were erased after 1932; fluctuations in the vote through 1948 affected all sections more or less evenly. Variations between metropolitan and nonmetropolitan counties were unimportant. Los Angeles County's vote usually cleaved close to the state mean, San Francisco County's slightly above and the seven southern counties outside Los Angeles and the Bay Area counties outside San Francisco several percentage points below. The Sacramento Valley, the sparsely populated mountain counties, and usually the San Joaquin Valley counties, were more Democratic than the state. The average deviation figure at the bottom of Table 27 is a convenient and simple measure of regional variations. The larger the figure, the greater the variation of the votes of the selected geographical areas around the Democratic mean.[23]

In summary, the foregoing analysis of the resurgence of the

Regional Distribution of
Democratic Presidential Vote,
1928-1948

	1928 % of Vote	1932 % of Vote	1936 % of Vote	1940 % of Vote	1944 % of Vote	1948 % of Vote
CALIFORNIA	34.2	58.4	67.0	57.4	56.5	47.6
Southern California	28.4	56.2	65.3	56.3	55.5	46.5
Northern California	40.4	61.1	68.8	58.7	57.6	48.9
Metropolitan counties	33.3	58.2	67.3	57.4	56.7	47.4
Nonmetropolitan	37.0	59.2	65.2	57.1	54.8	48.0
Los Angeles County	28.7	57.2	67.0	58.1	56.8	47.0
San Francisco County	49.4	64.8	74.1	59.5	60.5	47.8
Southern California minus Los Angeles	26.7	52.5	59.3	49.5	51.0	44.9
Bay Area minus San Francisco	35.1	52.8	63.8	54.3	56.5	46.3
San Joaquin Valley	38.1	67.2	72.8	60.5	56.4	55.1
Sacramento Valley	45.3	68.2	74.7	65.1	63.3	56.1
Mountain counties	45.0	68.8	71.6	64.7	58.6	53.0
Average deviation	6.36	4.90	4.00	3.00	1.81	2.54

NOTE: A metropolitan county is one that includes a city of 50,000 or more or is adjacent to such a county and has 10,000 or more persons in nonagricultural employment. From 1928 to 1936, these were Alameda, Contra Costa, Fresno, Los Angeles, Orange, Sacramento, San Bernardino, San Diego, San Francisco, San Joaquin, and Santa Clara. After 1940, Kern, Riverside, and San Mateo were added.

Bay Area counties are Alameda, Contra Costa, Marin, San Francisco, San Mateo, and Santa Clara.

San Joaquin Valley counties are Fresno, Kern, Kings, Madera, Merced, San Joaquin, Stanislaus, and Tulare. Sacramento Valley counties are Butte, Colusa, Glenn, Sacramento, Solano, Sutter, Yuba, and Yolo. Mountain counties are Alpine, Amador, Calaveras, El Dorado, Inyo, Lassen, Mariposa, Modoc, Nevada, Placer, Plumas, Shasta, Sierra, Siskiyou, Tehama, Trinity, and Tuolomne.

California Democratic party in presidential politics leads us to the following conclusions: (1) The major factor in the increase was the support of new voters. (2) Democratic strength rose most markedly in southern California and particularly in Los Angeles County. (3) Democratic gains were consolidated in 1936 into a pattern of distribution that remained relatively stable. (4) The causes of this increment were general; there was a substantial increase in Democratic strength in all major regional subdivisions. The regional variations in dispersion of the vote that remained were less than those in 1928.

The 1934 Election

The gubernatorial election of 1934 took place against a backdrop of social crisis that approached revolutionary proportions in California. Because of the radical program of the Democratic nominee, this election rubbed raw divisive social issues and polarized the state on class lines. Upton Sinclair lost the election, but out of the crisis period a new Democratic party constituency took shape. The alignments of 1934 marked out the arena for California state politics for two succeeding decades.

Roosevelt's decisive victory, the first Democratic majority in the California congressional delegation since 1896, and an increase in Democratic members of the assembly from seven in 1931 to twenty-five in 1933—all seemed harbingers of a Democratic renaissance in state government. Yet the party was ill-prepared to seize these opportunities. Its electoral strength was in an unassimilated protest vote; the victories of 1932 had failed to soothe the factional divisions inherited from the 1920s. Governor Roosevelt had intervened in September 1932 to urge upon Wardell and McAdoo the acceptance of Maurice Harrison of San Francisco, a "neutral," as state chairman. A year later it was clear the reconciliation had failed: both factions were jealously complaining that the other had been unduly rewarded with patronage in the newly created New Deal recovery agencies.[24]

In September 1933 Upton Sinclair, controversial author and perennial Socialist candidate for various California offices, changed his registration to Democrat and simultaneously announced that he was running for governor. Sinclair combined the tactics of an amateur social crusader with mature political strategy to inject a vigor and controversy into California politics more intense even than in Johnson's 1910 campaign.[25]

His plan to "End Poverty in California" was tempered during the year before the election, but its core remained essentially this: A California Authority for Land would condemn and purchase idle land where self-sufficient colonies of unemployed workers would be established. A California Authority for Production would buy unused factories and in conjunction with the Land Authority create an autonomous economic system within the existing capitalist structure. The agricultural products of the land colonies would be exchanged for the products of the factories by means of a barter scrip to be honored within the system. Supplemental benefits would include a monthly pension of fifty dollars for all persons over sixty.

The EPIC plan was to be initiated and underwritten by the state, but once the cooperatives achieved autonomy, the state would withdraw. To finance this plan, the recently enacted sales tax would be repealed and replaced by a graduated income tax starting with all incomes over $5,000 and rising to a 30 percent levy on incomes over $50,000; inheritance, utility and corporation taxes would be boosted and a 10 percent tax levied on all unimproved and uncultivated land. While the EPIC plan had antecedents in the self-help cooperatives that had mushroomed in southern California in the early 1930s, it was a visionary scheme; years later its author conceded his relief that he was never called upon to implement it.[26]

Sinclair took only a month respite from political organizing between November 1933 and the 1934 elections. By January, 255,000 copies of his *I, Candidate for Governor and How I Ended Poverty: A True Story of the Future,* were in circulation; by February, 300 EPIC clubs and by August more than 1,000 had been established. By the summer of 1934, Sinclair was widely regarded as the front-runner among the Democratic gubernatorial aspirants.[27]

The most promising contender who might unite the quarreling Democratic factions and checkmate the Sinclair drive was George Creel. A Democratic veteran who had served Woodrow Wilson as director of the wartime Committee on Public Information, Creel had achieved prominence in California as regional director for the National Recovery Act. He was a safe conservative who complained of too much centralization of power in the Washington offices of NRA and later in his career would support Republicans Earl Warren and Richard Nixon. Creel, who had moved to California only in 1926, was not stigmatized by too-close association with either the Wardell or McAdoo faction. Intransigence and confusion among the California Democratic leaders undermined the Creel candidacy and delivered the nomination to Sinclair. On April 19, Justus Wardell announced his candidacy for governor, indicating he did so in the belief that Creel would not be running. Almost simultaneously, John B. Elliott, perennial favorite of the McAdoo wing, disclaimed any political intentions. Then on April 25, Creel declared his candidacy. The suspicious Wardell-Dockweiler faction inferred that since Elliott had so inexplicably withdrawn, Creel must be in league with the McAdoo faction.[28] This was untrue. Creel was coolly received in southern California, and Elliott never openly supported him.[29]

More important than this political maneuvering, the depression reached its depth in California in the summer of 1934; social crisis convulsed the state. In June, 700,000 able workers were unemployed, half of them in Los Angeles County. One-fifth of the residents of the county were on relief, receiving an average monthly payment of $16.20 per family.[30] Longstanding exploitation of farm labor culminated in a series of strikes beginning in the fall of 1933, involving more than 14,000 workers in every important farming area of the state.[31] Vigilante groups (often with legal sanction) launched an offensive against labor organizers in the Central Valley. Strikers and their attorneys were frequently jailed and beaten. A waterfront strike that began in June tied up all but one California port and exploded into the violent San Francisco general strike in July. The Hearst Press led other less sensationalist newspapers in screaming "Red Menace"; headquarters of radical union groups were raided, and several were demolished by vengeful mobs.[32]

The political campaigns of 1934 became battlefields for the passions that social discontent had unleashed in California. The depression had created the environment in which a plan such as EPIC could germinate, but it generated the fears and suspicions that nourished bitter reactionary countermoves. The smear campaign against Upton Sinclair began when Justus Wardell charged that Sinclair was a "Communist." Creel was more circumspect, asserting only that EPIC would "Russianize California," but Sinclair suspected Creel's complicity in a faked pamphlet that purported to be a Communist endorsement of EPIC.[33]

Upton Sinclair's 52 percent vote in the Democratic primary gave him a clear majority among the nine contenders. Creel, the runner-up, won only 34 percent and Wardell a meager 6 percent. The EPIC slate nominated Sheridan Downey for lieutenant-governor, three candidates for the senate (including Culbert Olson for the Los Angeles County seat), and thirty-nine candidates for the assembly.

On the Republican ticket, Governor Frank Merriam, who had succeeded to the office on the death of "Sunny Jim" Rolph in June, won a plurality nomination (43 percent). A former speaker of the assembly, Merriam had long been associated with the standpat wing of the party.[34]

The third major candidate on the November ballot, Raymond Haight, had lost the Republican nomination for which he had cross-filed, but won the nomination of the newly formed Commonwealth party. A middle-ground candidate, Haight hoped to attract some of the nonpartisan Progressive following usually attached to Senator Hiram Johnson. Despite his lack of a party base, Haight's candidacy figured large in the strategy of his opponents. Various incentives, including money and promises of future support, were dangled before him by Republican leaders; Sinclair had offered him the EPIC nomination for attorney general and apparently, a short time before the November election, gave serious thought to withdrawing in Haight's favor.[35]

Sinclair was a vulnerable candidate. Selections from his extensive writings, wherein he had attacked organized religion, espoused vegetarianism and spoken approvingly of free love, provided rich grist for an opposition propaganda mill that commanded a near monopoly of the state's press. Sinclair was often tactless, as in his unfounded assertion that President Roosevelt planned to endorse him.[36] A statement that enactment of EPIC might draw some of the nation's unemployed to California touched off a wildly exaggerated rumor campaign describing the bums, itinerants, and Bolsheviks who were flooding California in anticipation of an EPIC victory.[37] With Sinclair for an opponent, Merriam could at once retain his conservative stance and praise Roosevelt's recovery program, support a legislative resolution commending the Townsend Plan, and endorse a compulsory thirty-hour work week.[38]

The primary victory handed formal control of the California Democratic party to EPIC. Culbert Olson became the new party chairman. To retain the support of the dispossessed leaders, the platform watered down the original EPIC plan: communal farms, the old-age pension, and the proposal to repeal the sales tax, among others, were eliminated. However, for the old-line party leaders, loyalty did not extend so far as to encompass even the modified EPIC proposals. First to defect were the San Francisco leaders. Justus Wardell disavowed Sinclair a few weeks after the state convention. Before the vindictive campaign had ended, EPIC had been abandoned by former state chairman Maurice Harrison and by George Creel and key members of the congressional delegation. Several associations of Democrats for Merriam had been formed.[39] Senator McAdoo was conspicuously absent from California during the campaign.[40] The national Democratic administration scrupulously avoided even routine endorsement of Sinclair. Jim Farley apparently inspired an eleventh-hour move to induce Sinclair to withdraw.[41] Sinclair was abandoned by his party and vilified by his opponents. By the conclusion of the campaign, Sinclair's new Democratic party consisted of little more than the EPIC following.

California voters defied a nationwide Democratic political trend in 1934. Sinclair won only 37.8 percent of the vote, while Merriam captured 48.9 percent, with 13.4 percent for Haight. The Democratic candidate carried only six counties, none by majority. His 879,000 vote total was only 4.4 percent greater than the Democratic primary vote for all candidates, while Merriam's 1,138,620 was a 29.1 percent increment from the vote in the August Republican primary.

From whence came the voter support that allowed Sinclair to win the 1934 Democratic nomination and with it gave EPIC control of the Democratic party? Why did California voters turn against Sinclair in the general election when they had voted so preponderantly for Roosevelt? Was the Democratic electoral constituency of 1934 an evanescent phenomenon, or did it mark a permanent realignment of Democratic party voter support?

The constituency that won Upton Sinclair the Democratic nomination in August 1934 was a unique combination of voters unlike any that appeared before or after in California politics. The primary vote for Sinclair correlated only .22 with Roosevelt's vote in 1932; .08 with that of the Democratic candidate for governor in 1930 and —.23 with Smith's vote in 1928.[42]

Southern California nominated Upton Sinclair. The eight counties there supplied 54 percent of the Democratic vote in the 1934 primary, but 67 percent of Sinclair's vote. Los Angeles County, which Sinclair swept by a 67 percent landslide, supplied 42 percent of the vote in the Democratic primary, but 54 percent of Sinclair's vote.[43]

Table 28 indicates two important qualities of the vote for Upton Sinclair in the 1934 Democratic primary. First, regional variations in the vote, particularly as between northern and southern California, were greater than in any other election considered here. Second, Sinclair made his best race in those areas where the most new voters had been added to the Democratic rolls.[44]

Sinclair failed to retain the loyalty of Democratic voters in the November election; the party's vote was greater than

TABLE 28
Regional Distribution
of Votes and Contributions,
1934 Democratic Primary

Area	Total Vote	Percent Contri- bution	Sinclair Vote	Percent Contri- bution	Percent Sinclair
CALIFORNIA	841,930		436,220		51.8
Southern California	452,970	53.8	290,784	66.6	64.1
Northern California	388,960	46.1	145,436	33.3	37.3
Metropolitan counties	643,798	76.4	362,691	83.1	56.3
Nonmetropolitan	198,132	23.5	75,531	17.3	37.1
Los Angeles County	354,506	42.1	238,308	54.6	67.2
San Francisco County	82,364	09.7	24,891	05.7	30.2
			Average deviation:		13.8

the total vote in the Democratic primary in only six counties, all of them metropolitan.[45] Who then were the Democratic voters that deserted Sinclair?

First, although regional variations in 1934 were less than those in 1930,[46] Sinclair was a stronger candidate in the general election in southern California than in the north. Part of this was because of the candidacy of Raymond Haight. Haight's center of strength (see Table 29) was in northern California outside the San Francisco Bay Area. He carried by plurality Fresno, Stanislaus, and Tulare counties and won more than a third of the votes in Yolo and Sacramento.[47] All five of these counties had exceeded the state Democratic percentage in 1932, and three had cast more than 66 percent of their votes for Roosevelt. The eight counties in the San Joa-

TABLE 29
Regional Distribution
of the Vote for Governor, 1934

	Democratic % of Vote	Republican % of Vote	Commonwealth % of Vote
CALIFORNIA	37.8	48.9	13.4
Southern California	40.2	49.2	9.0
Northern California	34.8	48.4	16.8
Metropolitan counties	38.6	48.0	13.4
Nonmetropolitan	34.4	51.7	13.9
Los Angeles County	42.0	47.5	10.5
San Francisco County	38.9	50.9	10.2
Southern California minus Los Angeles	34.1	55.8	10.1
Bay Area minus San Francisco	37.1	55.5	9.4
San Joaquin Valley	31.9	38.8	29.3
Sacramento Valley	30.0	42.1	27.9
Mountain counties	33.8	42.9	23.3

quin Valley, where Haight's 29 percent was his best showing in the state, had voted 67 percent for Roosevelt. The cost to Sinclair of the Haight candidacy can also be shown by a comparison of the Democratic vote for governor with that for Sheridan Downey, the EPIC-backed nominee for lieutenant-governor, who ran against a single Republican opponent. Downey's statewide percentage (45.0) exceeded Sinclair's by 7.2 percentage points. In Los Angeles, Downey bettered Sinclair by 7 points, in San Francisco by 3. But in the areas where Haight was most popular, Downey's percentage exceeded Sinclair's by 14 percentage points (in the San Joaquin Valley) and by 10 (in the Sacramento Valley). Like the Progressives a decade earlier, Haight's candidacy siphoned off potential Democratic votes.[48]

Second, Sinclair did not lose because of the defection of the newly recruited protest Democrats. Although Sinclair received only 66 votes for every 100 Roosevelt had received, the falloff was less marked in southern California and in Los Angeles County—the places where the party resurgence had been most pronounced. The 50 counties in northern California contributed 46.7 percent of the total votes cast in 1934, but accounted for 56.4 percent of the decrease in Democratic votes from 1932. Southern California supplied 53.5 percent of the total votes, but only 43.6 percent of the Democratic falloff. Los Angeles supplied 41.4 percent of the total votes, but 33.5 percent of the decrease; San Francisco, 9.6 percent of the total votes, but 12.6 percent of the Democratic falloff.

TABLE 30

Comparison of Democratic Vote,
General Elections, 1932 & 1934

	1932	*1934*	*Decrease*	*Contribution to Decrease* %	*1934/ 1932* %
CALIFORNIA	1,324,157	879,537	444,620		66.4
Southern California	694,625	500,481	194,144	43.6	72.0
Northern California	629,532	379,056	250,476	56.4	60.2
Metropolitan counties	1,135,763	702,128	333,635	75.0	67.7
Nonmetropolitan	288,394	177,409	110,985	25.0	61.5
Los Angeles County	544,476	405,331	149,145	33.5	73.1
San Francisco County	144,236	87,850	56,386	12.6	60.9

The Democratic vote in the general election of 1934 fell precipitously from that of 1932 in San Francisco, usually regarded as the center of Democratic strength in California. A study by George Higginbottom of the 1934 election there has related voting to ecological characteristics through identifying precincts with census tracts. He isolated thirteen census tracts in which the Democratic vote increased between the 1934 primary and general elections, 45 tracts in which the decrease was greatest, and 41 tracts with moderate decreases. The author found definite evidence of economic class differentials in the voting. The greater the proportion of laborers, service workers, operatives, craftsmen, and foremen in the population of a census tract, the less Democratic loss between the elections. The greater the number of professionals, proprietors and clerical workers, the sharper the falloff in Democratic votes.[49] Higginbottom concluded that a substantial portion of the vote for Creel in the primary was given to Merriam or Haight in the general election.[50]

The election of 1934 defined the arena for California state politics for two decades. The Democratic candidate in defeat polled 879,537 votes, two and one-half times the vote for the 1930 nominee and the greatest ever for a Democratic candidate for state office in California. A new party constituency emerged, although this can be attributed to the depression, not to the Sinclair candidacy.

Involvement of the electorate in the vigorous campaign and election was greater than in any immediately preceding gubernatorial race. In 1934, 606 of every 1,000 eligible voters cast ballots for governor compared to 445 in 1922, 420 in 1926, and 410 in 1930. This awakened political participation continued in 1938, when 631 of every 1,000 cast ballots, but in 1942 the ratio dropped to 455.[51]

The electoral groupings of 1934 remained essentially intact

TABLE 31
Regional Distribution
of Democratic Gubernatorial Vote,
1922-1942

	1922 % of Vote	1926 % of Vote	1930 % of Vote	1934 % of Vote	1938 % of Vote	1942 % of Vote
CALIFORNIA	35.9	24.6	24.1	37.8	52.5	41.8
Southern California	28.0	17.4	32.4	40.2	54.1	42.5
Northern California	40.8	30.2	12.9	34.8	50.5	40.8
Metropolitan counties	35.6	23.1	25.0	38.6	52.6	42.9
Nonmetropolitan	36.7	29.1	20.9	34.4	51.9	35.6
Los Angeles County	29.1	17.1	34.0	42.0	55.8	44.6
San Francisco County	53.2	38.1	10.0	38.9	53.4	45.9
Southern California minus Los Angeles	25.6	18.2	28.1	34.1	48.6	34.9
Bay Area minus San Francisco	43.5	25.6	14.4	37.1	49.1	41.3
San Joaquin Valley	34.4	29.5	24.3	31.9	53.3	37.1
Sacramento Valley	47.7	31.0	15.9	30.0	50.2	41.8
Mountain counties	42.3	28.4	16.5	33.8	59.8	37.7
Average Deviation	6.81	5.54	6.90	3.63	2.38	3.00

until 1958. As Table 31 shows, a new Democratic base, more or less evenly distributed across the state, and distinctly different from that of the 1920s, emerged in 1934 and remained stable through 1942. (For elections after 1942, see Table 36.)

The correlation matrices in Tables 32 and 33 point to 1934 as a realigning election in California. A linkage analysis[52] reveals three clusters in the Democratic matrix: 1910-1922; 1930; 1934-1938-1942. The low correlation of any election *before* 1934 with any election *after* 1934 indicates that a realignment took place in that year.[53] The Republican matrix is more complex. There are two distinct clusters: 1910-1922 and 1914-1930-1934-1938-1942. The lack of a Republican realignment in 1934 is not unexpected inasmuch as the major factor in the Democratic resurgence was the addition of new voters.

TABLE 32

Correlation Matrix:

California Democratic Governor's Vote

	1910	1922	1930	1934	1938	1942
1910						
1922	.66					
1930	.20	.04				
1934	—.05	.05	.34			
1938	.21	.21	.18	.57		
1942	—.09	—.07	—.12	.40	.65	

While voting analysis more confidently can identify the time when a transformation takes place than the groups making up the new constituency, the foregoing statistical analysis permits three generalizations.

(1) Regional factors were less important than factors op-

TABLE 33
Correlation Matrix:
California Republican Governor's Vote

	1910	1914	1922	1930	1934	1938	1942
1910							
1914	.33						
1922	.62	.18					
1930	.27	.14	—.04				
1934	.43	.57	.23	.30			
1938	.43	.47	.21	.18	.72		
1942	.11	.23	.07	—.12	.51	.65	

erating throughout the whole state in determining the fluctuations in the Democratic gubernatorial vote after 1934. Variation in party vote between elections was always greater than
any regional differences in a single election. The political folk
wisdom, based upon contemporary developments, that views
San Francisco County as a center of Democratic power and
Los Angeles County as rock-ribbed Republican, inaccurately
represents state voting patterns of 1934 to 1954. In three of
the five general state elections in this interval, Los Angeles was
actually more Democratic than San Francisco. If the Democratic vote in Los Angeles is included in the southern California totals, offsetting the stronger Republican counties of
the south, southern California was more Democratic than the
fifty northern counties in three elections and identical in percentage figures in the fourth. Northern California "failed" a
crucial test of party loyalty: when Earl Warren, a Republican,
cross-filed in the Democratic gubernatorial primaries of 1942
and 1946, winning the latter, he received a greater percentage
of Democratic votes from northern than from southern California.[54]

(2) The new voters who became Democrats in 1932 were not the volatile factor that accounts for the seesawing of party support through 1954. As with Sinclair's vote in the general election of 1934, the areas where increments in Democratic vote were the greatest in the early 1930s were slightly more Democratic than areas where the resurgence was less.

(3) Granting the tenuous qualities of ecological correlations, a comparison of the older Democratic electorate with the new one emerging after 1934 shows a trend toward a more urban-based constituency with greater labor support, greater sympathy for welfare measures, and less sensitivity to the prohibition question. Neither the old nor the new constituency showed any correlation with a sample civil rights issue.

TABLE 34

Ecological Factors
and the Democratic Party Vote
(in Correlation Coefficients)

Issues	Democratic Governor, 1922	Democratic Governor, 1938
Prohibition (1926)	—.38	—.17
Ham and Eggs (1938)	.21	.66
"No" on Hot Cargo (1942)	—.02	.39
FEPC (1942)	—.15	.02
Percent urban, 1930	—.17	.20

NOTE: The elections of 1922 and 1938 are "reference factors" based upon the matrix in Table 32. A "Yes" vote on Ham and Eggs is interpreted here as sympathy for pension and welfare measures; "No" on Hot Cargo as sympathy for organized labor; "Yes" on FEPC as sympathy for civil rights legislation; the prohibition factor is based upon the "No" vote for repeal of the Davis Act in 1926.

This discussion of the Democratic alignment after 1934 has ignored the extremely important fact that this was not a winning combination. Culbert Olson won 52.5 percent of the 1938 vote but earned a majority in only twenty-one counties. The governor's legislative program was inhibited by severe intra-party schisms. The Democratic party never gained control of the senate. Even in the assembly, which they did control during the four years of Olson's administration, the principal power bloc was an alliance of "economy bloc" Democrats and Republicans.[55] In 1942, the incumbent governor won only 41.8 percent of the votes as the Earl Warren landslide swept fifty-seven counties. Warren cross-filed in 1946 and won both party nominations. In 1950, the Democratic nominee James Roosevelt lost every county as Warren's victory margin surged to 64.8 percent. The Democrats lost control of the assembly in 1942, not to regain either house of the legislature until 1958. Despite lopsided Democratic predominance in registration, a Roosevelt landslide in 1944 and a narrow Truman victory in 1948, California state politics remained unassailably Republican.

Correlations between elections for President and elections for governor (Table 35) demonstrate the low relationship between the vote for Roosevelt and Truman and the vote for Democratic gubernatorial candidates. In particular, the election of 1934 does not correlate significantly with a single presidential election.

The system of 1934 began to disintegrate in 1954. The Democratic percentage of the vote for governor rose from 35 percent in 1950 to 43 percent as Richard Perrin Graves, an unknown and scarcely publicized candidate opposing an incumbent Republican, Goodwin Knight, won seventeen counties, none of which had voted Democratic four years earlier.

TABLE 35
Relation of Democratic Presidential
and Gubernatorial Vote, 1932-1952
(in Correlation Coefficients)

President	Governor 1934	Governor 1938	Governor 1942
1932	.16	.45	.26
1936	.21	.66	.51
1940	.28	.77	.60
1944	.29	.71	.74
1948	.30	.75	.79
1952	.33	.71	.77

Table 36 charts this upsurge in the 1950s and also indicates that it was short-lived. It reached meridian in 1958 with the election of Gov. Edmund Brown and Democratic control of both the assembly and senate. A decline began in 1962 that culminated in 1966 with the election of a Republican governor, Ronald Reagan. In 1968, Republicans regained control of the assembly, and the senate was divided 20-20 between the two parties.

Regional variations in voting, sharper than at any other time since the 1920s, reappeared in 1958. San Francisco emerged as more than ten percentage points more Democratic than the balance of the state—a position it retained through 1968. In 1962, the beginning of a Republican resurgence, southern California (except Los Angeles County) was more Republican than the rest of the state by margins greater than any since 1928.[56] California began in the 1960s a process of political realignment that promises to be as far-reaching as that of the early 1930s.

TABLE 36

Regional Distribution
of Democratic Gubernatorial Vote,
1950-1966

	1950 % of Vote	1954 % of Vote	1958 % of Vote	1962 % of Vote	1966 % of Vote
CALIFORNIA	35.1	43.2	59.7	51.8	42.3
Southern California	35.1	41.2	60.0	49.4	39.7
Northern California	35.1	45.4	59.6	55.2	45.9
Metropolitan counties	35.3	43.0	59.6	51.8	42.6
Nonmetropolitan	34.2	43.6	60.2	52.1	40.6
Los Angeles County	36.0	42.7	57.9	51.8	42.7
San Francisco County	34.8	44.0	70.8	62.1	59.0
Southern California minus Los Angeles	32.1	37.0	67.2	44.4	34.3
Bay Area minus San Francisco	34.5	45.2	62.7	54.1	46.5
San Joaquin Valley	36.0	48.6	63.9	53.6	42.2
Sacramento Valley	35.9	48.7	67.5	58.4	46.0
Mountain counties	39.7	49.0	66.1	57.5	41.5
Average deviation	.90	2.90	3.72	3.81	3.90

Conclusion

A two-party system was created in California in the early 1930s. Nevertheless, the party that claimed nearly 60 percent of the registered voters and won landslide victories in presidential contests remained the minority party at a state level.

Why did the Democratic party fail? Were there features in California registration and voting laws that caused the disparity between formal and actual party allegiance? Were there qualities in the California population or distinct features in the state's political history that operated to the disadvantage of the Democratic party?

The constitutional and legal ground rules for the conduct of politics in California, while they may be considered necessary, are not sufficient conditions for an explanation of Democratic ineffectiveness. Several structural features have had considerable influence on the conduct of party politics: the registration laws; the cross-filing law, repealed in 1958; the pattern of apportionment in the state legislature; and the provisions in the constitution regulating internal party government.

An important change in election laws preceded the critical election of 1934, and another significant modification preceded the Democratic revival in 1954. A permanent registration law—first effective in 1932—eliminated the necessity of reregistering every two years. The cross-filing law, which permitted a Democrat to vote in the primary for cross-filed Republican candidates, removed a major incentive for changing party affiliations. The permanent registration law, coupled with cross-filing, had the effect of freezing party registrations into the pattern of the early 1930s, the period of sharpest Democratic increments. Accordingly, the distribution of party strength as measured by number of registrations remained remarkably stable: the Democratic share was 57.8 percent in 1936 and 57.5 percent in 1960.[57] The election of 1954 was the first following an amendment to the cross-filing law, requiring party designations of candidates on primary ballots. Nevertheless, these structural factors alone do not explain the disparity between professed and actual party loyalty. There was no major realignment in party registration following the 1954 revision of the cross-filing laws or when the law was repealed in 1959.

Reapportionment, periodically a controversial issue in state politics, has had little effect upon the distribution of political power. The redistricting of 1951, carried out by a Republican legislature, was followed by a Democratic upsurge that won for the party control of both the senate and the assembly in 1958. In like fashion, after the Democrats reapportioned the state—allegedly in their favor—in 1961 and 1965, the Republicans increased their strength in Sacramento.

TABLE 37
Percentage of California Voters
Registered as Democrats

1952	1954	1956	1958	1960	1962	1964	1966
55.5	55.5	55.8	57.4	57.5	56.9	57.9	56.6

On the other hand, California's rigid constitutional requirements for party government, enacted in the Progressive period and embodying the reformer's distaste for strong, entrenched parties, have been important factors in maintaining the nonpartisan orientation of the state's politics. For example, the constitution requires that the state convention, the party's highest authority, shall consist of all nominees for elective office plus incumbent officeholders. As a result, legislators and legislative candidates make up the preponderant majority and use this advantage to control the official party committees and leadership posts. Accordingly, California legislators tend to be independent of governors elected from their own party. An executive can exercise leadership over his party only with difficulty.

Any explanation of the Democratic failure must include but go beyond structural dimensions. The factors that operated to produce surges and declines in Democratic voting strength also operated across the entire state, not in some particular regional substratum. Consistently, from 1934 to 1966, variations in votes between elections were greater than variations in any single election between regions, the major cities, or other geographical units. Given this demonstrable conclusion, several hypotheses that were advanced to explain California voting behavior must be rejected.

It seems doubtful that disparate rates of population growth, particularly as manifest in the burgeoning of Los Angeles County compared with the more modest expansion of San Francisco, relate in any way to party loyalty. Areas with rapid growth rates tended to vote much the same as areas with more moderate growth rates—at least until 1958.[58] Likewise, if regional variations in voting were unimportant between 1934 and 1958, any interpretation that links party loyalty in California to ethnic differences in the population must be questioned. Since various ethnic minorities in the state—for example, Irish, Italian, Negro, Mexican-American—are not distributed evenly among the counties or sectional substrata, ethnic differences should show up in regional differences. This was true in the 1920s when such issues as prohibition tended to segregate voters according to national or religious backgrounds. No evidence of regionally based ethnic differences in voting behavior appears after 1934.

In contrast to an ethnic hypothesis, one that relates the Democratic and Republican voter to economic class differences would appear to be more tenable. To avoid hasty generalizations based upon aggregate analysis, such a hypothesis would have to be carefully tested by comparative studies in several cities and rural counties of the state. Its potential plausibility is suggested, first, by the fact that class distinctions relate less to region and hence may be buried in aggregate statistics, and second, by the conclusions of three independent studies of California voting constituencies—two in San Francisco and one in Santa Clara County. All find Democratic party loyalty more evident among voters who are unskilled workers, live in lower rental units, and have less education.[59]

Beyond these broad generalizations, further attempts to explain the difference between professed and actual party loyalty in California and the accompanying weakness of the Democratic party become more impressionistic than empirical.[60]

By the 1930s, the nonpartisan heritage of progressivism had been firmly established in California. Party organization was weak, and the most effective party leaders, in particular Earl Warren, dissociated themselves from the official party machinery. Without strong parties to clarify and simplify alternatives, moderate conflict, and promote political consensus, extrapolitical organizations assumed an exaggerated importance.[61] The press in California, overwhelmingly Republican from the days of Hoover to the days of Eisenhower, was likely a more important factor in conditioning political sympathies than would have been possible in a state where parties were stronger and the population more deeply rooted. The influence of the press would be greater in state politics than in the more visible, dramatic, and widely publicized federal sphere. The role of powerful lobbies, supplying campaign funds to candidates irrespective of party, assumed scandalous proportions in the 1940s.[62]

It is difficult to link the political influence of lobbies with voting behavior except to infer that lobbies were likely forces for stability—an unchanging power base lending itself to manipulation more easily than one in transition.[63] Ineffective party organization magnified the effect of unidimensional volunteer groups espousing some particular reform. In the late 1930s and early 1940s, one such crusade, that for old-age pensions, came close to absorbing the political parties rather than the usual pattern of parties absorbing interest groups.[64] Major reforms within both California parties traditionally have been inaugurated by grassroots movements external to the party machinery—witness EPIC in 1934, the California Republican assembly a few years later, the California Democratic councils arising out of the volunteer movement in the Stevenson campaign of 1952, and the upsurge of conservative politics, beginning in 1958, that has gradually gained an upper hand in the Republican party.

The ineptness of party leadership bears an important responsibility for the fate of the Democratic party after 1934. Factional divisions shifted from the 1920s, but Democratic quarrels were still so intense as to sabotage the administration of the one Democratic governor. Sheridan Downey, Democratic U.S. Senator from 1938 to 1950, was notoriously indifferent, even hostile, to his California party compatriots. By the time of his retirement in 1950, Downey's political stance bore little resemblance to that of the EPIC nominee for lieutenant-governor in 1934. Attorney General Robert Kenny, by neglecting to campaign for the Democratic nomination in 1946, allowed his cross-filed Republican opponent, Earl Warren, to win by default. Democratic primary contests in the late 1940s and early 1950s were typically more vicious than even general election campaigns. For example, the red-baiting of Helen Gahagan Douglas, so prominent a feature of the 1950 campaign, was initiated in the primary by her conservative Democratic opponent, Manchester Boddy.[65]

Politically, California has been a mercurial state in which political change takes place in the form of dramatic surges rather than gradual and developmental transition. One postulates the existence of trends in California politics only with extreme caution; one predicts the outcome of these trends only with reckless intrepidity. A study of cyclical patterns in California voting gives few premonitions of such phenomena as the Earl Warren landslide that cut short a Democratic trend in 1942, the decisiveness by which Edmund G. Brown capped a Democratic trend in 1958 by winning fifty-four of the state's counties, or the emphatic Reagan victory in 1966. This dynamism of political change, which so complicates systematic study of California politics, is the very factor that makes California an important laboratory from which to view political processes. There seems little doubt that a major task of social and political analysis in the future will be to deal with dynamic, even impulsive, social change.

NOTES

1. Eugene C. Lee, *California Votes,* pp. A-30-A-32; State of California, Secretary of State, *Statement of Vote.* These are the sources for all statistics used in this paper. The latter is issued separately for every primary, general and special election and titled accordingly. Raw figures in the latter source have been transformed to percentages.

2. Robert E. Burke, *Olson's New Deal for California,* p. 5.

3. *New York Times,* 18 July 1924, p. 3.

4. Royce Delmatier, "The Rebirth of the Democratic Party in California" (Ph.D. dissertation), p. 224. The 9 Democratic victories in 66 contests for the House of Representatives and 11 out of 120 for the state Senate were all won in the primaries by cross-filing; of the 38 Democratic seats (of a possible 480) won in the Assembly, a Democrat defeated a Republican in a general election only 7 times.

5. Robert E. Hennings, "California Democratic Politics in the Period of Republican Ascendancy," *Pacific Historical Review* 31 (August, 1962):

267; Robert J. Pitchell, "Twentieth Century California Voting Behavior" (Ph.D. dissertation), p. 58.

6. William Gibbs McAdoo to Louis Untermeyer, 15 July 1924, McAdoo Papers, Library of Congress, Box 306.

7. Ronald E. Chinn, "An Analysis of the Structure and Function of the Democratic Party in California, 1920–1956" (Ph.D. dissertation), pp. 48–51.

8. Hennings, "California Democratic Politics," p. 276.

9. Clarence F. McIntosh, "Upton Sinclair and the Epic Movement, 1933–1936" (Ph.D. dissertation), p. 120; Chinn, "Democratic Party in California," pp. 39–40, 50–51.

10. Crinn, "Democratic Party in California," pp. 50–51.

11. Wilson's 1916 vote distribution correlated .50 with that of the Democratic candidate in 1922 and .03 with that of the 1930 gubernatorial candidate. Johnson's primary vote in 1922 correlated .58 with that of Wilson in 1916 and C. C. Young's Republican primary vote in 1926 correlated .38.

12. See Chap. 4 in this book. This is not to deny the importance of the Smith vote. However, 1928 was a better year for Republicans in California than 1924. La Follette and Davis together polled 42.7 percent of the state's vote; Smith polled 34.2 percent. The vote for La Follette correlated .73 with the Wilson 1916 vote, .80 with Smith's 1928 vote, and .67 with the Roosevelt vote in 1932. The La Follette correlations with Progressive Republicans was: Johnson, 1922: .58; Young, 1926: .35. It correlated .35 and —.13 with votes for Democratic governor in 1922 and 1930.

13. Franklin Hichborn, "California Politics, 1891–1939" (unpublished manuscript), pp. 2503–2505.

14. The Roosevelt vote in 1932 correlated .82 with that for Wilson. At the same time it correlated only .42 with that for the Democratic governor in 1922 and —.08 for the 1930 candidate. Hiram Johnson's vote in the 1922 Republican primary correlated .59 and C. C. Young's vote in the 1926 primary, .48 with Roosevelt's 1932 vote.

15. Russell M. Posner, "California's Role in the Nomination of Franklin D. Roosevelt," *California Historical Society Quarterly* 39 (June, 1960): 121–127; McIntosh, "Upton Sinclair," pp. 121–122.

16. Posner, "California's Role," p. 130; Delmatier, "Rebirth of the Democratic Party," pp. 111–112. The results in Los Angeles County were: Garner, 126,131; Roosevelt, 46,831; Smith, 58,743.

17. James MacGregor Burns, *Roosevelt: The Lion and the Fox*, p. 137; Posner, "California's Role," pp. 121–140.

18. *New York Times,* 18 June 1933, part 4, p. 6; McIntosh, "Upton Sinclair," pp. 123–125.

19. Lee, *California Votes,* p. 37.

20. For example, if the statewide vote differential was 60–40 and the registration differential was also 60–40, the voter/registration ratio would be 100. See Lee, *California Votes,* p. 78.

21. The comparison between votes actually cast for Roosevelt and the addition to Democratic vote totals since 1928 is introduced in order to hold constant the factor of population distribution; for example, the

fact there were more people in southern California. Hence the important statistic is the difference in percentage between contribution to the actual vote and contribution to the increase.

22. See Chap. 4, pp. 91–92.

23. The average deviation is the mean of the sum of the variations of each of the given units (1 . . . n) from the state mean.

24. McIntosh, "Upton Sinclair," pp. 123–125.

25. Turner Catledge gave this first hand description of the Sinclair constituency late in the campaign: "Its main support is not Communist, but the God-fearing, pure American and economically dispossessed thousands in Southern California. It is more than a political crusade; its roots are in religion, the "old time religion." Southern California is made up of thousands who migrated from the Middle West beginning about twenty years ago. In the depression these people suffered first and most. Savings were lost, they were caught in southern California's fantastic promotional schemes, banks failed on them back home, farm mortgages were foreclosed. They were changed from a proud middle-class to practical mendicants in the first few months of the collapse. They turned to religion and the numerous sects in southern California and then were caught up by Sinclair and his dream" (*New York Times*, 4 November 1934, part 2, p. 1).

26. McIntosh, "Upton Sinclair," pp. 9–17; Upton Sinclair, *I, Candidate for Governor and How I Got Licked*, pp. 16–59; Upton Sinclair, *The Autobiography of Upton Sinclair*, p. 276.

27. McIntosh, "Upton Sinclair," pp. 143–147.

28. *New York Times*, 26 April 1934, p. 17.

29. McIntosh, "Upton Sinclair," pp. 130–138.

30. Ibid., pp. 73–74. See also *New York Times*, 10 June 1934, part 4, p. 7.

31. Pitchell, "California Voting Behavior," pp. 157–165.

32. Ronald Chinn, "The Sinclair Campaign of 1934" (Master's thesis), pp. 8–10; *New York Times*, 24 June 1934, part 4, p. 6; ibid., 29 July 1934, part 2, p. 1; ibid., 5 August 1934, part 4, p. 6.

33. Chinn, "Sinclair Campaign," p. 46; McIntosh, "Upton Sinclair," p. 247; Sinclair, *I, Candidate*, pp. 52, 169.

34. Chinn, "Sinclair Campaign," pp. 49–52.

35. Bob Barger, "Raymond L. Haight and the Commonwealth Progressive Campaign of 1934," *The California Historical Society Quarterly* 43 (September, 1964): 219–230.

36. McIntosh, "Upton Sinclair," pp. 273–274; Sinclair, *I, Candidate*, pp. 181–183.

37. McIntosh, "Upton Sinclair," pp. 254–256; *New York Times*, 18 October 1934, p. 17; ibid., 29 October 1934, p. 4.

38. Chinn, "Sinclair Campaign," p. 103. These were all planks in the Republican state platform. See *New York Times*, 30 September 1934, part 4, p. 3.

39. McIntosh, "Upton Sinclair," p. 288; Chinn, "Sinclair Campaign," p. 94.

40. *New York Times*, 3 November 1934, p. 6. The defections in 1934

marked the end both of the McAdoo and the Dockweiler-Wardell factions. No prominent leader associated with either of the old-line factions was nominated by the party thereafter although some like Elliott, Dockweiler, and Creel appeared in delegations to presidential nominating conventions. McAdoo lost the senatorial nomination in 1938 to Sheridan Downey; John F. Dockweiler, son of Isidore, was defeated by Culbert Olson in the gubernatorial primary the same year.

41. Sinclair, *I, Candidate*, pp. 194–197; McIntosh, "Upton Sinclair," pp. 298–300.

42. In a series of fifty-seven electoral correlations compiled by the writer, the two highest correlations for the Sinclair primary vote were .52 with Sinclair's vote for Socialist senator in 1922 and .55 with Sheridan Downey's vote in the 1938 senatorial primary.

43. George Creel remarked in October 1934 that California as a whole was still Progressive, but Los Angeles had gone so far to the left that Hiram Johnson "in comparison looks like a hidebound conservative" (*New York Times*, 2 October 1934, p. 2).

44. For example, Los Angeles County contributed 49 percent of the new Democratic voters in 1932 and contributed 55 percent of Sinclair's 1934 primary vote; San Francisco accounted for 7 percent of the new Democrats and 6 percent of Sinclair's primary vote.

45. Actually, during the period 1922-1942, the vote of the minority party usually increased over the primary totals in the general election, while that of the majority party remained constant or declined.

46. An average deviation of 3.63 compared to 6.90 in 1930.

47. Ronald Chinn has demonstrated a remarkable parallel between the vote for Haight and the circulation of the McClatchy newspaper chain which had endorsed his candidacy. "Sinclair Campaign," Table VI.

48. Harold Gosnell found the vote for Sinclair to be approximately the same in the two sets of counties that he had classified "pro-New Deal" and "anti-New Deal." "However," he added, "this does not mean that the two groups reacted in the same way. The anti-New Deal counties strongly favored the conservative Republican, Merriam, giving him almost twice the vote they gave Sinclair, and paying almost no attention to Raymond L. Haight, the third major participant in the campaign. On the other hand, the New Deal counties, unwilling to support Sinclair, found Merriam almost as distasteful and hence voted strongly for Haight." (Harold Gosnell, *Grass Roots Politics: National Voting Behavior of Typical States*, p. 89)

49. George Higginbottom, "Epic By the Bay" (Master's thesis), p. 63.

50. Ibid., p. 76. Creel carried San Francisco in the primary.

51. Comparable figures for presidential elections were: 1928, 576; 1932, 628; 1936, 664; 1940, 741. Burton R. Brazil, "Voting in California, 1920-1946" (Master's thesis), pp. 72–73.

52. See Chap. 4, note 17.

53. The election of 1930, when traditional wet-dry divisions were reversed, stands out as a deviant election.

54. *Percentage Votes for Republican Earl Warren in Democratic Primaries, 1942–1946*

	1942	*1946*
CALIFORNIA	40.9	51.9
Southern California	37.9	45.4
Northern California	43.7	58.3
Los Angeles County	37.3	42.7
San Francisco	38.0	53.2

It should be noted, however, that in both instances the major Democratic nominee was from southern California.

55. New factional rivalries as intense as those of the twenties continued to plague the Democratic party. Robert E. Burke, in *Olson's New Deal in California*, p. 140, identifies four in the Olson administration:

1. The McAdoo-Creel group, consisting principally of federal office holders and their satellites, strongest in the San Francisco Bay Area, but badly crippled by the defeat of Senator McAdoo in the 1938 primary and the passage of the Hatch Act.

2. The right-wing group, consisting of anti-Olson Democratic legislators and other conservatives, numerically weak but well financed.

3. A left-wing group, consisting of CIO and Labor's Non Partisan League leaders as well as such mavericks as Lieutenant Governor Patterson and Senator Kenny.

4. The Olson group, consisting of members of the administration, AFL and Railroad Brotherhood leaders, and most Democratic members of the legislature.

In the late 1940s, the party polarized along liberal-conservative lines, a liberal faction including James Roosevelt, Ellis Patterson, Helen Gahagan Douglas, Jerry Voorhis, and usually Robert Kenny being opposed by a conservative group that included Edwin Pauley, John B. Elliott, Manchester Boddy, William M. Malone (chairman of the San Francisco central committee), Oliver Carter, and George Luckey of Los Angeles. Chinn, "Democratic Party in California," pp. 147–148.

56. Several writers have called attention to the current regional disparity in the California vote, but few have noted that it is on an upswing after a downturn of nearly two decades. See Raymond E. Wolfinger and Fred I. Greenstein, "Comparing Political Regions: The Case of California," *American Political Science Review* 63 (March, 1969): 74–85; Eugene C. Lee, "The Two Arenas and the Two Worlds of California Politics," in *The California Governmental Process*, ed. Eugene C. Lee, pp. 46–53; Lee, *California Votes*, pp. 59–77.

57. Lee, *California Votes*, p. 28.

58. This conclusion is supported in a recent study which concludes, "None of our 1964 data support the proposition that people new to California are more likely to be conservative" (Wolfinger and Greenstein, "The Case of California," p. 77).

59. George Higginbottom, "Epic By the Bay" (Master's thesis); Homer Bartlett Thompson, "An Analysis of Voting Behavior in San Francisco, 1936-1946" (Master's thesis); Dewey Anderson and Percy E. Davidson, *Ballots and the Democratic Class Struggle*.

60. Charles G. Bell, "A Study of Four Selected Factors Which Have Contributed to the Inability of the Democratic Party to Successfully Mobilize Its Latent Majority in California" (Master's thesis), identifies as his four selected factors: (1) registration patterns that froze the protest vote of the 1930s; (2) cross-filing; (3) the influence of the press; (4) gerrymandering of congressional districts. The importance of the latter point is questioned by Robert J. Pitchell, "Reapportionment as a Control of Voting in California," *Western Political Quarterly* 14 (March, 1961): 214–235. On the basis of my analysis, I would attach less credence than Bell to the first and fourth factors.

Chinn, "Democratic Party in California" (Ph.D. dissertation), concludes his comprehensive study by citing three major reasons for the Democratic party weakness in the period he considers: (1) the lack of leadership; (2) a Republican tradition in California and the fact that Republicans could take credit for the Progressive reforms (an interpretation suggested to Chinn by former Governor Culbert Olson); (3) the newspapers.

Robert J. Pitchell, "Twentieth Century California Voting Behavior" (Ph.D. dissertation), which studies voting through the early 1950s, concludes that the California voter has a preference for moderate candidates who do not take strong positions. Underlying this, he argues, is the urban white-collar, middle-class voter who reacts unfavorably to periodic social disturbances in labor and agriculture and tends to condemn the individuals and groups regarded as the perpetrators.

61. "If no party groups are active, then the hidden, difficult to identify political forces that thrive in the absence of strong party organization will dominate the politics of the state" (Dean R. Cresap, *Party Politics in the Golden State*, p. 29).

62. Dean E. McHenry, "The Pattern of California Politics," *Western Political Quarterly* 1 (March, 1948): 52–53.

63. H. R. Philbrick, *Legislative Investigation Report;* Lester Velie, "The Secret Boss of California," *Colliers* (13 August 1949): 11–13, 71–73; (20 August 1949): 12–13, 60–63; Robert T. Whalen, "Liquor Politics in California" (Master's thesis).

64. A comprehensive study of this interest group is Jackson K. Putnam, "The Influence of Older Age Groups on California Politics" (Ph.D. dissertation).

65. Chinn, "Democratic Party in California," p. 155.

6

Southern California:
Right-Wing Behavior and
Political Symbols

SOUTHERN California has enjoyed a shadowy presence in our analysis thus far. But the region's behavior in state politics is both crucial and puzzling. We have been forced, in each chapter, to return to southern California. It has importantly configured the support for (or opposition to) every protest movement in the years covered by our study and has played a key role in each major party realignment. We turn now to the political significance of southern California.

Southern California contains a substantial majority of the citizens of the state. That fact alone would be unimportant were there not a specific regional flavor to southern political behavior. A southern California political tradition has manifested itself with impressive continuity since the 1890s. That tradition is dominantly right-wing, with a short-lived, minority left-wing element appearing during hard times. How has this tradition developed, and how can it be explained?

This chapter undertakes three tasks. First, we shall review

voting patterns from 1892 to 1956, demonstrating the existence and character of the southern political tradition. Second, we shall show that this tradition came to dominate California politics in the 1960s, realigning major-party support and nominating and electing Gov. Ronald Reagan. Third, to understand the meaning of the tradition, we shall examine the southern California political culture.

The contemporary significance of southern California politics is not confined to the state. In a real sense the region is responsible not only for Reagan's effort to capture the 1968 Republican presidential nomination, but for Barry Goldwater's success four years earlier and Richard Nixon's ultimate presidential victory. Without southern California votes, Goldwater would have failed to win a single contested primary and might well have lost the Republican nomination. His debt to southern California also includes a father from the region and a summer home in Orange County. As for Nixon, he made his early career on southern California anticommunism. In 1968, Nixon lost the fifty counties of northern California by 144,000 votes, but his 367,000 plurality in the south gave him the state and with it a majority in the electoral college.

The importance of the southern California political tradition is thus heightened by its national impact. The national perspective forces us to examine the meaning of southern behavior as well. Politics in California has long seemed different from politics elsewhere. Party loyalty is weaker, nonpartisan and ideological appeals are stronger, social movements are more prominent, and bizarre candidates and political rhetoric recur. Southern California produces much of that uniqueness. How are we to comprehend its tradition? Why should it be right-wing? Why should it exist at all? The concepts with which contemporary political science explains voting behavior give us little help here. We shall be forced to investigate the southern California, right-wing symbolic world.

Right-wing symbols, we will argue, reflect aspects of the American national experience, magnified and distorted in the southern California setting. Discussions of meaning inevitably are less precise than descriptions of behavior. Nevertheless, we can draw on a rich tradition provided by observers of American culture in general and southern California life in particular. The "hard" data in this chapter consist of county election returns and census information. There are limits to what aggregate data can reveal about the meaning of political acts, but the statistics do permit an illuminating historical sweep.

The Right-Wing Political Tradition

The eight counties of southern California, separated from the rest of the state by the Tehachapi Mountains, form a sprawling urban and suburban concentration. There is immense agricultural wealth, but in this century farmers have been a small percentage of the population in most southern counties, and the metropolitan areas continue to expand rapidly into the countryside. For decades a majority of the state's residents have lived in the south, although the fifty northern counties comprise two-thirds of the state's land area. Los Angeles County alone contains 40 percent of the registered voters in the state.

Since the early 1900s, the southern population has grown at a fantastic rate. Between 1930 and 1960 the population of northern California increased from 2.7 million to 6.7 million, the southern population from 2.9 million to 9 million. (Only Imperial, the most agricultural county in the region, has not

kept pace with its southern neighbors.) Six of the eight southern counties, plus six of the fifty northern ones, make up the
twelve counties with the greatest rate of population growth
between 1950 and 1960. Orange County, now an extension of
suburban Los Angeles, led the state with a 226 percent population increase. Since newcomers continuously pour into the
area, native Californians have always been scarcer in the south
than in the north. In 1960, one-half to two-thirds of the population in each southern county had been born outside the
state.[1]

But the vast migrations to southern California have not
changed the character of the inhabitants. Southern California
was settled by respectable Protestants from the small towns and
cities of the Midwest. The "Okie" migration of the 1930s introduced a poorer element, but war prosperity eventually im-
proved their lot.[2] A community of wealthy, retired people has
grown in Santa Barbara, the northernmost southern county.
Ventura gained a substantial white working class, as war industries and large military bases came to the county in the
1940s. Many Negroes have migrated to Los Angeles since the
early 1940s, but they remain less than 10 percent of the county's population and are of insignificant numbers elsewhere in
the south. Ventura and Imperial have high percentages of
Mexican-Americans, with many nonvoting farm laborers in
the latter county. The city of Los Angeles has more Mexicans
than any other city in the world but Mexico City. Overall,
persons with Spanish surnames, Negroes, and other nonwhites
comprise 19 percent of the Los Angeles County population.
There is also a substantial Jewish minority. Nevertheless,
southern Californians remain overwhelmingly white, Anglo-
Saxon Protestants of native American stock. For a region that
has been predominantly urban for decades, the shortage of

Catholics and persons of European immigrant stock is particularly striking.

Catholics, and immigrants and their descendants, have always been more prominent in the San Francisco Bay Area, the
other metropolitan center of California population. In 1930,
for example, foreign-born whites and their children averaged
less than 15 percent of the population in the southern counties compared to 36 percent in the six Bay Area counties. In
1936 the southern counties averaged 12 percent Catholic, the
Bay Area counties 27 percent.[3] Most of California's remaining
forty-four counties are small or sparsely populated, although
a few have substantial urban concentrations, and others con-
tain immense agricultural wealth. The analysis here will generally contrast southern California with the Bay Area.

Los Angeles and its environs differ in significant respects
from the traditional American metropolitan area. At the
turn of the century, Los Angeles boasted the largest number
of churches per capita of any city in the country.[4] The atmosphere of low-church Protestantism has continued to dominate, with its distinctively southern California mixture of
puritanical respectability and garish display. "The growth of
large cities," writes Carey McWilliams, is "usually marked by
the rise of industry, the arrival of foreign immigrants, and the
spread of tenderloin districts. But the evolution of Los Angeles never followed the general pattern. The more it grew in
population . . . the more it resembled a village."[5] But even
this comparison is misleading, since it suggests precisely the
cultural integration lacking in southern California. Flagrant
self-seeking and corruption have coexisted with intense asser-
tions of moral purity since the early migrations to the south.
With its high mobility, rootless population, and church-sat-
urated atmosphere, southern California has long been seen as

the home of the "isms," which rise and disappear with such regularity in the politics of the state. Analysis of county voting returns over the past half-century tells a different story.

REFORM AND REACTION (1892–1928)

California populism, as we have seen, originated during hard times in southern California. But populism quickly lost its southern base, and was, in any case, weak throughout the state. From the rise of the Progressive movement to the coming of the New Deal, left-wing movements were not based in southern California. Los Angeles did have a powerful civic reform movement in the first decade of the twentieth century, but it was distinctly cool to left-wing social programs.[6] Progressive Hiram Johnson, winning the gubernatorial nomination in the 1910 Republican primary, ran no better in the south than in the north. By 1916, Johnson's program had won him impressive backing from workers and ethnic minorities in the Bay Area, but he was strongly opposed in the south. Johnson and other California Progressives remained in the 1920s weaker in the south than anywhere else in the state.[7]

Robert La Follette received 35 percent of the California vote in 1924, his best showing by far in a large, urban state. But both in 1924 and in the presidential primary of 1912, La Follette was even more strongly opposed in the south than Johnson. More radical than Johnson, La Follette is often considered the exemplar of native, petit bourgeois protest.[8] La Follette's vote, nevertheless, was almost entirely concentrated above the Tehachapis—particularly among San Francisco workers and in the mountain and lumbering counties of the north. The Socialist party elected some mayors in California during the Progressive era and ran fairly well in a few state elections. Socialists received support in several southern counties and almost elected the mayor of Los Angeles in 1911. But Socialists were also strong in the Bay Area. Socialist support was peculiarly urban and working class, not peculiarly southern.[9]

The southern counties, as we showed in Chapter 2, were distinctively conservative and Republican throughout the Progressive period. In opposition to Woodrow Wilson in 1916 and La Follette in 1924—both of whom received Progressive votes—Republican strength became even more concentrated in the south.[10]

Simple conservatism, however, does not tell the whole story. For two decades, the southern counties consistently supported prohibition. On a number of referenda from 1916 to 1933, six, seven, or all eight southern counties were in the top quartile of prohibitionist strength. The occasional county not in the top quartile was always in the second. Prohibition sentiment was also strong in native-stock, Protestant counties outside the south. But few such northern counties were as persistently and strongly prohibitionist as their southern neighbors. Orange, Riverside, and San Bernardino were always dry by margins unheard of in the rest of the state.[11] In some sense the desire for prohibition was "radical"; but it was intimately connected to the dominant, Anglo-Saxon, Protestant conservatism of southern California and to a suspicion of alien life styles and radical politics.[12]

THE DEPRESSION DECADE

The depression, as Chapter 5 indicated, transformed southern voting behavior. The region as a whole did not become left-wing, but important elements in the south (probably lower-middle and working class) broke with its conservative traditions.

To accomplish this change, the shock of economic disaster was required. In the 1920s, La Follette and Al Smith had received almost no southern support. The La Follette election is traditionally counterposed to Smith's—the last gasp of nineteenth century radicalism versus the pragmatic precursor of the New Deal.[13] But in California, Smith's vote was similar to La Follette's; both were strong among San Francisco workers, but neither could attract the lower-class southern support necessary to challenge Republican dominance.[14] With the elections of 1924 and 1928, the gap between north and south had become truly enormous. But in 1932, although Democratic strength increased throughout the state, it increased far more sharply in the south. Southern, depression-born sympathy for the Democrats enabled Roosevelt to carry California (see Figures 8 and 9).

The collapse of the 1920s boom had hit the south particularly hard. Formerly prosperous blue- and white-collar workers barely survived on the relief rolls. In 1933, former Socialist Upton Sinclair organized his movement to End Poverty in California. Almost overnight, EPIC received intense, widespread popular support. Democratic voters nominated Sinclair for governor in 1934 and EPIC-supporter Sheridan Downey for lieutenant-governor. Opposed by the entire state press and the national Democratic administration, EPIC was defeated in November. Four years later Downey, now supporting the "Ham and Eggs" old-age pension scheme, was elected to the senate.

Chapter 5 discussed the EPIC campaign of 1934 in some detail. Here it is necessary only to reiterate the southern California roots of the movement. EPIC clubs had sprung up at a phenomenal rate in southern California; there were far fewer clubs in the north.[15] The intense, widespread popular backing for EPIC included many Protestant clergymen, the

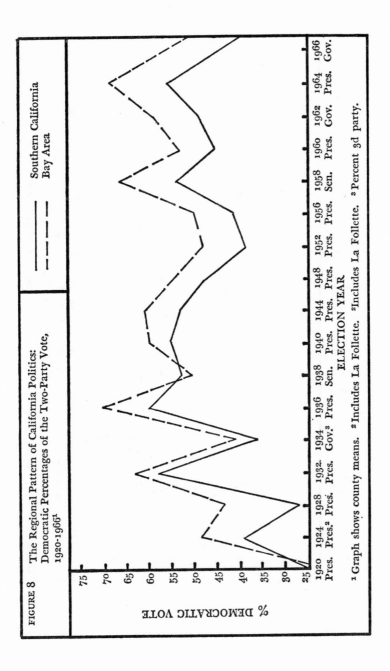

FIGURE 8   The Regional Pattern of California Politics: Democratic Percentages of the Two-Party Vote, 1920-1966[1]

Southern California
Bay Area

[1] Graph shows county means.   [2] Includes La Follette.   [3] Percent 3d party.

% DEMOCRATIC VOTE

ELECTION YEAR

1920 Pres.   1924 Pres.[2]   1928 Pres.   1932 Pres.   1934 Gov.[3]   1936 Pres.   1938 Sen.   1940 Pres.   1944 Pres.   1948 Pres.   1952 Pres.   1956 Pres.   1958 Sen.   1960 Pres.   1962 Gov.   1964 Pres.   1966 Gov.

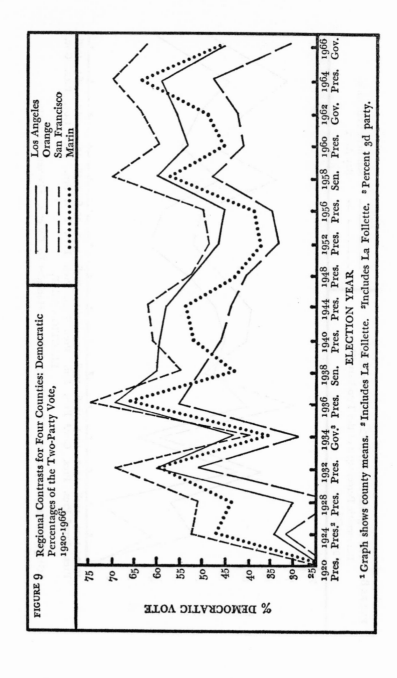

FIGURE 9   Regional Contrasts for Four Counties: Democratic Percentages of the Two-Party Vote, 1920-1966[1]

Los Angeles
Orange
San Francisco
Marin

% DEMOCRATIC VOTE

1920 1924 1928 1932 1934 1936 1938 1940 1944 1948 1952 1956 1958 1960 1962 1964 1966
Pres. Pres.[2] Pres. Pres. Gov.[3] Pres. Sen. Pres. Pres. Pres. Pres. Pres. Sen. Pres. Gov. Pres. Gov.

ELECTION YEAR

[1] Graph shows county means. [2] Includes La Follette. [3] Percent 3d party.

leader of the state Anti-Saloon League, and the former head of the Prohibition party. (Sinclair himself had been an ardent dry for years.)[16] The evangelical revivalism of southern California, politicized and radicalized by the depression, had found a home in EPIC.

EPIC electoral support was strongly southern-based. Southern voters nominated northerner Downey for the senate in 1938, although incumbent William Gibbs McAdoo was a Los Angeles resident and leader of the southern (dry) faction of the state Democratic party. Every southern county but Imperial was in the top quartile of Downey's strength in both his primary victories. Imperial and Ventura were in the second quartile in the Sinclair primary; the other southern counties were in the first. The Los Angeles support for Sinclair and Downey was even more striking. Sinclair received 67 percent of the Los Angeles vote, 44 percent and 36 percent of the remaining totals. Los Angeles was the top Downey county in both elections. Sinclair received far more support in Los Angeles County, San Diego County, and tiny Del Norte County in the north than in any other counties.[17] The proportions of the Los Angeles radical vote were unprecedented. No large county had ever behaved so differently from the rest of the state, except perhaps in support of a favorite son.[18]

Democratic primaries, however, do not tell the whole story. While Democratic registration increased astronomically between 1928 and 1934, surpassing Republican registration in Los Angeles and in the south as a whole for the first time, almost half the registered voters in the south remained Republican. In the general elections of 1934 and 1938, the radicalism of the south was severely muted. The EPIC ticket in 1934 ran well behind the Republicans in the south and did no better in the south than in the traditionally more Democratic Bay Area.[19] But our concern is with changes in southern voting behavior as well as with the absolute percentages of the EPIC vote. Under the impact of EPIC and the depression, the gap between north and south narrowed sharply. In both 1934 and 1938, the Democrats actually ran better in Los Angeles than in San Francisco; in 1938, they averaged better in the southern counties than in the Bay Area. These were unprecedented achievements for California Democrats.

Perhaps the southerners who voted Democratic in the 1930s were not Republican conservatives but new California arrivals without a Republican past. Since the migrants to southern California were, like the older residents, predominantly Anglo-Saxon Protestants, the shift in southern California voting patterns would still be significant. Chapter 5 did show the importance of new voters to Sinclair's 1934 primary victory. But it suggested that these were not depression migrants but older California residents who had not bothered to vote in preceding elections. In addition, the depression-bred migration from the southwestern dust bowl had barely begun at the time of the 1934 primary.[20] Okies did not nominate Sinclair. Moreover, registered Republicans as well as previous nonvoters supported EPIC. While the total registration in southern California increased by half a million between 1928 and 1934, Republican registration actually declined by more than 70,000. In Los Angeles between 1932 and 1934, Democratic registration increased by 180,000, Republican dropped by 100,000.[21] Apparently, former Republicans had moved into the Democratic primary to vote for Sinclair.

How were the southerners who became Democrats during the depression distinguished from the southerners who remained Republican? Without analysis of returns within the counties we cannot know for sure, but lower-income and working-class southerners were probably most likely to become Democrats. Los Angeles, the most working-class of the southern counties, experienced the biggest Democratic vote increase and the most precipitous drop in Republican registration. Orange County, the wealthiest and most middle-class in the south, supported Downey and Sinclair in the primaries. But most Orange County voters stayed Republican and in the general elections kept the county among the most Republican in the state (see Figure 10).

After EPIC and the pension schemes disappeared from California politics, the south became more conservative relative to the Bay Area. But the gap did not return to its 1920s level, and the south remained far more Democratic than it had been since the turn of the century. The shock of economic adversity had spawned left-wing radicalism in southern California; although the movements disappeared, the Democratic party loyalties remained. Thus the class politics of the depression permanently reoriented the party vote. Contemporary California party divisions were formed in the battles of the 1930s.[22]

MODERN PARTY POLITICS

The 1936 election ushered in a stable pattern of party competition, the first in California since progressivism. California party lines remained fairly stable for twenty-five years, the longest period in twentieth century state history (see Table 38).[23]

The north-south cleavage, as we showed in Chapter 5, did not dominate post-New Deal California party politics. In every presidential election from 1936 to 1960, Orange and Riverside were banner Republican counties, and four other southern counties were always among the top half of Republican counties in the state.[24] But after 1944, Ventura became strongly Democratic.[25] Los Angeles, with more votes than the other southern counties combined, was among the top twenty-nine

FIGURE 10   Regional Basis of the California Right: Seven Elections

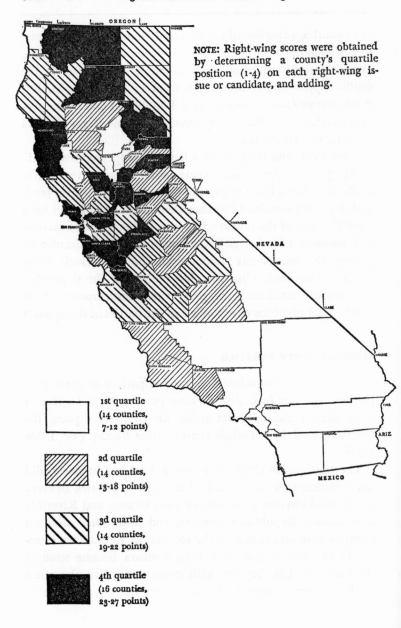

NOTE: Right-wing scores were obtained by determining a county's quartile position (1-4) on each right-wing issue or candidate, and adding.

1st quartile
(14 counties,
7-12 points)

2d quartile
(14 counties,
13-18 points)

3d quartile
(14 counties,
19-22 points)

4th quartile
(16 counties,
23-27 points)

TABLE 38
Intercorrelations among Counties in
California Presidential Elections, 1936-1960

	1936	1940	1944	1948	1952	1956
1940	.89					
1944	.81	.89				
1948	.78	.88	.93			
1952	.71	.77	.90	.95		
1956	.70	.79	.84	.93	.93	
1960	.64	.77	.84	.88	.89	.92

NOTE: In every year except 1948, the percentages of the two-party vote were used. Therefore, the intercorrelations among Democrats are identical to the Republican intercorrelations, except in 1948. The table uses Republican percentages of the three-party vote for that year because most Wallace-voters were Democrats. Democratic percentages would still give virtually the same correlations.

Republican counties only once in seven elections. The large Jewish, Negro, Mexican, and white working-class population kept the county more Democratic than its southern neighbors and only slightly less Democratic than San Francisco. At the same time, the Bay Area suburban counties of Marin and San Mateo, in spite of substantial Catholic and immigrant populations, remained strongly Republican. Party voting was firmly based on class divisions, which overcame, in part, any regional differences between north and south.[26]

THE CONTEMPORARY RIGHT

With the New Deal, the right-left contrast between southern California and the Bay Area lost its overwhelming partisan significance. But American interparty conflict from 1940 to 1960 was not highly ideological. Both parties nominated mod-

TABLE 39

Intercorrelations among Right-Wing Causes and Republican Candidates

	1952 Anti-subversive	1958 Right-to-work	1962 Anti-subversive	1964 (primary) Goldwater	1964 Anti-fair housing	1966 Reagan	1966 Anti-obscenity	1952 Rep. Pres.	1956 Rep. Pres.	1958 Rep. Gov.	1960 Rep. Pres.	1962 Rep. Gov.	1964 Rep. Pres.
1958 right-to-work	.55												
1962 anti-subversive	.58	.51											
1964 (primary) Goldwater	.54	.51	.69										
1964 anti-fair housing	.41	.45	.72	.62									
1966 (primary) Reagan	.49	.30	.78	.66	.59								
1966 anti-obscenity	.46	.47	.83	.78	.61	.68							
1952 Rep. Pres.	.43	.61	.43	.33	.27	−.11	.02						
1956 Rep. Pres.	.45	.62	.47	.34	.32	.06	.24	.93					
1958 Rep. Gov.	.60	.82	.64	.52	.50	.34	.15	.83	.89				
1960 Rep. Pres.	.44	.59	.50	.42	.45	.30	.50	.89	.92	.89			
1962 Rep. Gov.	.50	.60	.54	.47	.43	.32	.50	.85	.87	.88	.92		
1964 Rep. Pres.	.53	.74	.67	.82	.59	.48	.58	.77	.78	.61	.84	.82	
1966 Rep. Gov.	.43	.66	.63	.56	.58	.60	.54	.31	.58	.71	.92	.85	.85

erate presidential candidates; at the mass level, there was no party realignment and little intense commitment. For evidence of radical political sentiment, we must turn from party voting to primary and referendum campaigns which directly involved radical "ideologies." The present analysis was made from two antisubversive referenda, one in 1952, the other (the "Francis Amendment") in 1962; the 1958 "right-to-work" referendum; the 1964 anti-fair housing referendum (Proposition 14); the 1966 anti-obscenity referendum (Proposition 16); the Goldwater vote in the 1964 Republican presidential primary; and the 1966 Republican gubernatorial primary support for Ronald Reagan.

Analysis of electoral patterns in these contests revealed a general right-wing belief syndrome, extending over more than a decade.[27] Whether 60 percent of the population was supporting the right-wing cause (Proposition 14 and the 1952 antisubversive measure), or opposing it (Francis Amendment and right-to-work), the areas of right-wing support and opposition remained stable (see Table 39). The existence of such stability could not be predicted by survey findings, which have failed to locate developed ideologies at the mass level. Anti-Negro sentiment, opposition to unions, and fear of Communists may be found together among political leaders and activists, it is alleged, but not among ordinary citizens.[28] It is particularly impressive, therefore, that right-wing candidates and issues, whatever their specific content, should draw support from the same counties.[29]

Sometimes mass ideological consistency is a mere artifact of party tradition. Several studies have found right-wing sentiment stronger among Republicans than Democrats, and Republican counties in California were more right-wing than Democratic ones (see Table 39).[30] But while the normal party cleavage influenced right-wing patterns, it was not the overriding factor. By the 1960s, a right-wing constituency had emerged that bore little relation to the party vote of the previous decade. This constituency remained impressively stable from one campaign to another. The Francis Amendment, Propositions 14 and 16, and the Goldwater and Reagan primaries were more similar to one another than to the party vote (see Table 39). The intercorrelations are particularly striking, since these elections were not governed by traditional party loyalty. The consistency of right-wing ideological patterns approached party-induced stability.

The California regional cleavage, muted in normal party politics, reasserted itself in elections with right-wing candidates or issues. Year after year, right-wing support was more concentrated in the south than Republican strength, and less concentrated in the Bay Area.[31] The Bay Area counties of Marin and San Mateo, although heavily Republican, consistently opposed the right-wing causes.[32] Of the string of Republican coastal counties extending north and south of San Francisco, not one was consistently right-wing, while most were consistently liberal (see Figure 11).[33]

Seven of the eight southern counties were in the top quartile of both the Reagan and Goldwater primaries, and Santa Barbara was in the second quartile. On both antisubversive referenda Santa Barbara and Ventura were in the second quartile, all other southern counties being in the first. All southern counties except Santa Barbara were in the top half of the state in their support for Propositions 14 and 16. Only on the right-to-work referendum were three southern counties, including Los Angeles, in the third quartile. But even here, southern counties were far more right-wing than those in the Bay Area or in the state as a whole (see Figure 10 and Table 40).

Can the commonplace conflicts of American politics ex-

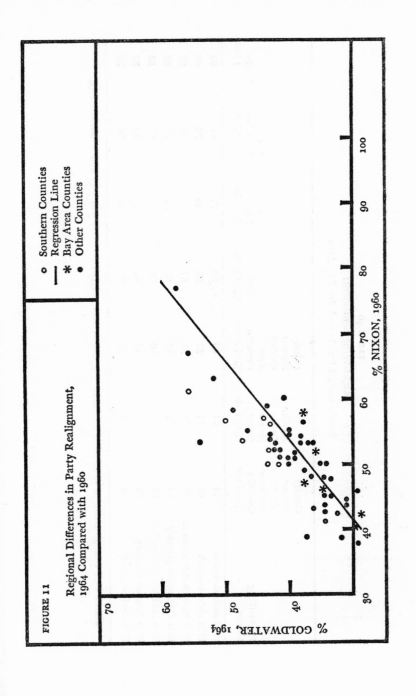

FIGURE 11

Regional Differences in Party Realignment,
1964 Compared with 1960

∘ Southern Counties
— Regression Line
* Bay Area Counties
• Other Counties

% GOLDWATER, 1964

% NIXON, 1960

TABLE 40

Right-Wing Sentiment:
Southern California and the Bay Area

Right-Wing Causes	County Means: Eight Southern Counties % of Vote	Median California County % of Vote	County Means: Six Bay Area Counties % of Vote	Orange % of Vote	Los Angeles % of Vote	San Francisco % of Vote	Marin % of Vote
1952 antisubversive	74	64	63	80	72	64	59
1958 right-to-work	46	41	37	53	40	32	48
1962 Francis Amendment	44	35	31	51	48	24	23
1964 Goldwater primary	56	42	37	66	60	34	33
1964 anti-fair housing[a]	69	64	60	78	67	53	53
1966 Reagan primary	77	63	46	81	79	30	30
1966 anti-obscenity	49	43	36	50	47	34	32

[a] Marin and Orange counties were both less than 3% Negro in 1960. Los Angeles was 9%, San Francisco 10%.

plain right-wing strength? Class and ethnic cleavages often determine voting patterns, but the relevant groups normally
have an obvious interest at stake. Thus, Germans deserted
the Democratic party during both world wars, Catholics supported Kennedy while Protestants opposed him, and workers
usually vote against the GOP because they regard it as the
party of the rich. Such pragmatic class and ethnic factors explain some of the support for Proposition 14 and right-to-
work, the two least southern-based, right-wing elections (see
Table 40). Right-to-work, which tapped attitudes toward unions, was the most class-based, the least southern, and the
closest to the normal party vote (see Table 39). Los Angeles
workers were more likely to vote against right-to-work than
against other right-wing causes, while middle-class Bay Area
Republicans were more likely to vote for it.[34] Proposition 14
also had a "pragmatic" component. Other research indicates
that anti-Negro sentiment among whites increases near the
centers of Negro population.[35] Therefore, we would expect
support for Proposition 14 to be more concentrated in the Bay
Area with its substantial Negro minority than the vote for the
other referenda. When county support for Proposition 14 is
plotted against support for the Francis Amendment, four of
the six Bay Area counties were significantly more for Proposition 14, while four southern counties were significantly more
for the Francis Amendment.[36]

Such class and ethnic divisions are the normal stuff of
American politics. But pragmatic group concerns cannot explain the southern base of Proposition 14 and right-to-work.
The south does have a special group composition: its residents
are primarily Anglo-Saxon Protestants, which is rare in a
metropolitan area. And right-wing California politics clearly
has a distinctive ethnic base. Reagan, Goldwater, the Francis
Amendment, and Proposition 16 were strong throughout Prot-

estant, Anglo-Saxon counties.[37] Since the last good statistics on county ethnic and religious backgrounds are a generation out of date, the correlations are particularly striking (see Table 41). Right-wing politics is ethnic politics with a vengeance, but it is not based on any tangible "group benefits" criterion that motivates the normal party politics of 45 percent of the American electorate.[38]

TABLE 41
The Ethnic Basis of the California Right

	1930 Percent Foreign White Stock	1936 Percent Catholic
1962 Francis Amendment	—.47	—.49
1964 Goldwater primary	—.59	—.51
1966 Reagan primary	—.59	—.43
1966 Anti-obscenity	—.64	—.50

Southern right-wing sentiment is not a product of normal group politics. What are the manifestly relevant variables analogous to working class opposition to right-to-work that would explain southern right-wing proclivities? Recent right-wing elections that have not tapped tangible class and ethnic interests have been particularly southern-based. The gap separating Los Angeles from San Francisco reached twenty-four percentage points for the Francis Amendment, twenty-six for Goldwater, and forty-nine for Reagan (see Table 40). Reagan obtained approximately 80 percent of the vote in five southern counties, including Los Angeles; no other county in the state supported him so strongly.[39] Right-wing targets must have special symbolic significance in southern California.

PARTY REALIGNMENT

Contemporary studies of electoral behavior either minimize the significance of mass ideological appeals or explain them in terms of pre-existing party cleavages. In California, however, right-wing sentiment is not only important in referenda and primaries—it has also reoriented the party vote. It is still too early to tell whether this reorientation will be durable. Its magnitude, however, matched for California the earlier national realignments of 1896 and 1928-1936. Farmers and populism configured the 1896 critical election; workers, immigrants, and the depression determined the character of the 1928-1936 realignment.[40] The California reorientation has focused around Negroes and related right-wing targets.

During a critical period, the electoral base of the major parties shifts markedly. Thus, elections during a time of normal party conflict are more similar to one another than they are to elections during a critical period. The California realignment began in 1958 when gubernatorial candidate William Knowland identified the GOP with right-to-work. It appeared more sharply in the 1964 Goldwater debacle and the 1966 Reagan triumph. The elections of 1958, 1964, and 1966, particularly the latter two, deviated from the normal party vote of the 1950s. Goldwater's vote was the least typically Republican of that given any GOP presidential candidate since World War II (see Tables 38 and 39).

However, correlations are determined mainly by small and sparsely populated counties. Since each county is treated as a unit, correlations obscure developments in the population centers. A comparison between the Bay Area and the south provides more substantial evidence that a realignment occurred and illustrates its nature as well.

The Republicans lost strength throughout the state in 1958. But their vote dropped far more precipitously in the Bay Area than in the south, creating the largest party gap between the regions since before the depression (see Figures 8 and 9).[41] The regional cleavage sharpened even further in 1964 and 1966. The gap between the metropolitan counties of San Francisco and Los Angeles, and between the suburban counties of Marin and Orange, is particularly remarkable. San Francisco, only five percentage points more Democratic than Los Angeles in 1956, was fourteen points more Democratic in 1964; the gap between Marin and Orange widened from three to eighteen (see Figure 9).

We can also illustrate the regional shift by comparing one of the right-wing elections, county by county, with a normal party vote. When the county percentages for Goldwater, for example, are plotted against those for Nixon in 1960 (Figure 11), thirteen counties are visibly below the regression line; these were less for Goldwater than their percentages for Nixon would have predicted. Three were in the Bay Area; nine of the remaining ten were contiguous counties to the north, south, and east. Of the fifteen comparable most pro-Goldwater counties, six were southern.[42] The contrast in regional behavior is striking.[43]

As the regional pattern suggests, the three elections of the critical period were rooted in ideological divisions. All were closer than normal Republican elections to the measures of right-wing sentiment (see Table 39). The 1958 vote, most closely related to right-to-work, had been an ideological realignment with class overtones. These tangible class appeals rooted Knowland's support in party normality and partly limited the ideological realignment.[44] The overtones for Goldwater and Reagan were ethnic and religious, reinforcing rather than counteracting the ideological shift. Protestant and native-stock counties most heavily supported the Francis Amendment and Proposition 16, and they nominated Goldwater and Reagan in the primaries. Normally Republican voters were not disproportionately native-stock Protestants; in 1962 the correlations were only .22 and .13.[45] They went up to .51 and .45 in 1964 and to .46 for both native stock and Protestant in 1966.[46]

How typical, and how significant, is the California party realignment? Examination of county returns within such states as Indiana and Wisconsin reveals no shift of critical election proportions in 1964. Nevertheless, there was a nationwide ideological realignment in 1964; it was regional rather than intrastate. Republican strength became more concentrated in the South, less in the East, than ever before in history.[47] Since California contains two populous regions with contrasting ideological patterns, the realignment shows up within the state itself. But California's 1964 voting response was not atypical. Like the deep South, but for less obvious reasons, southern California is peculiarly susceptible to right-wing appeals.[48] The area of northern California radiating out from San Francisco may be as anti-right wing as the northeast.

In 1964, as in 1958, the price of ideological politics was defeat for the right; even in southern California, Goldwater ran far worse than Nixon, Eisenhower, and Dewey. The years 1958 and 1964 saw two of the worst Republican defeats in California history.[49] But these were Democratic years across the country. The election year of 1966 demonstrated that new, politically salient issues—civil rights, Vietnam—could rejuvenate the California right. With Reagan, the right wing of the GOP achieved its long-sought mass base. Reagan, running on an openly antiuniversity, antiobscenity, antiwelfare, and antifair housing platform, amassed a one-million-vote plurality. At the very least a right-wing candidate running against an unpopular incumbent would not hurt the GOP in a year of Republican successes across the country.

When the symbolic political universe of southern California produces the governor of the nation's largest state, it is time to take that symbolic world seriously. Efforts to escape into party tradition, tangible group benefits, or the personal appeal of a particular candidate simply will not do. Right-wing politics has upset party loyalty, and its ethnic base lacks obvious political relevance. Reagan exhibited candidate appeal, but why did he appeal so peculiarly to southern Californians? We must confront the meaning of the cultural symbols themselves.

Culture and Politics in Southern California

Anthropologists assume that the round of daily activities in a society, from the cradle to the grave, takes form and meaning from shared symbolic attachments. Orienting symbols not only permeate the immediate daily concerns of a society's inhabitants, but they also dominate the response to distant events and new experiences. When anthropologists speak of culture, they have these symbols in mind. "Cultural patterns," writes Clifford Geertz, "are 'programs': they provide a template or blueprint for the organization of social and psychological processes, much as genetic systems provide such a template for the organization of organic processes."[50]

Cultural symbols provide meaning to human experience; they connect the individual to the world around him. These connections by their nature cannot be simply logical or "instrumental," since logic and utility alone cannot provide human meaning. At the same time, cultural symbols are more than brute preferences; they organize desires as they organize "reality." Symbols condense into affectively charged metaphors a world of associations, unconscious assumptions, and central beliefs.

What have cultural symbols to do with the political world of the ordinary voter? If we take the idea of political culture seriously, two things follow: the centrality of political symbols and their roots in broader cultural patterns.

Political symbols are one kind of cultural symbol. They make sense of the world of politics as symbols of family, work, and religion make sense of other human concerns. To believe that sophistication is required before citizens perceive political symbols is to miss the point. If passive voters relate to politics, it can only be through distant symbols somehow made personally relevant. "New frontier," "right to work," "law and order"—all these are efforts by politicians to create compelling political symbols that will influence mass behavior. Natural disasters, foreign countries, and visible groups also often take on symbolic political significance—think only of what Korea meant to mothers in 1952 and what drug addicts mean to them today. The import of such symbols can shift rapidly. Murray Edelman writes of the change in American consciousness following World War II: "In view of the changed perceptual world created by the symbols of the cold war, 'Germany' quickly took on a new meaning."[51]

Politicians themselves often acquire significant symbolic proportions. We need a richer, more powerful sense of the appeal of a Roosevelt, an Eisenhower, or a Reagan than the correct but meager assertion that many who voted for each were motivated by "candidate orientation." Did Eisenhower mean the same things to his adherents as Reagan meant to his? Voters preferring Reagan may have been more politically sophisticated or better at reasoning than those preferring Roosevelt.

But other dimensions seem more relevant in understanding and evaluating the appeals of both men.

> The mass public [writes Edelman] does not study and analyze detailed data about secondary boycotts, provisions for stock ownership and control in a proposed space communications system until political action and speeches make them symbolically threatening or reassuring, and then it responds to the cues furnished by the actions and the speeches, not to direct knowledge of the facts.[52]

Political sophistication is rare at the mass level, and worked-out political ideologies even rarer. As the authors of *The American Voter* conclude in their study of the 1956 election, "This profile of an electorate is not calculated to increase our confidence in interpretations of elections that presume widespread ideological concerns in the adult population."[53] But voters unaware of the abstract language of political leaders may still respond to concrete political symbols; absence of sophisticated content and absence of symbolic content are not the same thing. Confusion between the two leads Philip Converse, explaining Nazi strength in rural Germany, to argue that "the link between specific ideology and mass response was probably of the weakest."[54] Here an impoverished reading of "ideology" overlooks the symbolic connections between masses and political movements. Perhaps, as Converse argues, German Communists could equally well have mobilized the farmers had they persevered in their rural organizational efforts. But that assumes that anti-Semitism, anti-Communism, and other Nazi political symbols[55] had no affective meaning to German farmers in the 1930s, simply because farmers lacked political sophistication.

Converse has demonstrated that there is little consistency in the belief systems of ordinary voters. Individuals take contradictory stands on separate but related issues. They change their minds on a single issue from one year to the next, often in a way that can best be expressed mathematically by a random model of issue preference. But it makes little sense to evaluate the coherence of the voter's world by examples and standards drawn from the experience of political elites. Converse has also demonstrated that attitudes on certain issues—for example, FEPC and school segregation—are far more stable over a period of time than those toward such matters as public housing. Negroes, he explains, are significant objects to the electorate.[56] And V. O. Key has shown that single, dominant issues and candidates have considerable popular meaning in most elections.[57] Not all the symbols of politics are as irrelevant to most voters as government-built housing. What of the salience, in certain contexts and for certain subcultures, of Communists, atheists, and drug addicts? Of plutocrats and unions? We need to search for the set of political symbols relevant to a given group of voters, understand what these symbols mean to the voters, and explain why these particular symbols have become salient.

Discussions of electoral behavior rarely have explored the meaning of relevant political symbols to the ordinary voter. Perhaps this is because they have begun with the complex political issues central to the politician instead of the cultural patterns central to a voter's total life experience.[58] Politics is remote from the lives of most people. Is it surprising, therefore, that they organize their political perceptions around more familiar symbolic attachments? To understand how people think about politics, and why they vote as they do, we have to know how they live. This simple idea, foreign to most voting analysis, is second nature to those studying behavior in other contexts—delinquent gangs, ethnic ghettos, or legislatures.

We need to know, in short, what meanings ordinary voters attach to given political symbols. Under some circumstances and in some subcultures, the voter's connection with politics takes place through "candidate orientation," a self-interested notion of "group benefits," or a feeling of traditional party loyalty. It must be stressed that "Democrat," "worker," and "Eisenhower" are all political symbols, and to stop when we have given them names is only barely to comprehend their meaning. Old-fashioned, commonsense ideas about pragmatic group politics do explain much that goes on in mass American politics. However, under certain circumstances and in certain subcultures, political choices are made that prove refractory to analysis in terms of self-interested concern with tangible goals. How are we to understand, for example, the mass political appeals that have won favor in southern California for half a century or more?

We explore now the symbols of politics in southern California. The discussion treats voting behavior as saturated with cultural meaning, deriving from the whole world in which people live, not from an exclusively political universe. Southern Californians, when they vote, are trying to tell us something. Their electoral acts reveal the metaphorical meanings they attach to politics.

In the first part of this chapter, we found out what those acts were—that is, how southerners behaved politically. We showed that the electoral choices of southern Californians formed a historically, symbolically coherent regional pattern. Southerners are often alleged to support all forms of protest politics. The persistent strength of right- and left-wing radicalism in California is thus explained by southern characteristics.[59] But for more than half a century southern California has been the home of right-wing extremism, not radicalism in general. Southern radicalism is not visceral, mindless, and symbolically impoverished; we must explain what the symbols of right-wing politics mean, and why they have found a home in southern California.

Perhaps the most remarkable fact about California voting patterns is that they conform to the folk wisdom of the amateur political observer, and that this informed common sense owes more to art than to academic political science. For decades the contrast between northern and southern California has intrigued novelists, moviemakers, and critics, as well as political buffs. *The Maltese Falcon* and *The Thin Man Comes Home,* for example, are set in San Francisco; *The Loved One* and *The Day of the Locust* take place in Los Angeles. The south has not fared well in the comparison. Los Angeles was created, one writer explained in 1913, by the

> rural pietist obsessed with the spirit of village fellowship, of suburban respectability. . . . Hypocrisy, like a vast fungus, has spread over the city's surface. . . . And there is a good old medieval suspicion afloat in Los Angeles that all those things which charm by their grace and beauty are wiles of the devil, and only those things are decent which are depressing. . . . Los Angeles is overrun with militant moralists, connoisseurs of sin, experts of biological purity. . . . The inhabitants of Los Angeles are culled mainly from the smaller cities of the Middle West—"leading citizens" from Wichita; honorary pall bearers from Emmetsburg; Good Templars from Sedalia; honest Spinsters from Grundy Center. . . . These good folks brought with them a complete stock of rural beliefs, pieties, superstitions, and habits. . . . Everyone is interested in everyone else. Snooping is the popular pastime, gossiping the popular practice. Privacy is impossible.[60]

A generation later, George Creel, Upton Sinclair's opponent in the 1934 Democratic primary, expressed the trepidations civilized Californians have felt toward the southern part of the state. "Northern Californians offered no problem," said Creel, "for the hard-headed, hard-working native sons and daughters were in a majority, but when I crossed the Tehachapis into southern California, it was like plunging into darkest Africa without gun bearers."[61] More recently, the

Watts riots brought at least one curious New Yorker to the area. Elizabeth Hardwick found

> a strip of plastic and clapboard, decorated by skimpy palms. . . . This long, sunny nothingness, born yesterday. It turns out to be an exile, a stop-over from which there is no escape . . . infested with disappointments unmitigated by the year-round cook-out. Everything is small, but with no hint of neighborliness. The promise of Los Angeles, this beckoning openness, newness, freedom. But what is it? It is neither a great city nor a small town. Sheer impossibility of definition, of knowing what you are experiencing exhausts the mind. The intensity and diversity of small-town Main Streets have been stretched and pulled and thinned out so that not even a Kresge, a redecorated Walgreen's, or the old gray stone of the public library, the spitoons and insolence of the Court House stand to keep the memory intact. The past resides in old cars, five years old, if anywhere. . . . Without a car you are not truly alive.[62]

Such observations may seem out of place in a behavioral political science. But if the meaning of cultural experience affects the politics of a region, then exploring cultural meaning reveals much about political symbols. The voting returns indicate that Communists, saloons, Negroes, and pornography are charged with a special meaning in southern California. Why are Communists more of a menace in Los Angeles than in San Francisco? Why is the south so much more hospitable to Goldwater and Reagan? What is there about right-wing symbols that makes them so powerful south of the Tehachapis?

A full answer to these questions would require anthropological field work beyond the scope of this study. But such field work should begin with a tentative theoretical orientation toward the right-wing political symbols of southern California. The orientation proposed here draws upon studies of right-wing appeals, histories of California politics, analyses of American culture, and various renderings of life in the south.[63]

In *The Founding of New Societies,* Louis Hartz describes "fragment cultures" such as the United States, Latin America, and South Africa that fled at different stages from the ideological diversity of Europe. The American liberal tradition, he writes, "arose as a result of the extrication of a bourgeois fragment from the turmoil of seventeenth-century England, and it gave to the United States over three hundred years of liberal immobility, but now it confronts on the world plane, thrust back at it from places as distant as Russia and China, the very alien ideologies it managed to escape."[64] In the isolated "fragment world," explains Hartz, alien ideas disappear. The ideological fragment sinks to the level of basic, pervasive assumption, shifting from one value among many to a sole definition of reality. Acquiring "enormous new power . . . it is reborn, transformed into a new nationalism." Liberalism, for example, "comes back at us" as the American way of life.[65]

The southern California way of life comes back at us in right-wing symbols, which characteristically insist on conformity to Americanism. Indeed, chroniclers of life in Los Angeles, from Nathanael West to Carey McWilliams, generally caricature American life itself. Suppose we look at southern California as a distended fragment of the American fragment, magnifying certain aspects of liberal, bourgeois culture.

Los Angeles and its environs were settled and formed by the respectable, ambitious Protestants of late nineteenth-century America—"Good Templars from Sedalia; honest Spinsters from Grundy Center," "the middle-aged from the middle class of the middle west."[66] They personified traditional, small-town America, but southern California personified the Gilded Age. This "Great Barbecue," as Parrington called it, which shattered small-town traditions while fulfilling small-town dreams, created Los Angeles.

The late nineteenth century was a time of great dreams for many and great fortunes for some. The country was preoccupied with ambition and success; acquisitive capitalism had triumphed. We have come to associate this triumph with Horatio Alger, but rapid industrialization was not kind to the values that permeate the Alger stories. Alger's heroes lived by the Protestant ethic. They were boys of industry and virtue; they had a calling, worked hard, lived frugally, and luck came at the right moment to reward their good works. Episcopal Bishop of Massachusetts William Lawrence might insist at the end of the Gilded Age that morality still produced wealth, but he could not hide what all could see: the Gilded Age meant speculation, easy money, sharp practice, shortcuts to wealth, fantastic dreams, conspicuous consumption. Tempted, the virtuous, small-town Protestant had fallen.

Of course, the contrast is by no means as clear-cut as this. Speculation and boosterism accompanied the growth of frontier towns before the Civil War, and hard work and thrift did not disappear thereafter. But rapid industrialization provided examples and opportunities undreamed of in the first half of the nineteenth century. The climate and the transcontinental railroad produced expectations about southern California that were grandiose even for that time.

The Gilded Age created Los Angeles more completely than any other city in America. Frenzied boosterism and land speculation accompanied the Santa Fe Railroad to the city in 1886; population grew from 10,000 in 1880 to 80,000 in 1887.[67] Charles Dudley Warner, author with Mark Twain of the book that gave the Gilded Age its name, remarked, "I do not mean to say that everybody in southern California is rich—but everybody expects to be rich tomorrow."[68]

The railroad boom of 1886 quickly collapsed, but it left a permanent heritage. One historian writes, "The boom had, in fact, revolutionized southern California—it had swept away the vestiges of its Spanish origin and left it thoroughly American in land and spirit."[69] This first substantial boom also set the pattern for the settlement of southern California that followed. The area has a seventy-five-year history of population explosion. Hordes of new inhabitants constantly flood the south, called by "the promise of Los Angeles, this beckoning openness, newness, freedom." Once within the city, "infested by disappointments, unmitigated by the year-round cookout," they continue to move.[70] The paradise of their expectations seems always out of reach.

The cycle of optimism, restlessness, longing, and dissatisfaction is not peculiar to southern California. Its genesis lies in the egalitarian, capitalist society described by Tocqueville. "Men are in constant motion," he wrote of Jacksonian America, "rest is unknown there." There is no peace from the "tumultuous and constantly harassed life that equality makes men lead." External barriers to success seem eliminated, but with them go all inherited definitions of man's being. The individual must rely solely on himself, not only to succeed, but also to make his own world. It is left to "men alone" to achieve the final peace of satisfied aspirations. "At every moment they think they are about to grasp it; it escapes at every moment from their hold. They are near enough to see its charms, but too far off to enjoy them; and before they have fully tasted its delights, they die."[71]

Restlessness and dissatisfaction are not peculiar to southern California, but they are exaggerated there. The high hopes, formed in time by the Gilded Age and in space by southern California, have no real parallel outside the Southwest. But if the hopes are exaggerated, so also is their fulfillment. Southern California seems the perfect site on which to build an American paradise. Relics from the Old World are few. Other areas which so strongly assert Americanism are in the backwaters of the country, while southern California has expanded and prospered remarkably in the twentieth century. Nor can the restlessness be attributed to derelicts, outcasts, failures, or freaks. Right-wing southerners are respectable, substantial citizens who live in private houses and typify, in their own minds at least, the American way of life, the wave of the future. To use Hannah Arendt's distinction, they may be a mass, but they are surely not a mob.[72]

Southern California lacks the barriers to individual success that tradition, ethnic diversity, primitive technology, and engrained codes of prudent moral behavior all supply. But these limits to success also make failure bearable and enrich life, so that failure and success are not its only terms. Southern Californians, less protected from mobility than even Tocqueville could have imagined, are brought by their restlessness face to face with the American dream. Right-wing voting behavior, expressing fear of Communists, hippies, pornography, and Negroes, indicates the failure of the dream to provide comfort and security. Far from protecting southern Californians against alien forces, the American dream seems to conjure them up. The dynamic of that dream has somehow gotten out of hand, in just the uniform and prosperous region where it ought to work so well. It is as if a Frankenstein monster had been created by traditional American values themselves, transformed by the gilded modernity of Los Angeles.

Why, then, do southerners not turn against the dream? Why is there no evidence of sustained, radical attack on the citadels of Americanism, those truly powerful groups and institutions? Why blame Communists and Negroes for evils they lack the power to produce? Hartz points out that alien ideas are peculiarly threatening in a fragment universe, since they challenge the organizing principles of the symbolic world and its very definition of reality.[73] In their homogeneous surroundings, southerners have no place to turn but to their dream; to give up the dream would be to give up everything. As Edgar Z.

Friedenberg describes mobile, respectable Americans, "They cannot attack the system that has made their lives meaningless, for they are in collusion with it and want to rise within it."[74] Presences that make the southern California way of life seem anything less than inescapable threaten to open a pandora's box of alternatives whose existence cannot be admitted. Hence "the impulse of the fragment to flee in the face of new experience."[75] But southerners safe in the suburbs seem to need Negroes, long-haired youths, and drug addicts. These scapegoats permit frustrations to be deflected from the American dream onto its perceived enemies. Politics thus becomes hallucinatory, since the real source of the anxiety, southern California itself, can never be faced.

But we must face the question from which southerners run: what values underlie their American Dream? Tocqueville's analysis of American restlessness provides the best beginning. Equality of conditions, Tocqueville believed, set men in motion, emancipating them from the connections to the world provided by history, family loyalty, local tradition, codes of honor, class solidarity, and the other ties of an aristocratic age. A democratic era, according to Tocqueville, provided little protection for diversity; indeed, the democrat would too easily resent as pretension or privilege forms of experience different from his own.[76]

But ridding the country of aristocratic residues only made the real danger clearer. The human ties of traditional cultures had provided life with meaning; they formed a series of interconnected links in the great chain of being. But "democracy breaks that chain and severs every link of it."[77] In a world where human artifacts were blank and uniform, there was little to sustain the individual in an existence separate from, but related to, nature and his fellows. Seeking protection against their loneliness, men tried to immerse themselves totally in the world around them; they sought a kind of unity with the country.

In Tocqueville's description, this process simultaneously took two forms. Men sought through frenetic activity to control, dominate, and incorporate nature. They had to assert the power of their wills, expanding over, incorporating, and destroying the untouched earth to which they were otherwise not connected. At the same time, Tocqueville's Americans hoped to lose their lonely egos through immersion in the crowd.[78] To put it simply, exhausted by their constant striving and independence, men longed for unconditional love and security. In a world lacking cultural richness and diversity, the danger was that these longings could only be conceived of in totalistic terms. Passive desires for nurturance and obedience to authority could be seen beneath the American individualist. The submerged, egoless infant lay hidden behind and was the other side of the independent, unattached entrepreneur.

The longing for unity, with the death of consciousness and individual distinctness that it implied, seemed to Tocqueville the principal danger of equality of conditions. But he believed that free institutions could counteract the symbiotic feelings of loneliness and individual omnipotence. Political action would bring people out of themselves, teaching them their relatedness to and dependence on others; it would teach them what they could do and what they could not do. Politics would provide a safe, delimited field for the pursuit of honor and interest; it would teach men a skill.[79]

In the thinking of literate nineteenth century Americans, human action was not confined to politics. Work itself could be a kind of craft that would not shatter and dominate nature, but somehow coexist with it. Perhaps the classic statement here is Mark Twain's memoir of the Mississippi steamboat pilot. Situated quite precisely on the Mississippi, there was no place in the pilot's world for the unchained, romantic imagination. The pilot had to know every inch of the river; he could not safely disobey its rules, but he could learn to navigate by them. The pilot had a craft; he knew what was possible and what was not. The rules of his craft and the rules of the river placed him in the world. They gave the pilot a ritual based on his skill and limited by nature—the only kind of ritual democratic Americans could know—and Twain compares him to a squire. Like Tocqueville's villagers who became political to build roads, the pilot was an actor.[80]

With the Gilded Age, human action became far more difficult—in work as in politics. As usual, developments in the rest of the country were exaggerated in southern California. The absence of stable political institutions that involve masses of people has often been noted.[81] Even more basic was the disappearance of nature as a source of limits and values independent of the human will.

In urban America, unspoiled nature hardly delimits spheres for human action. But cities like New York and San Francisco, which grew haphazardly, building on past neighborhoods, came to have a kind of organic character.[82] Urban actors emerged with their special crafts, limited by the city's past, its ethnic diversity, it architecture, even its natural surroundings. Partial identifications insulated residents from universal goals; ethnic working-class cultures, for example, at least partially protected the poor from middle-class aspirations. It did not seem, in such cities, that everything was possible.

From the beginning, everything was possible in southern California. We have spoken of the extravagant dreams of the Gilded Age and their extravagant fulfillment in Los Angeles. Originally a desert, southern California is a triumph of technology over the limits of nature and history. Certainly the past has never been a barrier. The Spanish-Mexican heritage disappeared in the 1880s, returning as a kind of grotesque joke to provide names for suburban developments. These developments spring out of nowhere, and there is no reason to believe they will in time gain a past. The face of southern California changes almost daily. "If something is built wrong it doesn't matter much. Everyone expects it to come down in a decade or two."[83] "The past resides in old cars, five years old, if anywhere."

Like the Spanish names on suburban developments, political traditions survive only to remind the observer and mask from the resident their inappropriateness to the southern California world. As the voting returns show, there is a political tradition in southern California. But this right-wing tradition neither grows from and describes actual experience, nor limits human aspirations. Small-town, individualistic values had genuine political meaning in a rural Protestant environment. In southern California they function quite differently. Right-wingers attack government in an area that lives off the aerospace industry and has always depended on government water and land. Southern Californians demand a return to moral standards while engaging in orgies of credit buying, expense account living, and cutthroat office politics. They assert frontier individualism in a world dominated by giant bureaucratic corporations and complex technology. The south-western tradition of frontier individualism ought to recall, not settler victories in personal, small-scale Indian fights, but the triumphant march of the U.S. Cavalry.[84] But political traditions are not rooted in an experienced past and present. Instead politics creates fantasies in which the repressed actual character of southern California returns to public consciousness monstrously garbed.

If history falls before technology and fantasy, so also does nature. Nathanael West, through the eyes of his hero, captured the feeling of the buildings exactly: "When he noticed that they were all of plaster, lath, and paper, he was charitable and blamed their shape on the materials used. Steel, stone, and brick curb a builder's fancy a little, forcing him to distribute his stresses and weights to keep his corners plumb, but plaster and paper know no law, not even that of gravity."[85] It is as if the Mississippi River could be dynamited (like the southern California hills) and turned into a canal. Gone is the steamboat pilot with his laws, his craft, and his sense of the appropriate.[86]

When everything is possible, there is no field for human action. Man is thrown back on himself alone and, wanting to end that isolation, seeks to take over and incorporate the world or lose himself in it. But when that world is no longer a virgin land, but an enormous, man-made, synthetic universe, the dream of union becomes truly terrifying.

For Tocqueville, nature was simply something for Americans to conquer. Failing to find the traditional European reverence for the land, however, he overlooked its American counterpart. The land provided the kind of protection and source of value for lonely Americans that Tocqueville found only in the crowd. But the land seemed more concrete than the crowd, and it was not made by man. One could point, as Lincoln and so many others did, to the rivers, the valleys, the fields, the forests, and the frontier. The land existed independent of the human will, or as a cultivated "garden" that still had a life of its own. Worship of the land thus provided Americans with a stable source of value, a genuine connection with a world they had not created.

But while the popular culture of antebellum America romanticized the virgin land, the populace was mastering, transforming, and destroying it.[87] If the land was so important, what did human aggression against it signify? If the continent and the frontier made America a union, what did conquering the wilderness mean? By mixing his labor with the land, the American achieved a unity through mastery and incorporation, but he bought it at a great price. The desire for protection through immersion would not disappear. But one could only merge oneself, in that extreme case which concerns us here, with the synthetic landscape of southern California.

A technology made by man but emancipated from any humanly comprehensible purposes created that landscape. The world so created does away with one's sense of the real. Nothing can be used for its proper purpose or given its proper name; everything becomes synthetic, inappropriate, out of place. Modern buildings stand next to Okie shacks. The hero of *The Day of the Locust,* swarmed over by a mob hungry for Hollywood blood, cannot even remember the time when locusts lived off wheat. Instead he plans to add to his painting "a corinthian column that held up the palm-leaf roof of a nutburger stand."[88] Hollywood incorporates human action; Disneyland incorporates American traditions; senior citizens and their developments incorporate age; Forest Lawn incorporates death; a "disasterama" incorporates civil defense preparations for atomic attack.[89] Nothing can happen; nothing can be experienced; nothing can grow. Life must be totally congealed. "All those things which charm by their grace and beauty are wiles of the devil." Anger too must be bureaucratized before it can be safely experienced.[90] "Property values" permit the expression of prejudice in a way that open race hatred never could. "The intensity and diversity of small-town Main Streets have been stretched and pulled and thinned out so that not even a Kresge, a redecorated Walgreen's, or the old gray stone of the public library, the spitoons and insolence of the Court House, stand to keep the memory intact."

This is conspicuous consumption on a scale and for a purpose that even Veblen did not imagine. Status seeking is an important element, and, as Veblen recognized, the more impersonal, anonymous, and unstable the environment, the greater the need for public display, and the larger the feats of waste needed to make an impact.[91] But conspicuous consumption occurs also for its own sake, not for display. It perpetuates the infant dream of omnipotence, the hunger for total union with the world. Unincorporated experience reminds the right-wing southerner that the world has an existence independent of his will and desire. The southern California Great Barbecue fills the world with incorporated, mastered objects that will not demand that, in experiencing the autonomous reality of others, one experience also himself.

William Carlos Williams' beautiful lines, from the poem "To Elsie," embody the relations we have tried to develop here:

> The pure products of America
> go crazy . . .
> From imaginations which have no
> peasant traditions to give them
> character . . .
> Expressing with broken
> brain the truth about us . . .
> as if the earth under our feet
> were an excrement of some sky
> and we degraded prisoners
> destined
> to hunger until we eat filth
> while the imagination strains
> after deer
> going by fields of goldenrod in
> the stifling heat of September
> Somehow

it seems to destroy us . . .
No one
to witness
and adjust, no one to drive the car.[92]

All that is personal and unique is burned out of the southern California landscape. It seems hardly surprising that, in
the face of a bureaucratic, impersonal, and unmanageable outside world, southern Californians assert the values of home
and family all the more strongly. Again the experience here
seems only to exaggerate that which is found elsewhere in the
country. Talcott Parsons has pointed out, for example, that
the modern American nuclear family has become isolated
both from extended kinship relations and from productive
economic activity. Sick people go to hospitals, and old folks
go to homes, further shrinking the family-controlled sphere
of life. But where some have viewed the isolation of the nuclear family as a step towards its disappearance, Parsons finds
it an evermore important source of sustenance to its members.
In southern California, the extended family is often a continent away, and the nuclear family is isolated from neighbors
as well as the old and sick. As if in fulfillment of Parsons'
prophecy, nowhere are personal and family values more prominent.[93]

Indeed, family values in southern California are projected
back onto the public area. According to one writer, the California right-wing simply offers a philosophic justification for
the pursuit of private happiness.[94] Another has demonstrated
that the political judgments of Goldwater supporters were
based entirely on standards of personal virtue.[95] The street
railway system created in the early 1900s made the suburbs—
already called "bedroom communities"—possible. H. E. Huntington, father of the street railways, said he was going to "join

the whole region into one big family."[96] The folksy helicopter pilots who gossip about freeway traffic to miles of motorists, like the listener-participation talk shows, suggest a drive for human contact in a depersonalized public world.[97]

Cities are not families, and the inappropriateness of trying to turn them into families adds to the dreamlike quality of the southern California atmosphere. But the trouble goes deeper. For what the family itself has become is no more appropriate to a genuine family than to a city. Family life has internalized the values of southern California public life; the allegedly personal standards reenter politics as the return of the repressed.

In theory, the southern California family is a refuge from the competitive, anonymous outside world. Here the child (or the father) is supposed to be loved for himself alone, not for anything he does; here the running, the striving, and the mobility should stop. But the claim to a family-centered, child-centered existence has a hidden meaning. Family love in fact is not unconditional, but a tool in the fashioning of the child; he learns what he must do to earn it. Like their parents, children learn feverishly to work and consume objects in the search for love. Worse yet, "child-centered" suggests the unnaturally great hopes placed on the children. Family self-esteem depends on what children, as well as fathers, achieve. If children reach heights that parents only imagine, parental striving is justified.

American middle-class family life has always had elements of this investment in children, but less is left to chance in southern California. Right-wing politics attacks social planning—not truly to assert family spontaneity, but to deny the social planning that has entered the home. The small-town front porch, where spectators participated in the life of the street, is replaced by the fenced-in backyard. Indeed, there is no unplanned street life at all; school playgrounds stand empty; and in some sections of Los Angeles pedestrians without dogs court arrest for loitering. Social life is far less neighborhood-centered than in the nineteenth century small town or in the traditional working-class community. There is more planning, more inviting, more traveling to entertainment— and less "dropping in." The neighbor is the man whose unmowed lawn threatens the image of one's block and the value of one's house. The house is less a home than an investment; the lawns are occasionally acquired before the less visible living room furniture.[98] Boosterism moves from the marketplace into the family.

The ideal child thus is not meant to grow and become a separate and distinct person from his parents, any more than the neighbor can have ivy rather than grass on his lawn. Even room partitions and doors, protectors of privacy, disappear.[99] The goal is an unnatural family unity, in which mastery and striving aim at the total security already lost to infants denied the breast, and unattainable thereafter.[100] The manufactured southern California home thus is no alternative to the synthetic southern California landscape. The right-wing model for the state is an unnatural family, not a genuine one. The demand for rigid, coercive standards of morality, which prevent growth, is as life-denying in the home as in politics. Indeed, in the fury against children who will not be mastered and incorporated, the southern California family enters politics with a vengeance. That ideal, applied to student rebels, hippies, and drugs, helped elect Ronald Reagan.[101]

Intolerance of the youth culture, like other characteristics of the symbolic world of right-wing southern California, finds roots in broader American historical experience. Other visible minorities, Indians and Negroes, also have seemed to challenge the American way of life. Groups so different from the bourgeois liberal fragment had to be incorporated or mastered, cured or imprisoned, made safe or destroyed. As Tocqueville accurately saw, they could not be permitted to enjoy a secure and separate existence.[102]

Indians were largely destroyed. As Hartz puts it, "the violence involved in the external elimination of the Indian permitted a heightened degree of peace within the American community."[103] With Negroes and slavery the relation was more complex. Feudal culture, writes Hartz, "had a concept of status that could be revamped for the purpose" of slavery. Slaves could be less than free but more than property; they could marry, go to church, get educated. "The moral polarity of the egalitarian idea" permitted no such adjustments in America. Slavery must be totally abolished, or slaves were no different from other property. Negroes must be treated like white Americans, or they could not be human at all.[104]

But few in the North who opposed slavery believe that Negroes could be incorporated into white America. Subversive qualities of sensuality, endurance, savagery, violence, and religious ecstasy were fixed upon Negroes. Some whites hoped that Negroes would transform what Harriet Beecher Stowe called "the hard, dominant, Anglo-Saxon race."[105] More, with Jefferson, feared this transformation. Anxious to protect self-government of the passions as well as political democracy, Jefferson feared "staining the blood" through "mixture" and hoped Negroes would return to Africa.[106] Once slavery ended and Negroes did not disappear into Africa, they had to become invisible within America. Visible once again in recent years, Negroes have returned to plague liberal uniformity. While increasing numbers of whites subscribe abstractly to a belief in equal rights, few believe in practice that the Negro can become like them. Insofar as Negroes cannot be incorporated or assimilated, they must be excluded or destroyed.

The symbolic significance of Negroes has been intensified in southern California, it appears, and transferred to other groups as well. The need to cure or eliminate is extended to cover Communists, the young, drugs, pornography—targets that seem to express relations of sensuality, rebellion, and acknowledged dependence not permitted in the southern world. Thus the students who want to leave home threaten family unity, bringing the southerner out of "himself alone" and forcing him to acknowledge those within his family as separate and distinct from himself. The Negro threat to property values, the students' rejection of property, and the Communists' desire to take it away—all metaphorically threaten ownership and control of the self, that is, self-government, self-mastery, and protection against the world of significant objects.[107]

Equally serious, in southern California there is little faith in the cure or in the power of the American dream to make over and incorporate these minorities. The Southwest was always the home of unassimilable minorities—Mexicans, Indians, Orientals—rather than the melting pot immigrants of European stock. Not believing in assimilation, the right-wing southerner turns to elimination.[108] He turns from the ambivalent and guilt-ridden pattern of Negro-white relationships to the heroic sagas of the Indian wars.[109] But the actual cowboy, Barry Goldwater, still suggests "the intensity and diversity of small town Main Streets"; he threatens to "keep the memory uncomfortably intact."[110] Unlike the southern California dream come true, Goldwater has too many real ties to the past; he is not synthetic enough to be truly safe. Goldwater calls things by their real names; he still sees wars in terms of real bombs, not disasteramas. He lacks the imagination to contemplate turning Vietnam into an enormous parking lot.[111] He is not yet quite a robot, a sleepwalker, an image on a screen, whose acts are dissociated from his being. In the twentieth century reenactment of the nineteenth century drama, the most compelling hero is not the real cowboy but Ronald Reagan, the man who plays cowboys.

NOTES

1. Carey McWilliams, *Southern California Country*, pp. 4–5; Donald J. Bogue and Calvin L. Beale, *Economic Areas of the United States*, pp. 555–558; U.S., Department of Commerce, Bureau of the Census, *Eighteenth Census of the United States Taken in the Year 1960*, vol. 1, part 6, pp. 227–228. Southern counties comprised five of the top six, and seven of the top ten, counties in the percentage of non-native California residents. Only one Bay Area county was included in the top ten.

2. In 1940, one-third of the population in Los Angeles County had been born in the "great heartland" states of the Midwest, Great Plains, Southwest, and Rocky Mountains. The comparable figure in San Francisco was less than 10 percent. Between 1920 and 1940, 400,000 people born in the heartland moved to Los Angeles; less than one-tenth as many came to San Francisco. See James Q. Wilson, "A Guide to Reagan Country: The Political Culture of Southern California," *Commentary* 43 (May, 1967). The 1930s migration, it should be noted, was far smaller than the migrations of the 1920s and 1940s.

3. See McWilliams, *Southern California Country*, pp. 12–16, 316; U.S., Department of Commerce, Bureau of the Census, *Fifteenth Census of the United States Taken in the Year 1930*, pp. 251–255, 267–272; U.S., Department of Commerce, Bureau of the Census, *Religious Bodies 1936* 1: 725–726; U.S., Department of Commerce, Bureau of the Census, *U.S. Census of Population and Housing: 1960, Census Tracts, Final Report PHC (1)-82*, p. 25.

In 1930, the Bay Area had 24 percent of the state's population, the south 52 percent. In 1960, the proportions were 18 percent and 57 percent, respectively. In 1960, all eight southern counties were more than 60 percent urban. The percentage living on farms in Imperial, 7.6 percent, was more than twice as high as in any other southern county. In 1930, 41 percent of the Imperial population lived on farms; the other southern counties ranged from 2 percent to 22 percent, and all were in the bottom half of the state in the percentage rural-farm. But although the percentage of farmers has long been low, the economy of Imperial, and to a lesser extent some other southern counties, is dominated by corporate agriculture.

The last religious census was taken in 1936. The ethnic figures are taken from the 1930 census; more recent censuses, by counting third generation immigrants as "native born of native parents," minimize the ethnic heterogeneity of the Bay Area counties. Note that right-wing support among Anglo-Saxons of Los Angeles County is considerably higher than the overall county percentages, which include the vote of substantial ethnic minorities, reveal.

4. McWilliams, *Southern California Country*, p. 157.

5. Ibid., p. 159.

6. George E. Mowry, *The California Progressives*, pp. 34–56, 64–104; Remi Nadeau, *Los Angeles: From Mission to Modern City*, pp. 253–258.

7. See Chap. 2 in this book.

8. Richard Hofstadter, *The Age of Reform*, pp. 178, 246–247, 279.

9. See Chaps. 2 and 3 in this book. The Socialist county percentages in several statewide elections were divided into quartiles. Bay Area counties were as often in the top quartiles as southern ones.

10. See Chaps. 2 and 3 in this book.

11. In 1933, for example, Californians finally voted by a large majority to repeal prohibition; the median county gave only 18 percent of its support to the drys. But Orange, Riverside, and San Bernardino remained more than twice as dry as the state median, a feat matched by only two other counties. These were both in the San Joaquin Valley (the agricultural region extending north from the Tehachapis), the other center of dry strength. But southern California was more universally and strongly prohibitionist than the San Joaquin Valley.

The analysis of prohibitionist strength is based on the referenda of 1916, 1918, 1926, and 1933. See also Gilman M. Ostrander, *The Prohibition Movement in California, 1848–1933*; Harold F. Gosnell, *Grass Roots Politics*, p. 81.

12. Prohibitionist sentiment, however, could be allied with progressivism, as in the San Joaquin Valley.

13. Hofstadter, *Age of Reform*, pp. 281–282, 295–299; Samuel Lubell, *The Future of American Politics*, pp. 35–43, 138, 149, 151, 218.

14. See Chaps. 2–5 in this book.

15. Ronald E. Chinn, "The Sinclair Campaign of 1934" (Master's thesis), pp. 30–35; McWilliams, *Southern California Country*, pp. 297–299.

16. Chinn, "Sinclair Campaign of 1934," pp. 21–23, 64.

17. In 1934, Downey received less than 60 percent of the vote in every county but Los Angeles; in 1938 he received less than 55 percent. Only Los Angeles, San Diego, and Del Norte gave Sinclair more than 60 percent of their votes. (The 1938 Downey vote was correlated .64 with both the 1934 Sinclair and Downey showings, indicating the continuity in radical sentiment.)

18. See also Chap. 5 in this book.

19. The various pension schemes of the late 1930s also foundered on southern conservatism. Consider the "Ham and Eggs" plan, rejected in 1938 in a close vote. The support for Ham and Eggs was by no means as southern as the support for Sinclair and Downey. Three of the eight southern counties were in the bottom half of Ham and Eggs strength.

While the south was more for the plan than the Bay Area, the San Joaquin Valley was the most consistently pro-pension.

20. Even from 1935–1940, a higher percentage of the migrants to California came from the west-north-central than from the west-south-central states (25.2 percent to 22.9 percent). In the city of Los Angeles, the figures were 25.9 percent and 15.9 percent. Most of the Okies settled not in southern California but in the agricultural counties of the Great Valley. See Davis E. McEntire, "An Economic and Social Study of Population Movements in California, 1850–1944" (Ph.D. dissertation), pp. 109–110; Walter Stein, "California and the 'Dust Bowl' Migration" (Ph.D. dissertation), pp. 78, 97, 109–110.

21. See tables in Eugene C. Lee, *California Votes 1928–1960*, pp. A29–A32. The entire volume is an invaluable source of electoral data.

22. See Chap. 5 in this book. It should be noted that Roosevelt and the depression rather than EPIC probably reoriented the party vote. The gap between north and south had actually decreased to its post-depression level by 1932. However, EPIC does appear responsible for a more minor-party reorientation. In 1934, Raymond Haight ran as a Progressive candidate against Sinclair and Republican Frank Merriam. Haight was far stronger in the Sacramento and San Joaquin valleys than elsewhere in the state. The influential *Bee* papers supported Haight, and the correlation between *Bee* circulation and the Haight vote was high (Chinn, "Sinclair Campaign of 1934," pp. 120–122). Perhaps because *Bee* circulation was generally stronger in the San Joaquin than in the Sacramento Valley or because of the traditional progressivism of the San Joaquin Valley, the San Joaquin counties were more for Haight and the Sacramento Valley counties more for Merriam. Since 1934, but not before, the Sacramento Valley has been more Republican than the San Joaquin Valley. In the 1960s it gave greater support to right-wing referenda and candidates.

23. See Chap. 5 in this book. The intercorrelations between California presidential elections from 1936 to 1960 fell below .7 only once. Among the elections of 1944 to 1960, the correlations ran from .84 to .95. The off-year correlations, although lower, were always above .7. Party patterns have remained stable in spite of the tremendous migration to California since 1930. This is what we would expect, since our concern is not with particular individuals but with the type of people who live in southern California. Since the area itself, and the type of people living there, have not fundamentally changed, we would not expect massive population turnover alone to change the political patterns.

24. The single exception is that San Bernardino was in the third Republican quartile in 1952. Imperial, San Diego, and Santa Barbara, on the other hand, have often been in the first quartile.

25. The movement of workers into Ventura during the war probably explains this. Note also that Ventura has many Mexican-Americans, although it is not clear why they would first exert Democratic influence in 1944.

26. For the impact of class on California party allegiances, see Homer

Bartlett Thompson, "An Analysis of Voting Behavior in San Francisco, 1936–1946" (Master's thesis), pp. 27–44; Dewey Anderson and Percy E. Davidson, *Ballots and the Democratic Class Struggle*, pp. 116–143. See also Chap. 5 in this book.

27. Three elections failed to fall in the right-wing syndrome; the reasons are illuminating. First, a 1952 old-age pension scheme bore no relation to the orthodox expressions of right-wing sentiment. Right-wing leadership ideology does not include a statist element; the same seems true at the mass level. Even in 1938 many southern conservatives had not supported pension schemes. By 1952, a year of prosperity, the pension issue was even less popular in the south. Second, the vote for right-winger Joseph Shell against Richard Nixon in the 1962 gubernatorial primary was not similar to other right-wing indicators. Although Shell was a Los Angeles state assemblyman, Nixon continued to receive strong southern support. Nixon's roots, after all, were in right-wing ideological politics. The Communist issue played a major role in his 1946 congressional and 1950 senatorial victories. Indeed, there was a greater north-south split in 1950 than in all party elections but one between 1936 and 1956 (see Figure 1).

The November 1962 vote for Max Rafferty may also not fit into the general right-wing pattern. Although the vote is correlated with the other measures of right-wing sentiment, Rafferty as a Republican had right-wing correlations generally lower than those of Nixon, the Republican gubernatorial candidate. Further analysis of the Rafferty vote was not attempted.

28. See Angus Campbell et al., *The American Voter*, pp. 188–265; V. O. Key, Jr., *Public Opinion and American Democracy*, pp. 153–201; Herbert McClosky, "Issue Conflict and Issue Consensus Among Party Leaders and Followers," *American Political Science Review* 54 (June, 1960): 419–426; idem, "Consensus and Ideology in American Politics," *American Political Science Review*, 58 (June, 1964): 372–374; Philip E. Converse, "The Nature of Belief Systems in Mass Publics," in *Ideology and Discontent*, ed. David E. Apter, pp. 214–241; Martin A. Trow, "Right-Wing Radicalism and Political Intolerance: A Study of Support for McCarthy in a New England Town" (Ph.D. dissertation), pp. 94–100, 281, and the references cited in the note on p. 281.

29. How can we explain the apparent contradiction between survey findings and California electoral data? In part the contradiction may be spurious. Right-wing coherence may exist solely among the better educated and politically sophisticated, a fact obscured by aggregate data. Thus a right-wing constituency probably contains an atypically high proportion of politically sophisticated voters. See Philip E. Converse et al., "Electoral Myth and Reality: The 1964 Election," *American Political Science Review*, 59 (June, 1965): 332–335. Moreover, an analysis of poll data on Proposition 14 revealed that differences between northern and southern Californians were much greater for the better educated than the less educated. See Raymond E. Wolfinger and Fred I. Greenstein, "The Repeal of Fair-Housing in California: An Analysis of Referendum Voting," *American Political Science Review* 62 (September, 1968): 762.

If differences largely among the better educated can create political patterns like those in California, then ideology is more significant at the mass level than survey researchers generally argue. Survey findings themselves may also minimize mass ideological sensitivity. In the first place, low consistency on attitudes defined by the observer as right-wing proves little; we want to know what attitudes, if any, voters themselves find related. Second, attitude surveys alone reveal little about propensity to act. A poll of attitudes on race relations six months before the vote on Proposition 14 showed no differences between northern and southern inhabitants. But, as we shall see, many more southerners voted against fair housing. Apparently the live issue of Negro housing tapped symbolic dimensions in the south unrevealed in the attitude survey. See Wolfinger and Greenstein, "Repeal of Fair-Housing in California," p. 762. Finally, the survey picture is static; changes in the political significance of issues or groups may give them a new meaning at the mass level. Negroes and Communists may be connected today in the minds of many who never would have made this connection ten years ago. A rudimentary right-wing ideology can develop; to ignore this is to ignore politics.

30. Nelson Polsby, "Towards an Explanation of McCarthyism," *Political Studies* 8 (October, 1960): 262; Raymond E. Wolfinger et al., "America's Radical Right: Politics and Ideology," in *Ideology and Discontent*, ed. David E. Apter, pp. 267–269; Michael Paul Rogin, *The Intellectuals and McCarthy: The Radical Specter*, pp. 233–234.

31. Right-wing sentiment was also strong in the agricultural, Anglo-Saxon, Protestant counties of the Sacramento Valley.

32. San Mateo was in the fourth quartile of right-wing strength in five elections and the third quartile in two. Marin was in the fourth quartile on all elections but right-to-work, when it was in the first.

33. These eight counties, except for San Francisco, were consistently in the top half of Republican strength from 1936 to 1960. At least four, and often six or seven, were in the bottom quartile of right-wing strength in the five right-wing elections of the 1960s.

34. The right-to-work referendum had the highest right-wing correlation (−.42) with the percentage of males in manufacturing.

35. V. O. Key, Jr., *Southern Politics in State and Nation*, pp. 5–12, 42–43, 215–216, 344, 531, 666–667; Michael P. Rogin, "Politics, Emotion, and the Wallace Vote," *British Journal of Sociology* 20 (March, 1969): 28–32; idem, "Wallace and the Middle Class: The White Backlash in Wisconsin," *Public Opinion Quarterly* 30 (Spring, 1966): 106. In addition, the white suburbs near Watts in Los Angeles County supported Proposition 14 most strongly, with more than 85 percent of their votes. And this was before the Watts uprising.

36. In other words, the Bay Area counties were significantly above the Francis Amendment/14 regression line, and the southern counties significantly below it. The four southern counties were among thirteen counties; the four Bay Area counties were among twelve. Negroes probably contributed more anti-14 than anti-Francis Amendment votes; therefore, counties with a substantial Negro minority might be more opposed to 14 than their vote on the Francis Amendment would predict. This was

true of Alameda County, with the highest Negro percentage in the Bay Area; it was also true of Los Angeles.

37. This was not true of the 1952 antisubversive referendum, which had drawn almost equally from Protestants and Catholics, perhaps because of the prominence of Catholic Joseph McCarthy. McCarthy had attracted more Catholic than Protestant support throughout the country. See Seymour Martin Lipset, "Three Decades of the Radical Right: Coughlinites, McCarthyites, and Birchers (1962)," in *The Radical Right,* ed. Daniel Bell, p. 404; Louis Bean, *Influences in the 1954 Midterm Elections,* p. 26; Rogin, *Intellectuals and McCarthy,* pp. 91–94, 164, 246.

38. See Campbell, et al., *American Voter,* p. 249; Wolfinger et al., "America's Radical Right," p. 279.

39. Regional polarization was exacerbated because Christopher had been mayor of San Francisco, and Reagan was produced by Los Angeles. But clearly the pattern transcends the fact of residence.

40. V. O. Key, Jr., "A Theory of Critical Elections," *Journal of Politics* 18 (February, 1955); Duncan MacRae, Jr., and James A. Meldrum, "Critical Elections in Illinois, 1888–1958," *American Political Science Review* 54 (September, 1960). See also chaps. 1 and 4 in this book.

41. In 1960 and 1962, the gap between southern and northern counties returned to pre-1958 levels. But the gap between the population centers of San Francisco and Los Angeles remained wider than at any time since the 1930s (see Figures 8 and 9). Perhaps this was a lasting effect of the 1958 election; more likely, it reflected Nixon's appeal in Los Angeles and John F. Kennedy's and Governor Brown's in San Francisco.

42. The 1960 election, the presidential contest most recently preceding that of 1964, was used as a measure of the normal party vote, and it is striking that Goldwater's Catholic opposition and Protestant support show even in comparison with the Kennedy election. (The 1952 election was also plotted against 1964, with similar results.) Determination of which counties' votes in 1964 are least predicted by the regular party vote is not arbitrary, as examination of Figure 11 will disclose. Where to draw the line between typical and atypical counties is a matter of judgment, but inclusion of more counties as "atypical" would not change the picture.

43. Southern failure to desert Goldwater made California the thirteenth most Republican northern state in 1964; in 1960, it had ranked twenty-first, in 1956 twenty-ninth. See U.S., Bureau of the Census, *Statistical Abstract of the United States: 1965,* (86th ed.), pp. 374–375.

44. See Table 39. The elections of 1948 to 1954, not reported in Table 39, were correlated from .58 to .70 with right-to-work.

45. The correlations are with percentage of foreign-born whites and their children and percentage of Catholics (see note 3 above). The figures are —.13 and —.16 in 1956, —.22 and —.13 in 1962.

46. The pro-Goldwater counties on the Nixon-Goldwater scattergram supported Goldwater in the primary and the Francis Amendment far more than the anti-Goldwater counties. The pro-Goldwater counties ranged from 1 to 14 percent Catholic, averaging 9 percent; the anti-

Goldwater counties ranged from 15 to 33 percent, averaging 23 percent. The pro-Goldwater counties ranged from 8 to 29 percent foreign stock (in 1930), averaging 19 percent; the anti-Goldwater counties ranged from 23 to 43 percent, averaging 35 percent.

47. State voting returns alone make this clear. In addition, see Irving Crespi, "The Structural Basis for Right-Wing Conservatism: The Goldwater Case," *Public Opinion Quarterly* 29 (Winter, 1965). Southern California may now behave politically as part of a distinctive southwestern region.

48. The religious overtones of the California realignment were matched in Indiana, where Goldwater antagonized Catholics (outside of metropolitan Lake County where the race issue was salient) more than Protestants. See Rogin, "Politics, Emotion, and the Wallace Vote," pp. 30–32, 36–38. For further evidence of the fundamentalist, Protestant character of the contemporary American right, see David Danzig, "The Radical Right and the Rise of the Fundamentalist Majority," *Commentary* 33 (April, 1962): 291–298; Wolfinger et al., "America's Radical Right," pp. 267, 279, 281–283.

49. The 1958 election was the biggest Democratic landslide in California history; 1964 was third, behind 1958 and 1936.

50. See Clifford Geertz, "Ideology as a Cultural System," in *Ideology and Discontent*, ed. David E. Apter, p. 62.

51. See Murray Edelman, *The Symbolic Uses of Politics*, pp. 173–174; Geertz, "Ideology as a Cultural System," pp. 47–76; Lucian W. Pye and Sidney Verba, eds., *Political Culture and Political Development*.

52. Edelman, *Symbolic Uses of Politics*, p. 172.

53. See Campbell et al., *American Voter*, p. 249. See also note 28 above.

54. See Converse, "Nature of Belief Systems," p. 254.

55. Not to mention the orienting role of locally important reference groups—pastors, local newspapers, businessmen, and the like. It seems rash to argue that the political traditions of an area are, with respect to the mass of ordinary voters, more or less accidental.

56. Converse, "Nature of Belief Systems," pp. 214–241.

57. V. O. Key, Jr., *The Responsible Electorate*, pp. 35–148.

58. See Robert Lane, *Political Ideology*, Chap. 26.

59. McWilliams, *Southern California Country*, pp. 293, 304; Carey McWilliams, *California: The Great Exception*, pp. 172–173, 182–194; Chinn, "Sinclair Campaign of 1934," pp. 5–6; Gosnell, *Grass Roots Politics*, pp. 75–77, 82–83.

60. Quoted in McWilliams, *Southern California Country*, pp. 157–158.

61. Quoted in Robert E. Burke, *Olson's New Deal for California*, p. 3.

62. Elizabeth Hardwick, "After Watts," *New York Review of Books* 6 (31 March 1966): 3–4.

63. What will be suggested is an ideal type of right-wing, southern California political culture. It does not claim to be the sole explanation of southern political behavior. Other factors than those which organize life around right-wing symbols are at work in southern California, but they are not the concern of the discussion that follows. The extent to which

right-wing symbols will engage public attention varies considerably, depending on such situational factors as the issue involved, the salience of other issues, the level of discontent, the role of political elites, and so forth. Individuals will also vary in their adherence to this symbolic world, certainly far more developed among right-wing activists than ordinary voters. Some right-wing causes will fail to obtain majority support in the south, as Goldwater did in November, 1964. On the other hand, the support for Proposition 14 in the Los Angeles and Orange county suburbs—75 to 85 percent—approached consensus, and Reagan's primary strength was at least as high. In what follows, no effort is made to specify the conditions for the dominance of right-wing politics. The connections between politics and life are assumed; in real political life the connections have to be created. Insofar as they are created, it is argued that they look as they are pictured here.

64. Louis Hartz, *The Founding of New Societies*, p. 4.

65. Ibid., pp. 5–6, passim.

66. A popular phrase during the settlement of Los Angeles, quoted in Nadeau, *Los Angeles*, p. 75.

67. Ibid., pp. 64–80.

68. Quoted in Nadeau, *Los Angeles*, p. 71.

69. Ibid., p. 80.

70. This is not to argue that upwardly, downwardly, or geographically mobile people are more right-wing than individuals with stable homes or statuses. Although their measures are inexact, several studies suggest this is not the case. By the same token, simple short-run population growth in a relatively stable region need not produce right-wing sentiment. But mobility and restlessness are cultural experiences in southern California, extending outward in space for hundreds of miles and backward in time for seventy-five years. Such lack of stability will affect not only those who move, but also those who remain fixed while all is flux around them. The experience of instability may well support right-wing politics.
On individual mobility and right-wing proclivities see Trow, "Right-Wing Radicalism," pp. 94–100; Wolfinger et al., "America's Radical Right," pp. 278–281; Lipset, "Radical Right," pp. 402–403; Raymond E. Wolfinger and Fred I. Greenstein, "Comparing Political Regions: the Case of California," *American Political Science Review* 63 (March, 1969): 75–81. On the other hand, several essays in the volume, *The American Right Wing*, edited by Robert A. Schoenberger (New York: Holt, Rinehart and Winston, Inc., 1969) definitely establish a relation between both vertical and horizontal mobility and right-wing behavior, in California, and in the nation as a whole.

71. See Alexis de Tocqueville, *Democracy in America* 2: 147, 219, 270, 271, passim.

72. See Hannah Arendt, *The Origins of Totalitarianism*, pp. 305–318, 334–339.

73. Hartz, *Founding of New Societies*, pp. 19–24.

74. Edgar Z. Friedenberg, *The Dignity of Youth and Other Atavisms*, p. 121.

75. Hartz, *Founding of New Societies*, p. 47.

76. Tocqueville, *Democracy in America*. The whole of vol. 2 is a commentary on this theme.

77. Ibid., 2: 104–106, is the best single statement.

78. The tyranny of public opinion and the importance of the crowd are perhaps the most familiar of Tocqueville's themes. See Tocqueville, *Democracy in America* 2: 275–276, 311–312.

79. Ibid., 1: 73, 95–98, 198–205, 251–261; ibid., 2: 109–128.

80. See Mark Twain, "Life on the Mississippi," in *Selected Shorter Writings of Mark Twain*, ed. Walter Blair. In terms of Hannah Arendt's conceptions, which have influenced the formulation here, it would be more precise to call the pilot *homo faber;* but for our purposes the similarities between makers and actors, compared to laborers/consumers, are crucial. See Hannah Arendt, *The Human Condition.* See also note 86 below.

81. Whatever the realities in Tocqueville's time, mass political participation today does not play the role he envisioned. Tocqueville had in mind concrete activity in local associations, which must not be confused with mere membership in giant interests groups or with activity in right-wing movements. (Right-wing southerners may well feel politically efficacious and belong to several groups.) Mass participatory politics is absent in southern California, as in the rest of the country. In addition, southern California lacks stable political institutions, such as the urban machine, which provide concrete political focus and stability without Tocquevillian participation. But the machine was never important in middle-class communities, and their right-wing proclivities in southern California cannot be attributed to its absence.

82. "Real cities," complained Philip Marlowe about Los Angeles, "have something else, some individual bony structure under the muck" (Raymond Chandler, *The Little Sister*, p. 181).

83. An Angeleno, quoted in Christopher Rand, "The Ultimate City-I," *New Yorker*, 1 October 1966, p. 56.

84. See Christopher Rand, "The Ultimate City-III," *New Yorker*, 15 October 1966, pp. 64–65, 94, 97–100; and "The Ultimate City-II," *New Yorker*, 8 October 1966, pp. 86, 110–111.

85. Nathanael West, *The Day of the Locust*, pp. 3–4.

86. On the triumph of consumption, laboring, and technology over work and human activity, see Arendt, *Human Condition.* Southern Californians may develop a sense of individual accomplishment through the hobbies that flourish there. But hobbies fail, as work once did, to connect the individual to an independent but manageable external reality. Hobbies are a withdrawal from the world out there; they do not determine the conditions of existence. Hobbies are private; work is public.

87. See Perry Miller, *Errand Into the Wilderness*, pp. 204–216; Leo Marx, *The Machine in the Garden;* Henry Nash Smith, *Virgin Land.*

88. West, *Day of the Locust*, p. 166.

89. The "disasterama" is reported in Cynthia Lindsay, *The Natives Are Restless*, p. 203.

90. Friedenberg, *Dignity of Youth*, pp. 120–123.

91. "Consumption becomes a larger element in the standard of living in the city than in the country. Among the country population its place is to some extent taken by savings and home comforts known through the medium of neighborhood gossip sufficiently to serve the like general purpose of pecuniary repute . . . the community or social group is small enough to be reached by common notoriety alone . . .

"The serviceability of consumption as a means of repute, as well as the insistence on it as an element of decency, is at its best in those portions of the community where the human contact of the individual is widest and the mobility of the population is greatest. . . . The means of communication and the mobility of the population now expose the individual to the observation of many persons who have no other means of judging of his reputability than the display of goods . . . which he is able to make while he is under their direct observation. . . . One's neighbors, mechanically speaking, often are not socially one's neighbors, or even acquaintances; and still their transient good opinion has a high degree of utility. The only practicable means of impressing one's pecuniary ability on these unsympathetic observers of one's everyday life is an unremitting demonstration of ability to pay. . . . In order to impress these transient observers, and to retain one's self-complacency under their observation, the signature of one's pecuniary strength should be written in characters which he who runs may read" (Thorstein Veblen, *The Theory of the Leisure Class*, pp. 71–73).

92. William Carlos Williams, "To Elsie," in *Selected Poems*, pp. 36–38.

93. See Talcott Parsons, *Essays in Sociological Theory*, pp. 177–196; Remi Nadeau, *California: The New Society*, pp. 103–104, 177–207, 278–280, passim. Hannah Arendt also sees a personal retreat into "intimacy" as the social realm of *homo laborans* expands its boundaries. See Arendt, *Human Condition*, pp. 35–38, 188.

94. Nadeau, *California*, p. 282.

95. Aaron Wildavsky, "The Goldwater Phenomenon: Purists, Politicians, and the Two-Party System," *The Review of Politics* 27 (July, 1965): 393–410. Wildavsky calls this "the privatization of politics."

96. Quoted in Nadeau, *Los Angeles*, p. 116.

97. See Rand, "The Ultimate City-I," p. 110.

98. On the southern California family, see Nadeau, *California*, pp. 59, 103–104, 174–207, 254–278. We are also indebted for material in this paragraph to interviews in a southern California suburb by sociologists Jerry Mandel and Carl Werthman.

99. Ibid., p. 186.

100. "His knees were drawn up almost to his chin, his elbows were tucked in close and his hands were against his chest. But he wasn't relaxed. Some inner force of nerve and muscle was straining to make the ball tighter and still tighter. He was like a steel spring which has been freed of its function in a machine and allowed to use all its strength centripetally. While part of a machine the pull of the spring had been used against other and stronger forces, but now, free at last, it was striving to attain the shape of its original coil.

"Original coil . . . In a book of abnormal psychology borrowed from the college library he had once seen a picture of a woman sleeping in a net hammock whose posture was much like Homer's. 'Uterine Flight,' or something like that, had been the caption under the photograph" (West, *Day of the Locust*, p. 148). See also Geza Roheim, *Magic and Schizophrenia*, pp. 93–227; Melanie Klein, *Contributions to Psychoanalysis*.

101. The treatment of teenagers on Sunset Strip shortly after the election illustrates the violence felt by the southern California adult world toward nonconforming youth. See Edgar Z. Friedenberg and Anthony Bernhard, "The Sunset Strip," *New York Review of Books* 8 (9 March 1967): 8–14.

This thinking about the centrality of the American family in right-wing political symbolism owes much to the comments of John Schaar after he had read an earlier draft of this chapter. He also points out that the targets of right-wing politics are all stereotyped as enemies of the family: Communists and hippies believe in free love; people on welfare are sexually abandoned and then don't care for their children; Negro family life is a mess; children must be protected from smut, neighborhoods from the influx of dirty people, and so forth.

102. For Tocqueville's comments on Indians and Negroes in America, see Tocqueville, *Democracy in America* 1: 343–397, 411.

103. Hartz, *Founding of New Societies*, p. 95.

104. Ibid., pp. 50–51. See also Stanley Elkins, *Slavery*, pp. 27–139; Gunnar Myrdal, *An American Dilemma*, esp. chaps. 1 and 2.

105. Harriet Beecher Stowe, *Uncle Tom's Cabin*, p. xix. Mrs. Stowe connected the special qualities of Negroes with mother love. To accept Negroes was to accept maternal love; both, she hoped, would redeem America. The therapeutic role of Negroes in changing white America came sharply into focus with northern white student involvement in the Student Non-violent Coordinating Committee (SNCC). SNCC leader Stokely Carmichael defends the shift to black power because the slogan asks what Negroes want, not what whites want from Negroes. He is saying, in effect, that Negroes will no longer be therapy for white Americans. Stokely Carmichael, "What We Want," *New York Review of Books* 8 (22 September 1966): 5–8.

106. See Adrienne Koch and William Peden, eds., *The Life and Selected Writings of Thomas Jefferson*, pp. 255–262, 278, 693–697.

107. We are now better able to see why southern California prefers right-wing to left-wing "radicalism." Left-wing protest has been much more willing to confront authorities. It has sought or relied on the partial loyalties provided by traditions, class consciousness, ethnic affiliations, and cultural insulation to provide values in opposition to the dominant ones. Thus left-wing protest avoids the duality of self-reliance and submergence in homogeneity. Moreover, left-wing protest emphasizes reality difficulties in the environment, not aiding so easily in the right-wing effort to evade reality. Here lies one significance of the economic focus of the left.

Right-wing protest is an authoritarian extension of tendencies in the mainstream American tradition. Normally left-wing protest, like La

Follette's, while offering alternatives to dominant American practices, has been quite as civilized as the society under attack. La Follette was apparently too tolerant of a variety of life-styles and too intolerant of powerful groups to suit the mood of southern California. However, in times of severe, tangible distress, when reality difficulties in the environment cannot be avoided, traditional right-wing constituencies have supported "left-wing" movements. It is these which have been most similar to normal right-wing protest. This explains EPIC and the pension schemes in depression-ridden southern California. EPIC bordered on the panacea—the pension schemes were simple flights of fancy. Pension politics publicly sought scapegoats; privately, it was riddled with financial manipulation.

Moreover, southern California political leaders, left-wing under atypical depression conditions, moved right rather quickly. Sheridan Downey became a conservative United States senator, and liberal Californians eventually forced his retirement. Jack Tenney and Samuel Yorty were both prominent in left-wing southern California depression politics, undeterred by association with pro-Communists. Tenney became prominent as the McCarthy of California, investigating Communist subversion in the 1950s. Yorty became mayor of Los Angeles, capitalizing on the subversive issue, anti-intellectualism, and a know-nothing political style. In the 1960s he easily incorporated racist resentments into his appeal. Finally, Reagan himself was originally a left-winger, active in union affairs. The progression of these men from the popular front to an anti-radical, anti-intellectual, implicitly anti-Negro style of politics too accurately reflects the evolution of their constituents. For other examples of the atypically left-wing behavior of normally right-wing constituencies, and fuller discussion of the relation between right- and left-wing protest, see Rogin, *Intellectuals and McCarthy.*

108. At the same time, many radical youths, no longer hoping to transform America through integration (see note 105), have identified themselves with Indian tribalism.

109. See Rand, *The Ultimate City-III,* pp. 64–65.

110. Consider Goldwater's clear-cut opposition to the welfare state in this light. Many observers find Reagan more "moderate" than Goldwater because he is less concerned with such traditional right-wing issues; the interpretation here is quite the opposite.

111. The thought came to Reagan during the 1966 campaign. In 1969, Reagan and the University of California Regents turned Berkeley "People's Park" into a parking lot, following police violence in the community. Told that the blood of the people of Berkeley would be on his hands, Reagan responded, "Fine. I'll wash it off with baraxo." (University of California, Berkeley, *Daily Californian,* 24 June 1969)

Bibliography

Manuscript and Data Collections

Berkeley. Bancroft Library. Hiram Johnson Papers.

Berkeley. Bancroft Library. Chester Rowell Papers.

City and County of San Francisco. "Official Statement of Vote." Files of Registrar of Voters, San Francisco City Hall.

County of Los Angeles. "Minutes of the Board of Supervisors: Record of Elections." Files Section, Board of Supervisors, County Administration Building, Los Angeles.

HAVENNER, FRANCK R. "Franck Roberts Havenner Reminiscences." Transcript of tape-recorded interviews, Bancroft Library, Berkeley, 1953.

SCHARRENBERG, PAUL. "Paul Scharrenberg Reminiscences." Transcript of tape-recorded interviews, Bancroft Library, Berkeley, 1954.

Washington, D.C. Library of Congress. William Gibbs McAdoo Papers.

Unpublished Materials

BELL, CHARLES GORDON. "A Study of Four Selected Factors Which Have Contributed to the Inability of the Democratic Party to

Successfully Mobilize Its Latent Majority in California."
Master's thesis, University of Southern California, 1958.

BICKMORE, JEAN. "Voting in Urban Counties in the United States:
1880–1944." Master's thesis, University of California at Los
Angeles, 1949.

BRAZIL, BURTON R. "Voting in California, 1920–1946." Master's thesis,
University of California at Los Angeles, 1948.

CHINN, RONALD E. "An Analysis of the Structure and Function of the
Democratic Party in California, 1920–1956." Ph.D. dissertation, University of California, Berkeley, 1957.

————. "The Sinclair Campaign of 1934." Master's thesis, Stanford
University, 1937.

DELMATIER, ROYCE D. "The Rebirth of the Democratic Party in California." Ph.D. dissertation, University of California at Berkeley, 1955.

HENNINGS, ROBERT EDWARD. "James D. Phelan and the Wilson Progressives of California." Ph.D. dissertation, University of California at Berkeley, 1961.

HICHBORN, FRANKLIN. "California Politics, 1891–1939." Unpublished
manuscript, Haynes Foundation, Los Angeles.

HIGGINBOTTOM, GEORGE. "Epic by the Bay." Master's thesis, San Francisco State College, 1965.

LIPOW, ARTHUR. "Edward Bellamy and the Nationalist Movement:
A Study in the Sociology of Authoritarian Ideological Cur-
rents in American Socialism." Master's thesis, University of
California at Berkeley, 1965.

MCENTIRE, DAVIS E. "An Economic and Social Study of Population
Movements in California, 1850–1944." Ph.D. dissertation,
Harvard University, 1947.

MCINTOSH, CLARENCE F. "Upton Sinclair and the Epic Movement,
1933–1936." Ph.D. dissertation, Stanford University, 1955.

OLIN, SPENCER C., JR. "The Social Conscience of the Hiram Johnson
Administration." Paper delivered at the Annual Meeting of
the Organization of American Historians, Chicago, 1967.

PITCHELL, ROBERT JOSEPH. "Twentieth Century California Voting
Behavior." Ph.D. dissertation, University of California at
Berkeley, 1955.

PUTNAM, JACKSON KEITH. "The Influence of the Older Age Groups on California Politics, 1920–1940." Ph.D. dissertation, Stanford University, 1964.

ROSE, ALICE. "The Rise of California Insurgency." Ph.D. dissertation, Stanford University, 1942.

SHAFFER, RALPH EDWARD. "Radicalism in California." Ph.D. dissertation, University of California at Berkeley, 1962.

SHANE, JOYCE ANN. "The Religious Factor in the Voting Behavior of San Franciscans." Master's thesis, University of California at Berkeley, 1960.

TAGGART, HAROLD F. "The Free Silver Movement in California." Ph.D. dissertation, Stanford University, 1936.

THOMPSON, HOMER BARTLETT. "An Analysis of Voting Behavior in San Francisco, 1930–1946." Master's thesis, Stanford University, 1947.

WALTERS, DONALD E. "Populism in California: 1889–1900." Ph.D. dissertation, University of California at Berkeley, 1952.

WEINTRAUB, HYMAN. "The I.W.W. in California, 1905–1931." Master's thesis, University of California at Los Angeles, 1947.

WHALEN, ROBERT T. "Liquor Politics in California." Master's thesis, University of California at Berkeley, 1955.

Newspapers

Sacramento Bee, 1924.
San Francisco Chronicle, 1920.
The New York Times, 1924, 1933–1944.
The Labor Clarion, 1913–1916.
The Southern California Labor Press, 1924.

Public Documents

ALLEN, DON A., SR. *Legislative Sourcebook: The California Legislature and Reapportionment, 1849–1965.* Sacramento: Assembly of the State of California, 1966.

California, Secretary of State. *Statement of Vote.*

California Statistical Abstract, 1965.

U.S. Bureau of the Census. *Population: 1890.* Vol. I. U.S. Government Printing Office, Washington, D.C., 1891.

————. *Statistics of Agriculture: 1890.* U.S. Government Printing Office, Washington, D.C., 1891.

————. *Report on Farms and Homes: Property and Indebtedness: 1890.* U.S. Government Printing Office, Washington, D.C., 1891.

————. *Report on Statistics of Churches: 1890.* U.S. Government Printing Office, Washington, D.C., 1891.

————. *Agriculture: 1909–10.* Vol. VI. U.S. Government Printing Office, Washington, D.C., 1911.

————. *Population: 1910.* Vol. II. U.S. Government Printing Office, Washington, D.C., 1913.

————. *Religious Bodies: 1916.* Vols. I & II. U.S. Government Printing Office, Washington, D.C., 1919.

————. *Population: 1920.* Vol. II. U.S. Government Printing Office, Washington, D.C., 1922.

————. *State Compendium, 1920: California.* U.S. Government Printing Office, Washington, D.C., 1922.

————. *Population: 1923.* Vol. II. U.S. Government Printing Office, Washington, D.C., 1933.

————. *Religious Bodies: 1936.* Vol. I. U.S. Government Printing Office, Washington, D.C., 1941.

————. *Population: 1940.* Vol. II. U.S. Government Printing Office, Washington, D.C., 1943.

————. *Characteristics of the Population: 1950.* Vol. II. Part 5, California. U.S. Government Printing Office, Washington, D.C., 1953.

————. *U.S. Census of Population and Housing: 1960. Final Report PHC (1)-82. Los Angeles–Long Beach Standard Metropolitan Statistical Areas.* U.S. Government Printing Office, Washington, D.C., 1962.

Books

ANDERSON, DEWEY, and DAVIDSON, PERCY E. *Ballots and the Democratic Class Struggle.* Stanford: Stanford University Press, 1943.

APTER, DAVID E., ed. *Ideology and Discontent*. New York: The Free Press, 1964.

ARENDT, HANNAH. *The Human Condition*. Garden City, N.Y. Doubleday, Anchor Books, 1959.

————. *The Origins of Totalitarianism*. New York: Meridian Books, 1958.

BEAN, WALTON E. *Boss Reuf's San Francisco*. Berkeley: University of California Press, 1952.

BENSON, LEE. *The Concept of Jacksonian Democracy*. Princeton: Princeton University Press, 1961.

BLAIR, WALTER, ed. *Selected Shorter Writings of Mark Twain*. Boston: Houghton Mifflin Co., 1962.

BOGUE, DONALD J., and BEALE, CALVIN L. *Economic Areas of the United States*. New York: The Free Press, 1961.

BURKE, ROBERT E. *Olson's New Deal for California*. Berkeley: University of California Press, 1953.

BURNS, JAMES MACGREGOR. *Roosevelt: The Lion and the Fox*. New York: Harcourt, Brace & Company, 1956.

CAMPBELL, ANGUS et al. *The American Voter*. New York: John Wiley & Sons, 1960.

CARNEY, FRANCIS. *The Rise of the Democratic Clubs in California*. New York: Holt, Rinehart & Winston, Eagleton Institute, 1958.

CHAMBERS, CLARKE A. *California Farm Organizations*. Berkeley: University of California Press, 1951.

CHANDLER, RAYMOND. *The Little Sister*. London: Penguin Books, 1955.

CLEMENS, SAMUEL [Mark Twain]. *Life on the Mississippi*. New York: Harper & Bros., 1905.

CRESAP, DEAN E. *Party Politics in the Golden State*. Los Angeles: Haynes Foundation, 1954.

EDELMAN, MURRAY. The Symbolic Uses of Politics. Urbana, Ill.: University of Illinois Press, 1964.

FARRELLY, DAVID, and HINDERAKER, IVAN, eds. *The Politics of California: A Book of Readings*. New York: Ronald Press Co., 1951.

FISHER, LLOYD H. *The Harvest Labor Market in California*. Cambridge, Mass.: Harvard University Press, 1953.

FORCEY, CHARLES. *The Crossroads of American Liberalism.* New York: Oxford University Press, 1961.

FRIEDENBERG, EDGAR Z. *The Dignity of Youth and Other Atavisms.* Boston: Beacon Press, 1965.

GOSNELL, HAROLD F. *Grass Roots Politics: National Voting Behavior of Typical States.* Washington, D.C.: American Council on Public Affairs, 1942.

HABER, SAM. *Efficiency and Uplift.* Chicago: University of Chicago Press, 1964.

HAGOOD, MARGARET JARMON. *Farm-Operator Family Level-of-Living Indexes for Counties of the United States, 1930, 1940, 1945, and 1950.* Washington, D.C.: Government Printing Office, 1952.

HARTZ, LOUIS. *The Founding of New Societies.* New York: Harcourt, Brace & World, 1964.

HAYS, SAMUEL P. *Conservation and the Gospel of Efficiency.* Cambridge, Mass.: Harvard University Press, 1959.

HICKS, JOHN D. *The Populist Revolt.* Lincoln: University of Nebraska Press, 1961.

HOFSTADTER, RICHARD. *The Age of Reform: From Bryan to F.D.R.* New York: Alfred A. Knopf, 1955.

HUTCHISON, CLAUDE B., ed. *California Agriculture.* Berkeley: University of California Press, 1954.

KEY, V. O., JR. *A Primer of Statistics for Political Scientists.* New York: Thomas Y. Crowell Co., 1954.

————. *Public Opinion and American Democracy.* New York: Alfred A. Knopf, 1961.

————. *The Responsible Electorate.* Cambridge, Mass.: Harvard University Press, 1966.

KIDNER, FRANK L. *California Business Cycles.* Berkeley: University of California Press, 1946.

KLEIN, MELANIE. *Contributions to Psychoanalysis.* London: Hogarth Press, 1948.

KNIGHT, ROBERT EDWARD LEE. *Industrial Relations in the San Francisco Bay Area, 1900–1918.* Berkeley: University of California Press, 1960.

KOMAROVSKY, MIRRA, ed. *Common Frontiers of the Social Sciences.* Glencoe, Ill.: The Free Press, 1957.

LEE, EUGENE C., ed. *The California Governmental Process.* Boston: Little, Brown & Co., 1966.

——. *California Votes, 1920–1960.* Berkeley: Institute of Governmental Studies, University of California, 1963.

LINDSAY, CYNTHIA. *The Natives Are Restless.* Philadelphia: J. B. Lippincott Co., 1960.

LUBELL, SAMUEL. *The Future of American Politics.* New York: Harper & Bros., 1951.

MCWILLIAMS, CAREY. *California: The Great Exception.* New York: Current Books, 1949.

——. *Factories in the Field.* Boston: Little, Brown & Co., 1939.

——. *Southern California Country.* New York: Duell, Sloan & Pearce, 1946.

MARTIN, ROSCOE C. *The People's Party in Texas.* Austin, Texas: University of Texas Press, 1933.

MARX, LEO. *The Machine in the Garden.* New York: Oxford University Press, 1964.

MAY, HENRY F. *The End of American Innocence.* New York: Alfred A. Knopf, 1959.

MILLER, PERRY. *Errand Into the Wilderness.* New York: Harper & Row, 1964.

MOWRY, GEORGE E. *The California Progressives.* Chicago: Quadrangle Books, 1963.

NADEAU, REMI. *California: The New Society.* New York: David McKay, 1963.

——. *Los Angeles: From Mission to Modern City.* New York: Longmans, Green & Co., 1960.

NEPRASH, JERRY ALVIN. *The Brookhart Campaigns in Iowa, 1920–26.* New York: Columbia University Press, 1932.

NEUMANN, SIGMUND, ed. *Modern Political Parties.* Chicago: University of Chicago Press, 1956.

NUGENT, WALTER. *The Tolerant Populists.* Chicago: University of Chicago Press, 1963.

OLDER, FREMONT. *My Own Story.* Oakland: The Post–Enquirer Publishing Co., 1925.

OLIN, SPENCER C., JR. *California's Prodigal Sons: Hiram Johnson and the Progressives, 1911–1917.* Berkeley: University of California Press, 1968.

OSTRANDER, GILMAN M. *The Prohibition Movement in California, 1848–1933.* Berkeley: University of California Press, 1957.

PERRY, LOUIS B., and PERRY, RICHARD S. *A History of the Los Angeles Labor Movement, 1911–1941.* Berkeley: University of California Press, 1963.

PHILBRICK, H. R. *Legislative Investigation Report.* Sacramento: Premier Publications, 1949.

POLLACK, NORMAN K. *The Populist Response to Industrial America.* Cambridge, Mass.: Harvard University Press, 1962.

PYE, LUCIAN W., and VERBA, SIDNEY, eds. *Political Culture and Political Development.* Princeton: Princeton University Press, 1965.

RAND, CHRISTOPHER. *Los Angeles, The Ultimate City.* New York: Oxford University Press, 1967.

RICE, STUART A. *Farmers and Workers in American Politics.* New York: Columbia University Press, 1924.

ROGIN, MICHAEL PAUL. *The Intellectuals and McCarthy: The Radical Specter.* Cambridge: M. I. T. Press, 1967.

ROHEIM, GEZA. *Magic and Schizophrenia.* New York: International Universities Press, 1955.

ROLLE, ANDREW F. *California: A History.* New York: Thomas Y. Crowell Co., 1963.

SINCLAIR, UPTON. *The Autobiography of Upton Sinclair.* New York: Harcourt, Brace and World, 1962.

———. *I, Candidate for Governor and How I Got Licked.* Los Angeles: End Poverty League, 1935.

SMITH, HENRY NASH. *Virgin Land: The American West as Symbol and Myth.* Cambridge, Mass.: Harvard University Press, 1950.

THOMPSON, WARREN S. *Growth and Changes in California's Population.* Los Angeles: Haynes Foundation, 1955.

TOCQUEVILLE, ALEXIS DE. *Democracy in America.* 2 vols. New York: Random House, Vintage Books, 1959.

WEST, NATHANAEL. *The Day of the Locust.* 1939. New York: New Directions, 1962.

WILLIAMS, WILLIAM CARLOS. *Selected Poems.* New York: New Directions, 1963.

Articles

ANDERSON, TOTTEN J. "Bibliography on California Politics," *Western Political Quarterly*, Supplement 11 (December, 1958): 23–51.
———. "The 1956 Election in California," *Western Political Quarterly* 10 (March, 1957): 102–116.
———. "The 1958 Election in California," *Western Political Quarterly* 12 (December, 1958): 276–300.
BAILEY, THOMAS A. "California, Japan and the Alien Land Legislation of 1913," *Pacific Historical Review* 1 (March, 1932): 36–59.
BARCLAY, THOMAS S. "Reapportionment in California," *Pacific Historical Review* 5 (June, 1936): 93–129.
———. "The Reapportionment Struggle in California in 1948," *Western Political Quarterly* 4 (June, 1951): 313–324.
———. "The 1954 Election in California," *Western Political Quarterly* 7 (December, 1954): 597–604.
BARGER, BOB. "Raymond L. Haight and the Commonwealth Progressive Campaign of 1934," *California Historical Society Quarterly* 43 (September, 1964): 219–230.
BONE, HUGH A. "New Party Associations in the West," *American Political Science Review* 45 (December, 1951): 1115–1125.
BUENKER, JOHN D. "The Urban Political Machine and the Seventeenth Amendment," *Journal of American History* 56 (September, 1969): 305–322.
BURNHAM, WALTER DEAN. "The Changing Shape of the American Political Universe," *American Political Science Review* 69 (March, 1965): 7–28.
CAMPBELL, EARL C. "Party Nominations in California: 1860–1909," *Southwestern Social Science Quarterly* 12 (December, 1931): 245–257.
CONVERSE, PHILIP E. et al. "Electoral Myth and Reality: The 1964 Election," *American Political Science Review* 59 (June, 1965): 321–336.
CROUCH, WINSTON W. "The Constitutional Initiative in Operation," *American Political Science Review* 33 (August, 1939): 634–645.
FINDLEY, JAMES C. "Cross-Filing and the Progressive Movement in

California Politics," *Western Political Quarterly* 12 (September, 1959): 699–711.

FLINN, THOMAS A. "The Outline of Ohio Politics," *Western Political Quarterly* 13 (September, 1960): 702–721.

FLOURNOY, HOUSTON I. "The 1958 Knowland Campaign in California —Design for Defeat," *Western Political Quarterly* 12 (June, 1959): 571–572.

FRIEDENBERG, EDGAR Z., and BERNHARD, ANTHONY. "The Sunset Strip," *New York Review of Books,* 9 March 1967, pp. 8–14.

GILB, CORINNE LATHROP. "Justice Jesse W. Carter, An American Individualist," *Pacific Historical Review* 29 (May, 1960): 145–157.

HAMILTON, MARTY. "Bull Moose Plays An Encore: Hiram Johnson and the Presidential Campaign of 1932," *California Historical Society Quarterly* 41 (September, 1962): 211–221.

HARDWICK, ELIZABETH. "After Watts," *New York Review of Books,* 31 March 1966, pp. 3–7.

HENNINGS, ROBERT E. "California Democratic Politics in the Period of Republican Ascendancy," *Pacific Historical Review* 31 (August, 1962): 267–280.

HIGHAM, JOHN. "The American Party, 1886–1891," *Pacific Historical Review* 19 (February, 1950): 37–46.

HOFFMAN, PAUL J., and FERGUSON, JENNIELLEN W. "Voting Behavior: The Vote on the Francis Amendment in the 1962 California Election," *Western Political Quarterly* 17 (December, 1964): 770–777.

HOLLINGSWORTH, J. ROGERS. "Populism: The Problem of Rhetoric and Reality," *Agricultural History* 29 (April, 1965): 81–85.

HUCKSHORN, ROBERT J., and YOUNG, CHARLES E. "Study of Voting Splits on City Councils in Los Angeles County," *Western Political Quarterly* 13 (June, 1960): 479–497.

HUNDLEY, NORRIS C., JR. "Katherine Phillips Edson and the Fight for California Minimum Wage, 1912–1923," *Pacific Historical Review* 29 (August, 1960): 271–285.

HUTCHINSON, W. H. "Prologue to Reform: The California Anti-Railroad Republicans, 1899–1905," *Southern California Quarterly* 44 (September, 1962): 180–208.

HUTHMACHER, J. JOSEPH. "Urban Liberalism and the Age of Reform," *Mississippi Valley Historical Review* 49 (September, 1962): 231–241.

HYINK, BERNARD L. "The California Legislature Looks at the State Constitution," *Western Political Quarterly* 15 (March, 1962): 157–169.

KAUER, RALPH. "The Workingmen's Party of California," *Pacific Historical Review* 13 (September, 1944): 278–291.

KELLEY, ROBERT L. "The Mining Debris Controversy in the Sacramento Valley," *Pacific Historical Review* 25 (November, 1956): 331–346.

KEY, V. O., JR. "Secular Realignment and the Party System," *Journal of Politics* 21 (May, 1959): 198–210.

———. "A Theory of Critical Elections," *Journal of Politics* 17 (February, 1955): 3–18.

——— and MUNGER, FRANK. "Social Determinism and Electoral Decision: The Case of Indiana." In *American Voting Behavior*, edited by Eugene Burdick and Arthur J. Brodbeck. Glencoe, Ill.: The Free Press, 1950.

KNOLES, GEORGE HARMON. "Populism and Socialism with Special Reference to the Election of 1892," *Pacific Historical Review* 12 (September, 1943): 295–304.

LAYNE, J. GREGG. "The Lincoln–Roosevelt League: Its Origins and Accomplishments," *Southern California Quarterly* 25 (September, 1943): 79–101.

LEE, EUGENE C., and BUCHANAN, WILLIAM. "The 1960 Election in California," *Western Political Quarterly* 14 (March, 1961): 309–326.

LINCOLN, A. "My Dear Governor: Letters Exchanged by Theodore Roosevelt and Hiram Johnson," *California Historical Society Quarterly* 38 (September, 1959): 229–247.

MCHENRY, DEAN R. "The Pattern of California Politics," *Western Political Quarterly* 1 (March, 1948): 44–53.

MCKEE, IRVING. "The Background and Early Career of Hiram Warren Johnson, 1866–1910," *Pacific Historical Review* 19 (February, 1950): 17–30.

MCQUITTY, LOUIS L. "Elementary Factor Analysis," *Psychological Reports* 9 (1951): 71–78.

MACRAE, DUNCAN, JR., and MELDRUM, JAMES A. "Critical Elections in Illinois, 1888–1958," *American Political Science Review* 54 (September, 1960): 669–683.

MOWRY, GEORGE E. "The California Progressive and His Rationale: A

Study in Middle Class Politics," *Mississippi Valley Historical Review* 36 (September, 1949): 239–250.

NASH, GERALD D. "The Influence of Labor on State Policy, 1860–1920: The Experience of California," *California Historical Society Quarterly* 47 (September, 1965): 241–257.

OLIN, SPENCER C., JR. "Hiram Johnson, the California Progressive, and the Hughes Campaign of 1916," *Pacific Historical Review* 31 (November, 1962): 403–412.

PITCHELL, ROBERT J. "Reapportionment as a Control of Voting in California," *Western Political Quarterly* 14 (March, 1961): 214–235.

———. "The Electoral System and Voting Behavior: The Case of California's Cross-filing," *Western Political Quarterly* 12 (June, 1959): 459–484.

POMPER, GERALD. "A Classification of Presidential Elections," *Journal of Politics* 29 (August, 1967): 535–566.

POSNER, RUSSELL M. "California's Role in the Nomination of Franklin D. Roosevelt," *California Historical Society Quarterly* 39 (June, 1960): 121–127.

———. "The Progressive Voters League, 1923–26," *California Historical Society Quarterly* 36 (September, 1957): 251–261.

QUINT, HOWARD H. "Gaylord Wilshire and Socialism's First Congressional Campaign," *Pacific Historical Review* 26 (November, 1959): 327–340.

SAXTON, ALEXANDER. "San Francisco Labor and the Populist and Progressive Insurgencies," *Pacific Historical Review* 34 (November, 1965): 421–438.

SEAGER, ROBERT II. "Some Denominational Reactions to Chinese Immigration to California, 1856–1892," *Pacific Historical Review* 28 (February, 1959): 49–66.

SELLERS, CHARLES G., JR. "The Equilibrium Cycle in Two-Party Politics," *Public Opinion Quarterly* 29 (Spring, 1965): 16–37.

SHIELDS, CURRIN V. "A Note on Party Organization: The Democrats in California," *Western Political Quarterly* 7 (December, 1954): 673–683.

TAGGART, HAROLD F. "California and the Silver Question in 1895," *Pacific Historical Review* 6 (September, 1937): 249–269.

———. "The Election of 1898 in California," *Pacific Historical Review* 19 (August, 1950): 357–368.

———. "The Party Realignment of 1896 in California," *Pacific Historical Review* 8 (December, 1939): 435–452.

———. "The Silver Republican Club of Los Angeles," *Southern California Quarterly* 25 (September, 1943): 102–116.

———. "Thomas Vincent Cator, Populist Leader," *California Historical Society Quarterly* 30 (December, 1948): 311–318; (March, 1949): 47–55.

TITUS, CHARLES H. "Rural Voting in California, 1900–1926," *Southwestern Social Science Quarterly* 9 (September, 1928): 198–215.

———. "Voting in California Cities, 1900–1925," *Southwestern Social Science Quarterly* 8 (March, 1928): 383–399.

———and NIXON, CHARLES R. "The 1948 Elections in California," *Western Political Quarterly* 2 (March, 1949): 97–102.

VELIE, LESTER. "The Secret Boss of California," *Collier's* 13 August 1949, 11–13, 71–73; 20 August 1949, 12–13, 60–63.

WILDAVSKY, AARON B. "The Goldwater Phenomenon: Purists, Politicians, and the Two-Party System," *The Review of Politics* 27 (July, 1965): 393–410.

WILSON, JAMES Q. "A Guide to Reagan Country: The Political Culture of Southern California," *Commentary* 43 (May, 1967): 37–45.

WOLFINGER, RAYMOND E., and GREENSTEIN, FRED I. "Comparing Political Regions: The Case of California," *American Political Science Review* 63 (March, 1969): 74–85.

———. "The Repeal of Fair-Housing in California: An Analysis of Referendum Voting," *American Political Science Review* 62 (September, 1968): 753–769.

Index

Alameda County, 17
Alger, Horatio, 186
Alpine County, xvii
American Protective Association, 8, 16–17
American Railway Union, 18
Anti-Saloon League, 160
Arendt, Hannah, 188

Bard, Thomas, 54
Bay Area, San Francisco, 38, 39, 43, 44, 45, 46–47, 48, 49, 55, 118, 122, 131, 157, 158, 159, 163–164, 165, 167, 170–173, 175–176
Bell, Theodore, 66
Bellamy, Edward, 15
Billings, Warren, 48
Boddy, Manchester, 146
Brown, Edmund P., 140, 147
Bryan, William Jennings, xv, 5, 6, 7, 20, 21, 24–26, 27, 50, 103
Building Trades Council, 69

California Democratic Council, 146
California Federation of Labor, 66, 67

California Republican Assembly, 146
Carter, Jesse, 52, 54
Civil War, 4, 5, 6, 186
Commonwealth party, 128
Converse, Philip E., 180–181
Coolidge, Calvin, 100
Creel, George, 126, 127, 129, 134, 183

Davis, John W., 100, 106, 107, 114
Debs, Eugene V., 75
Del Norte County, 163
Democratic party, xv, 5, 7, 16, 19–29, 44, 49, 50–51, 53, 66, 71, 79, 82, 91–95, 97, 100, 101, 103, 106–109, 112–147, 160, 163–169, 173, 176, 177, 182
Dewey, Thomas E., 177
Disneyland, 194
Dockweiler, Isidore, 114, 115, 117, 118, 126–127
Douglas, Helen Gahagan, 146
Downey, Sheridan, 128, 132, 146, 160, 163, 165

Edelman, Murray, 179–180
Eisenhower, Dwight D., 145, 177, 179, 182

227

Elections: 1884, 19–20, 103; 1888, 19–20, 26, 103; 1890, 5; 1892, 5, 7, 10, 13, 15, 20, 100, 103; 1894, 5, 7, 12–13, 16–18, 21, 24; 1896, xiv, xv, 4–7, 19–27, 50, 95, 175; 1902, 24, 26; 1906, 24, 26; 1908, 19–20, 44, 103; 1910, 37–39, 43–44, 53, 65, 70, 78, 79, 80, 125, 136, 158; 1912, 37, 38, 45, 65, 72, 75, 103, 158; 1914, 29, 38, 46–48, 65, 67, 71, 72, 75, 79; 1916, xv, 29, 38, 46–51, 65, 67, 75–76, 80, 91, 92, 95, 97, 100, 103, 106, 107, 109, 122, 158, 159; 1918, 29, 65; 1920, 37, 51, 65, 75, 91, 92, 97, 100, 103, 106, 107; 1922, 51, 65, 72, 134, 136; 1924, xv, 51, 65, 66, 67, 72, 75, 76, 91, 92, 93, 97, 100, 103, 106, 107, 109, 116, 122, 158, 159, 160; 1926, 51, 114, 117, 134; 1928, 85, 90–109, 120, 122, 124, 130, 140, 160; 1930, 115, 117, 130, 134, 136; 1932, 90, 91, 103, 106, 109, 112, 117–120, 124, 130, 131, 160; 1934, 112, 124–138, 142, 144, 160, 163–165; 1936, 103, 112, 120, 124, 165; 1938, 112, 134, 136, 139, 163–165; 1940, 103, 107, 112; 1942, 134, 136, 137, 139, 147; 1944, 97, 100, 139; 1946, 137, 139, 146; 1948, 139; 1950, 139; 1954, 137, 139, 142; 1956, 176; 1958, 136, 140, 144, 147, 175–177; 1960, 165, 176; 1962, 140, 177; 1964, 169, 174, 175–177; 1966, 140, 144, 147, 169, 174, 175–177; 1968, 140, 154
Elliot, John B., 114, 115, 126
End Poverty in California movement (EPIC), xvi, 16, 125–132, 146, 160, 163–165

Farley, James, 129
Forest Lawn, 194

Francis Amendment, 169–170, 174, 177
Fresno County, 131
Friedenberg, Edgar Z., 188–189

Garner, John Nance, 117–118
Geertz, Clifford, 178
Germany, 179, 180
Goldwater, Barry, 154, 169–170, 173–177, 184, 196, 200–201
Gosnell, Harold F., 100
Graves, Richard P., 139

Haight, Raymond, 128, 129, 131–133, 134
Harding, Warren G., 101
Hardwick, Elizabeth, 184
Harriman, Job, 69
Harrison, Maurice, 124–125, 129
Hartz, Louis, 184–185, 188, 199
Havenner, Franck, 66
Hearst, William Randolph, 117, 118, 127
Heney, Francis J., 116
Higginbottom, George, 134
Hofstadter, Richard, 64
Hollywood, 194
Hoover, Herbert, 67, 115, 145
Hughes, Charles Evans, 49–50, 76, 100, 101
Huntington, H. E., 195–196

Industrial Workers of the World (IWW), 64
Imperial County, 155, 156, 163
Indiana, 177

Jefferson, Thomas, 199
Johnson, Hiram, xvii, 37–39, 43–49, 51, 52, 53, 55, 63, 64–68, 69, 70–72, 75–76, 78–80, 82–83, 85, 114, 125, 128, 158

Kansas, 9
Kelley, Charles T., 64
Kennedy, John F., 173
Kenny, Robert, 146
Key, V. O., Jr., xiii–xvi, 3, 19, 90, 91, 94, 95, 100–101, 106, 181
Knight, Goodwin, 139
Knowland, William, 175, 176
Korea, 179

La Follette, Robert M., 45, 50–51, 75, 76, 79, 85, 92, 101, 106, 107, 116, 122, 158, 159, 160
Lawrence, William, 186
League of Nations, 37, 67, 100
Lincoln, Abraham, 193
Lincoln–Roosevelt League, 36
Long Beach, 80, 82, 83
Los Angeles, 8, 15, 17, 37, 43, 44, 48, 65, 67–68, 69, 70, 71, 72, 79–80, 82–83, 114, 115, 118, 120, 122, 124, 127, 129, 130, 132, 133, 137, 140, 144, 155–158, 163–167, 170, 173, 174, 176, 183–201
Los Angeles Times, 55, 63
Lubell, Samuel, 90–91, 92, 93–94

McAdoo, William Gibbs, 114–115, 117, 124, 126, 129, 163
McCarthy, P. H., 69
McKinley, William, 7
McLaughlin, John P., 66
MacRae, Duncan, Jr., 100, 102, 107
McWilliams, Carey, 157, 185
Marin County, 167, 170, 176
Marina District, San Francisco, 93
Market Street, 69–71, 76, 93
Massachusetts, 91
Meldrum, James A., 101, 102, 107
Merriam, Frank, 128, 129, 134
Mission District, San Francisco, 69–71, 76, 93
Mississippi River, 5, 7, 8, 190–191, 193
Modoc County, xvii

Mooney, Tom, 48
Mowry, George, 36–38, 39, 54, 63, 64, 66

Nebraska, 9
New Deal, xvi, 4, 27, 38, 52, 55, 56, 103, 106, 107, 125, 158, 160, 165, 167
New England, 90, 95
New York, 191
Nixon, Richard M., 126, 154, 176, 177
Nob Hill, San Francisco, 68–69, 72
Non-Partisan League, 48
Norbeck, Peter, 48
North Beach, San Francisco, 71–72, 93–94
North Dakota, 9, 48

Oakland, 17
Olson, Culbert, 54, 112, 116, 128, 129, 139
Orange County, 43, 114, 154, 156, 159, 165, 176
Ostrander, Gilman M., 37, 38

Pacific Heights, San Francisco, 70–72, 83, 93
Parrington, Vernon L., 185
Parsons, Talcott, 196
Pasadena, 80, 82, 83
Phelan, James D., 114
Plumas County, 95
Populism, xv, xvi, 5, 7–27, 36, 158
Potrero Hill, San Francisco, 71
Progressivism, xv, xvi, 6, 27, 29, 35–55, 62–85, 108, 115–116, 117, 128, 133, 143, 145, 158–159
Prohibition party, 79, 163
Proposition 14, 169–170, 173
Proposition 16, 169–170, 177
Pullman boycott, 17–18

Reagan, Ronald, 140, 147, 154, 169–
170, 173–178, 179, 184, 198, 200–
201
Republican party, xv, 9, 20–27, 35,
43–44, 45, 46, 48, 50–51, 55, 65,
67, 70, 72, 75, 79, 80, 91, 93, 95,
101, 103, 108, 112, 113, 114, 115,
117, 119, 120, 128, 130, 132, 136,
137, 139–140, 142–147, 154, 159,
160, 163–170, 173, 175–178
Reuf, Abraham, 68, 70
Richmond District, San Francisco,
70–72, 83
Right-to-work referendum, 1958,
169–170, 173, 174, 175, 176, 179
Riverside County, 95, 114, 159, 165
Rolph, James D., 114, 115, 128
Roosevelt, Franklin D., 90, 112,
117–118, 120, 124, 128–129, 130,
131–132, 133, 139, 160, 179
Roosevelt, James, 189
Roosevelt, Theodore, 37, 38, 45–46,
72, 103
Rowell, Chester, 67
Russian Hill, San Francisco, 70–72

Sacramento, 17, 64, 69, 112, 131, 143
Sacramento Bee, 68
Sacramento Valley, 122, 133
San Bernadino County, 159
San Diego, 163
San Francisco, xviii, 8, 10, 17–18, 26,
37, 38, 39, 46–47, 49, 53, 55, 56,
63, 65, 66, 67, 68–72, 75–76, 78,
79, 80, 82, 83, 93, 114, 120, 122,
125, 127, 132, 133–134, 137, 140,
144, 145, 158, 160, 164, 167, 170,
174, 176, 177, 183, 184, 191
San Francisco Labor Clarion, 67
San Francisco Labor Council, 69
San Joaquin County, 17
San Joaquin Valley, 37, 39, 48, 122,
131–132
San Jose, 17
San Mateo County, 167, 170
Santa Barbara County, 156, 170

Santa Clara County, 17, 145
Sante Fe Railroad, 8, 186
Saxton, Alexander, 84
Scharrenberg, Paul, 65–66, 67
Sinclair, Upton, xvi, 16, 54, 124–134,
138, 160, 163–165, 183
Smith, Alfred E., 55, 85, 90, 92, 93,
97, 100, 107, 109, 113, 114–115,
117–118, 122, 130, 160
Socialist party, 47, 63, 69, 70–71, 75,
79, 80, 82, 84, 97, 106, 107, 125,
158, 160
South Dakota, 9, 48
Southern California, xv, xvi, 8, 9,
10, 15–16, 26, 36–38, 43–44,
45–46, 48, 50, 51, 53–54, 55, 63,
67, 79, 85, 115, 118, 119–120,
122, 124, 127, 130–131, 133, 137,
140, 153–178, 182–201
Southern California Labor Press, 67
Southern Pacific Railroad, 24, 53,
54, 70, 85
Stanislaus County, 131
Stanton, Philip, 43
Stevenson, Adlai E., 146
Stockton, 17
Stowe, Harriet Beecher, 199
Sunset District, San Francisco, 70–72

Taft, William Howard, 44, 45
Tehachapi Mountains, 43, 155, 158,
183, 184
de Tocqueville, Alexis, 6, 187–191,
193, 199
Townsend plan, 129
Truman, Harry S., 139
Tulare County, xvii, 131
Twain, Mark, 186, 190–191

Union Labor party, 53, 68

Veblen, Thorstein, 195
Ventura County, 156, 163, 165, 170
Vietnam, 177, 200–201

Walsh, Thomas J., 114
Walters, Donald E., 9
Wardell, Justus, 114, 115, 117, 118, 124, 126, 127, 128, 129
Warner, Charles Dudley, 186
Warren, Earl, 112, 126, 137, 139, 145, 146, 147
West, Nathanael, 185, 192–193, 194
Western addition, 71
Wheatland, 64
Wichita, Kan., 8, 183
Williams, William Carlos, 194–195

Wilson, J. Stitt, 80
Wilson, Woodrow, 29, 47–51, 55, 75–76, 79, 80, 85, 92, 100, 106, 107, 115, 117, 122, 126, 159
Wisconsin, 177
World War I, 29, 46, 48, 51
World War II, 175

Yolo County, 131
Young, C. C., 50–51
Young, Milton, 115